THE CHILD IN SHAKESPEARE

Charlotte Scott has written widely on Shakespeare, including two books, *Shakespeare and the Idea of the Book* (OUP, 2007) and *Shakespeare's Nature: From Cultivation to Culture* (OUP, 2014) as well as articles and essays. She reviews for *Shakespeare Survey* and is a frequent contributor to literary festivals and public events. She has taught at Goldsmiths for over 14 years.

Praise for *The Child in Shakespeare*

'In this capacious study, Charlotte Scott of course discusses Mamillius, Arthur, and the changeling boy—children by age—but she also considers hundreds of others of Shakespeare's characters—children by association. No matter their years, they are defined by their relations to their siblings, their kin, and especially their parents. Scott shows that the 'child' is a vehicle for Shakespeare to explore themes of alliance, conflict, hierarchy, socialization, morality, agency, interiority, memory, possibility, and more. Read this book as a survey of the meaning and significance of children in Shakespeare. Or read it as a meditation on the human condition, inspired by Shakespeare and filtered through Scott's intelligence, learning, and empathy.'

Lena Cowen Orlin, Georgetown University

'Scott's style is reader friendly, even poetic. Recommended.'

J.S. Carducci, *CHOICE*

'Organized by genre, and surveying Shakespeare's career-long interest in all phases of childhood, from infancy to adolescence, Scott's book opens with a vivid account of royal children in the early history plays, who, she argues, are forced to enter an 'adult world' of political intrigue for which they are hopelessly ill-equipped.'

Laura Kolb, *Times Literary Supplement*

The Child in Shakespeare

CHARLOTTE SCOTT

OXFORD

UNIVERSITY PRESS

OXFORD

UNIVERSITY PRESS

Great Clarendon Street, Oxford, OX2 6DP,
United Kingdom

Oxford University Press is a department of the University of Oxford.
It furthers the University's objective of excellence in research, scholarship,
and education by publishing worldwide. Oxford is a registered trade mark of
Oxford University Press in the UK and in certain other countries

© Charlotte Scott 2018

The moral rights of the author have been asserted

First published 2018
Published in paperback 2021

All rights reserved. No part of this publication may be reproduced, stored in
a retrieval system, or transmitted, in any form or by any means, without the
prior permission in writing of Oxford University Press, or as expressly permitted
by law, by licence or under terms agreed with the appropriate reprographics
rights organization. Enquiries concerning reproduction outside the scope of the
above should be sent to the Rights Department, Oxford University Press, at the
address above

You must not circulate this work in any other form
and you must impose this same condition on any acquirer

Published in the United States of America by Oxford University Press
198 Madison Avenue, New York, NY 10016, United States of America

British Library Cataloguing in Publication Data
Data available

Library of Congress Cataloging in Publication Data
Data available

ISBN 978–0–19–882855–6 (Hbk.)
ISBN 978–0–19–284307–4 (Pbk.)

Links to third party websites are provided by Oxford in good faith and
for information only. Oxford disclaims any responsibility for the materials
contained in any third party website referenced in this work.

For Ruby

Acknowledgements

There is no doubt that every book written is the sum of a great many more voices and influences than those who are directly referenced. This book carries the traces of the many extraordinary people who have shaped my understanding of literature and of the intersections between the head and the heart where so much that is important begins. There would have been no *Child in Shakespeare* were it not for Peter Holland and Stanley Wells, who set me on this path. Later joined by Lena Orlin, as series editors for the Oxford Shakespeare Topics, I was supremely privileged to work with these great Shakespeareans as the book developed in a different direction. Without exception, they have, in different, but powerful, ways, made it a better book and I am profoundly grateful for their perspicacity and unerring good judgement. I hope that the anonymous readers for Oxford University Press will see how important their guidance and encouragement has been to the manuscript and that I have learned a great deal from their wisdom. The many conversations I have had with Laurie Maguire have shaped this book more than she knows; from her extraordinary ability to see to the point of something in an instant to her breadth of knowledge, generosity and vibrant mind. Deanne Williams' invitation to contribute to her and Richard Preiss's edited collection, *Childhood, Education and the Stage in Early Modern England* (CUP, 2017) was a great gift for me and I am very grateful to her for that. I am very lucky to have exceptional friends who are also great intellects and I know that whether we talk about Shakespeare or shopping I am made vastly better by being in their presence. For more than this I am always thankful to Ruth Morse, Farah Karim-Cooper, Jaqueline Norton, Gordon McMullan, Lucy Hanington, Richard Scholar, Flip Gibbons, Tess McPherson, Beatrice Rose, Sophie Scott, James Lambe, Rachel Bliss, and my late and much-loved colleague, Russ McDonald. Peter Holland, Patrick Cheney and David Scott Kastan have supported me unfailingly throughout my career and I remain indebted to them for their intellectual and professional generosity.

I am also very lucky to have wonderful colleagues at Goldsmiths, in particular Michael Simpson for his tenacity and engagement with our research culture, and my head of department, Lucia Boldrini, for her support and compassion, as well as her vision in developing Shakespeare's studies at Goldsmiths College. My daily life at work is always made easier (and nicer) by the presence and hard work of Marian Perez, Rushmi Ahmed and Richard Bolley.

The writing of this book has been formed and defined by my children. Because I love them more than will ever be possible to tell them and because being a parent has taught me to find sermons in stones and books in the running brooks. But so, too, does being a child. And there is no doubt that I go on learning from my wonderful mother and the hope she brings that there is good in everything. I dedicate this book to my family, my extraordinary and brilliant husband, Jerry Brotton, and our children Ruby, Hardie, and Honey. Ruby, as my eldest, is my greatest and littlest Shakespeare companion who shows me something new every time we go to the theatre together: 'Into which state comes Love, the crowning sun: Beneath whose light the shadow loses form.' They are 'the lords of life, and life is warm'.

Contents

1

'And all my children?'

The best of mortals, and those who are not, love children; they may differ in means, the haves and have-nots, but all love children.

(Euripides, *Herakles*, 634–6)[1]

This quotation, from Euripides' 5th-century BC play, focuses the audience's imagination on the power of children to produce emotion. The love felt for children, as the best of mortals or the worst of them, signifies the power that children have to bind communities and individuals, as well as to destroy them. In Euripides' play, the hero is tormented into mistakenly killing his own children by Hera, Zeus's vengeful wife. Prevented from killing himself or even burying his children, Herakles leaves his city and his play a broken and desperate figure. Children, according to Euripides, can transcend the limits of individual moralities to become the dramatist's greatest weapon of feeling: nothing breaks a hero more than the destruction of love; and nothing reflects failure more than severing the ties that bind. But what is it about children that makes them such powerful registers of human emotion, and what does this power mean to the contexts in which it is explored? When King Lear looks at his youngest daughter and admits: 'I loved her most, and thought to set my rest | On her kind nursery' (1.1.121–2, F) we feel a tremor of the magnitude of the tragedy that will follow. Only the ferocity of that love will match the force with which Cordelia is punished. What binds the play-worlds of Euripides and Shakespeare is the love of children; whether unconditional or contingent, violent or nurturing, the child represents the single most powerful relationship in Shakespeare's drama, and the question that this book asks is, why?

One of the most emotive children in Shakespeare's canon never actually appears on stage but haunts the drama as a spectre of the limits of female

---

[1] Euripides, *Medea and Other Plays*, trans. Philip Vellacott (London: Penguin, 1963). As quoted by John Boswell, *The Kindness of Strangers: The Abandonment of Children in Western Europe from Late Antiquity to the Renaissance* (Chicago: University of Chicago, 1988), p. 37 n. 86.

monstrosity. The suckling infant that Lady Macbeth invokes to measure the strength of her commitment to murder has preoccupied critical interpretations of the play. Railing on her husband's wavering pledge to kill Duncan, she exclaims:

> What beast was't then
> That made you break this enterprise to me?
> When you durst do it, then you were a man;
> And to be more than what you were, you would
> Be so much more the man. Nor time nor place
> Did then adhere, and yet you would make both.
> They have made themselves, and that their fitness now
> Does unmake you. I have given suck, and know
> How tender 'tis to love the babe that milks me;
> I would while it was smiling in my face
> Have plucked my nipple from his boneless gums
> And dashed the brains out, had I so sworn as you
> Have done to this.   (1.7.47–58)

Considering this remarkable speech through different approaches to the narrative, whether psychological, historical, character, or plot based, L. C. Knight's now famous question, 'How many children had Lady Macbeth?' has come to represent the many divisive and productive approaches to Shakespeare criticism.[2] In a play so fascinated by the limits of what is natural, Lady Macbeth's speech presents a powerful example of her own terms of dehumanization. The lengths to which she is prepared to go, so explicitly outlined in her call to be 'unsex[ed]', are exemplified in the image of a smiling, nursing baby who will shortly have his brains dashed out by the woman who nourished him. Despite the many gruesome murders in *Macbeth*, this speculative image has come to dominate the play's reception as well as the characterization of Lady Macbeth.[3] Understanding her to be

---

[2] The critical responses to this scene are too many to list here, but the most formative approaches to character, motivation, gender, and maternity are outlined in the following works: A. C. Bradley, *Shakespearean Tragedy: Lectures on Hamlet, Othello, Lear and Macbeth* (London: Macmillan, 1905); L. C. Knights, 'How Many Children Had Lady Macbeth?', in *Explorations* (London: Chatto, 1946); Carol Chillington Rutter, 'Remind Me: How Many Children Had Lady Macbeth?', *Shakespeare Survey*, 57 (2004); Janet Adelman, 'Born of Woman: Fantasies of Maternal Power in Macbeth', in Marjorie Garber (ed.), *Cannibals, Witches and Divorce: Estranging the Renaissance* (Baltimore: Johns Hopkins, 1985); Kate Aughterson (ed.), *Renaissance Women: Constrictions of Femininity in England* (London: Routledge, 1995); Susan Frye, 'Maternal Textualities', in Naomi Miller and Naomi Yavneh (eds), *Maternal Measures: Figuring Caregiving in the Early Modern Period* (Aldershot: Ashgate, 2001).

[3] Justin Kurzel's film adaptation of the play, *Macbeth* (2015), starring Michael Fassbender, begins with the funeral of the Macbeths' child, suggesting that the 'missing baby', as Rutter calls it, defines and stands behind much of the play's action.

a woman capable of infanticide or as a woman who has suffered the most profound of griefs in the loss of a child positions her within a particular narrative within the play that makes her either accessible or irreprehensible. Whatever motivation we, as readers and audience members, want to ascribe to this image there is no doubt that within the context of the scene, and of the play world more generally, Lady Macbeth is talking about the frontiers of human commitment. She presents her husband with the scenario of the murdered baby as a marker of the limits to which she would go to 'had I so sworn as you | Have done to this'. Lady Macbeth's studied attempts to dehumanize herself in order to participate in the murder of Duncan largely revolve around her identity as a woman, and the maternal body. The speech which precedes this conversation with her husband in which she calls on 'you murdering ministers' to 'come to my woman's breasts | And take my milk for gall' to 'make thick my blood; | Stop up the access and passage to remorse' focuses our attention on her body as female, lactating and menstruating. To deny her body the right to childbirth and nursing is to simultaneously, so the play-world suggests, render her unnatural and therefore capable of anything, including regicide. The play has consistently generated a great deal of interest in the terms through which we may discover early modern conceptions of the natural, including the role that women and witches play in organizing structures of aberration and conformity. Despite the bearded women who inhabit the air, the men who murder, the images of bloodied bodies and ghosts, it is Lady Macbeth's imagined baby that remains as the play's most powerful marker of human horror. The focus of this book is those children, visible and imagined, who map the values, agonies, pleasures, and conflicts of the play-worlds they inhabit.

Early modern records of infanticide attest to the socially powerful ways in which women are cast as natural or unnatural according to their maternal identities. Frances Dolan's work has shown the staggering inequality that presides in cases of child murder where women are always more rapaciously and violently condemned than men.[4] Within the social imagination, mothers are understood to occupy a less powerful but in many ways more

[4] Frances Dolan, *Dangerous Familiars: Representations of Domestic Crime in England, 1550–1700* (Ithaca, NY: Cornell University Press, 1994); Peter Hull and N. E. H. Hull, *Murdering Mothers: Infanticide in England and New England, 1558–1803* (New York: New York University Press, 1981); Laura Gowing, 'Secret Births and Infanticide in Seventeenth Century England', *Past and Present*, 156 (1997), pp. 87–115; Keith Wrightson, 'Infanticide in European History', *Criminal Justice History*, 3 (1982); J. Sharpe, 'Domestic Homicide in Early Modern England', *The Historical Journal*, 24.1 (1981), pp. 24–48; Linda Pollock, 'Childbearing and Female Bonding in Early Modern England', *Social History*, 22 (1997), pp. 286–306; Randall Martin, *Women and Murder in Early Modern News Pamphlets and Broadside Ballads, 1573–1697* (Aldershot: Ashgate, 2005).

profound role than fathers: deviation from that role ruptures the entire fabric of social relations. Lady Macbeth's assertion that she is hypothetically capable of killing her own child supports her wider commitment to dehumanization. To kill your child is to sever all relationships with a functioning society. Lady Macbeth's imagined infanticide sets the tone for a play in search of the limits of human nature, a limit she defines in the presence of the child.[5] Much of the interest in Lady Macbeth's maternity has focused on the representation of gender and its pivotal role in the play's value system. Her particular references to her female body and the emotive context of breast-feeding make her an unusual and compelling symbol of failed maternity. A number of early modern texts, some written by women, support maternal breast-feeding as a god-given marker of the duties of procreation: some of these texts go further to suggest that a refusal or inability to suckle your own child is a profound rupture in a Christianized view of human order. Elizabeth Clinton's book *The Countess of Lincoln's Nurserie* (1622) attests to the social and emotional importance of breast-feeding, 'In setting downe whereof, I wil first shew, that every woman ought to nurse her owne childe'—whereby the mother's character is understood in relation to her abilities to nurse:

> I pray you, who that judges aright, the suckling of her owne childe the part of a true mother, of an honest mother, of a iust mother, of a syncere mother, of a mother worthy of loue, of a mother deseruing good report, of a vertuous mother, of a mother winning praise for it? All this is assented to by any of good vnderstanding. Therefore this is also a Precept, as for other duties, so for This of mothers to their children; which saith, whatsoeuer things are true...whatsoeuer things are honest, whatsoeuer things are iust, whatsoeuer things are pure, whatsoeuer things be worthy of loue, whatsoeuer things be of good report, if there be any virtue, if there be any praise think on these things, these things do and the God of peace shall be with you.[6]

Clinton's rhetoric reflects the socially powerful ways in which maternal breast-feeding is associated with 'virtue', 'honesty', 'love', 'justice', and 'worth'. To refuse to breast-feed, as some women of 'higher and the richer sort' do, is 'unthankful' and 'unnatural'.[7] Jacques Guillemeau, in his book *Childbirth, or The Happy Delivery of Women* (1612), goes even further when he claims that there is 'no difference betweene a woman that refuses to nurse her owne childe; and one that kills her child'.[8] Lady Macbeth continues to

---

[5] I discuss the role of nature, human and organic, in *Macbeth* in *Shakespeare's Nature: From Cultivation to Culture* (Oxford: Oxford University Press, 2014).

[6] Elizabeth Clinton, *The Countess of Lincoln's Nurserie* (London, 1622), pp. 6–7.

[7] Clinton, *The Countess of Lincoln's Nurseries*, p. 11.

[8] Guillemeau, *Child Birth* (London, 1612), Li2r.

confound expectations, since not only is it unusual for an aristocratic mother to nurse her own child but she then rehearses the destruction of an act or a bond that would have been unlikely to fall to her anyway. The image that Shakespeare constructs is less concerned with Lady Macbeth as a nursing mother and more about the moral landscape that the play confronts. The child of Lady Macbeth's imagined assault marks her as profane and unnatural because it enables her to review a value system and then to destroy it. More broadly, the entire play is concerned with such absolute distinctions between right and wrong, natural and unnatural, action and intention, and the image of the child, both in our shared imagination with Lady Macbeth, as well as Fleance and the little MacDuffs, supports a moral context of socio-political obligation. No amount of unsexing, so the play suggests, will render Lady Macbeth as appalling as the idea that she would kill her own child. The play sets up the expectation that Lady Macbeth can transcend her own terms of humanity but in fact she fails: she does not kill her baby and she cannot, in the end, kill the King because he resembled her father as he slept. Macbeth's murdering mind will take him to the limits of his fantasies of infallibility; Lady Macbeth's mind, on the other hand, will destroy her and in doing so return her to the organizing structures of right and wrong. Condemning the 'fiend-like queen' though her suicide, Malcolm's final speech looks forward to a future where the past is buried with its dead. Describing Macbeth as a 'butcher' but Lady Macbeth as 'fiend-like' sends her to hell as an inhumane copy of what she should have been. The play never actually commits to or presents such inhumanity but the legacy of the imagined death of an imagined infant will never, much like her desperate candle in the dark, leave her side.

How societies recognize, define, locate, treat, and represent children reveals a great deal about their cultural formation and socio-political identities.[9] Definitions of childhood vary depending on whether you follow chronological, lexical, philosophical, or legal boundaries. These boundaries change according to the impact of both lexical and social structures

---

[9] In the autumn of 2016, for example, 14 refugee children were allowed into the UK, from the Calais 'jungle', to be reunited with their families. *The Telegraph* newspaper ran the headline, 'These don't look like children to me', apparently recording a widespread anxiety about the status of these young people: these children were not what the right-wing press expected—they were too old, or tall, or well built, well dressed, too cheerful, or functional. One newspaper even went so far as to suggest that the children should have their teeth checked to prove they were under 18. So what kind of children were they expecting? The question is an important one because it reveals now, as for the sixteenth century, that the idea of the child is something culturally specific; and that the figure of the child adheres to certain historically precise expectations.

on terms of definition. Considering the challenges the historian faces in attempting to recover early modern perceptions of the child, John Boswell writes:

> Two sets of problems overlap: the semantic variability of terms for children and childhood, and historical changes in social structures and expectations regarding both. . . . Terms for 'child', 'boy' and 'girl', for example, are regularly employed to mean 'slave' or 'servant' in Greek, Latin, Arabic, Syriac, and many medieval languages. This is both a philological subtlety and a social one. In modern western democracies, everyone of sound mind achieves independent adult status on attaining a prescribed age: the primary distinction in social and political capacity is between children and adults, and everyone normally occupies each position in succession. But during most of western history only a minority of grown-ups ever achieved such independence: the rest of the population remain throughout their lives in a juridical state more comparable to 'childhood', in the sense that they remained under someone else's control—a father, a lord, a master, a husband etc.[10]

These networks of control define all of the Shakespeare's children on the early modern stage, whatever age they may be. Cordelia is one of Shakespeare's most famous children; like her sisters', her role is vilified, cursed, denigrated, and parodied by Lear throughout the play: from the serpent's tooth to the mock trial, the word 'child' and 'daughter' haunts the play as the last bastion of hope: like Pandora's box, perhaps, the child is the image on which all hope, as well as destruction, rests.[11] But this raises another question central to this book, and to Shakespeare's drama, which is what constitutes a child on the early modern stage? Cordelia is, to all intents and purposes, an adult in terms of her age, but she is a child in terms of her status and that is what drives the tragedy of the play. If we understand children through the contexts of power relations then it is perhaps no surprise that they become so central to Shakespeare's play-worlds.[12] If we also accept that the prevailing distinction between child and adult, based on independence, is a modern one, we can begin to appreciate that the dramatic fascination with children is not only about size or age, but it is also, and at times, overwhelmingly, about status: as Frances Dolan writes: 'even long after birth, after a child was physically and

---

[10] *The Kindness of Strangers* (Chicago: University of Chicago Press, 1988), pp. 27–8.

[11] Lear's vituperation, 'How sharper than a serpent's tooth it is | To have a thankless child' (1.4.251–2) observes his fatal and deeply held belief in the role of duty and obligation beyond that of individual feeling. The mock trial appears in the quarto only (3.6). The words daughter and child appear over 40 times within the play.

[12] As Boswell notes: 'The layers of complexity in Latin become ponderous. All humans were designated in the Latin Bible as the *pueri* of God (e.g. Isaiah 8:18, Wisdom 12:7, Hebrews 2:13), meaning both "children" and "slaves", drawing deliberately on the conflations underlying the word', *The Kindness of Strangers*, p. 29 n. 60.

legally distinct from its mother, both parents' relation to and responsibility for their offspring remained uncertain and contested.'[13] It is precisely this tension that remains so contested in *Hamlet*, where the scholar prince is increasingly defined as his dead father's son, suffering the agony of his mother's betrayal, and a remarriage that makes him 'a little more than kin, and less than kind' (1.2.65). It is this contested and uncertain relation that appears to fascinate Shakespeare's stage, and which will be the focus of this book.

To be a child in the early modern period was not, we might imagine, under so much scrutiny or of so much interest as it is today. The majority of familial records, historical and literary, focus on the parent, and give little or no consideration to the representation of the child in their own right. In her discussion of child murder, Betty Travitsky notes that: 'The woman who had broken out of bounds had great fascination for a society with rigidly ordered hierarchy in which women's subordination to men and their inferiority were axiomatic. But there were limitations to this interest. The drama therefore concerned itself with women as central actors in domestic crimes when those crimes involved other adults rather than infants who have traditionally been less valued under law than older persons.'[14] Travitsky's point is that the children themselves are not as interesting, or, as she puts it, 'beneath the notice of the playwright or the fascination of the playgoer', because they were accorded little status in the Elizabethan imagination. The status of the child was not privileged or suggestive of any entitlement beyond that of an inferior or slave.[15] Similarly, what it meant to be an Elizabethan parent was less about the quality of the adult position and more about the conformity of the child's role to certain Christian codes of behaviour. There are a surprisingly large number of books of this period which address children's behaviour, parenting, and education but they are all, without exception, mediated though a Christian narrative that supports the mantra, 'He who spareth

---

[13] *Dangerous Familiars: Representations of Domestic Crime in England, 1550–1700* (Ithaca, NY: Cornell University Press, 1994), p. 139.

[14] 'Child Murder in English Renaissance Life and Drama', *Medieval and Renaissance Drama*, 6 (1993), p. 76.

[15] Boswell notes how the conflation of child and slave retains traces of its philological heritage: Words for 'children' designate adults well into the high Middle Ages, and it is often impossible to be sure, without adequate context, whether the appellation is based on age or status, or both. ('Boy' is still used in English in the United States to disparage an adult male, particularly as a racial slur. In pre-modern Europe it was not precisely a insult but it was a negative and disempowering observation.) *The Kindness of Strangers*, p. 28. Many of the books which seek to address the relationship between father and child also address the relationship between master and servant; William Cotes's *A Dialogue of Diverse Questions demanded of the children to their father* (1585) is a typical example of such texts which produce conversational templates for the power relations which they represent where the superior (father/master) asserts themselves through a knowledge of scripture.

the rod, hateth his son' (Proverbs 13:24). Even the more liberal humanist writers like Roger Ascham, Erasmus, and Richard Mulcaster, while urging restraint in punishment and pleasure in learning, recognize that discipline is one of the most important conditions through which a child must develop.[16] In modern western cultures, being a mother or father is understood to be something of a privilege, and more, to be fulfilling in itself. But such value systems were not expressed as such in the early modern period. That is not to say that early modern parents were not fulfilled by their roles as parents, but comparable expectations were not in place: producing and bringing up children was a necessary hazard of sexual relationships and although a great deal of doctrinal writings considered the moral and religious 'office' of the parent, none represented it as an emotionally or socially fulfilling experience.

Perhaps unsurprisingly social history does not offer a consistent perspective on the status of the child in the early modern period. Lawrence Stone infamously argued that parental, and especially maternal, relationships were modulated by high infant mortality rates which necessarily adapted the emotional bonds of the family.[17] Linda Pollock and Keith Wrightson have been rigorous in their attack on Stone's thesis and shown that, while cultures of parenting change from one generation to the next, love remains a consistent marker in the evolution and development of the human species. Or, as Boswell states: 'Everywhere in Western culture, from religious literature to secular poetry, parental love is invoked as the ultimate standard of selfless and untiring devotion, central metaphors of theology and ethics presuppose this love as a universal point of reference and

[16] John Lyster's *A Rule on how to Bring up Children* (London, 1588) is unflinching in its commitment to physical punishment and forced obedience. Mulcaster's *Positions* (1581) asserts that children have a 'variety of wits' and must be understood to respond differently to the learning environment, to which they should not be brought too young: 'and we that teach do meet with to much toile, when poore young babes be committed to our charge, before they be ripe. Whom if we beat we do the children wrong in those tender years to plant any hatred, when love should take route and learning grow by liking', p. 24. Ascham, in *The Schoolmaster* (1570), notes that children should be taught 'cheerfully and plainly', p. 1v.
[17] The critical debate of the place and perception of childhood has moved on considerably in the last twenty years and some of the most significant contributions to this debate include Lawrence Stone, *The Family, Sex and Marriage, 1500–1800* (New York: Harper and Row, 1977), Philipp Aries, *Centuries of Childhood: A Social History of Family Life*, trans. Robert Baldick (New York: Knopf, 1962), Keith Wrightson, *English Society: 1580–1630* (London: Hutchinson, 1982); Linda Pollock, *Forgotten Children* (Cambridge: Cambridge University Press, 1983), Ralph Houlbrooke, *The English Family: 1450–1700* (London: Longman, 1984), Anthony Fletcher, *Gender, Sex and Subordination* (New Haven: Yale University Press, 1995), Gillian Avery and Julia Briggs (eds), *Children and their Books* (Oxford: Oxford University Press, 1989), Iona Opie and Peter Opie, *The Lore and Language of Schoolchildren* (Oxford: Oxford University Press, 1977); Lena Cowen Orlin, 'Rewriting Stone's Renaissance', *Huntington Library Quarterly*, 64.1–2 (2002), pp. 189–230.

language must devise special terms to characterise persons "wanting" in this natural affection.'[18] What does change most powerfully from one historical moment to another, however, is how cultures support the terms of 'natural affection'—corrective, punitive, educative, restrictive, devoted, or nurturing—how parents treat their children is a route map for the geography of social values.[19] Dorothy Leigh's *The Mother's Blessing* is one of the more unusual texts of the period, not only in being written by a woman but in the ways in which it understands maternal devotion as universal. A highly popular text, it went through over four editions in twenty years; it is offered by its author as a legacy to her children after her death and as a guide to ensuring their spiritual salvation. As Leigh sets out the importance of reading, for both male and female children, explaining why she has written the book and what she hopes to achieve, she reveals her perception of the role of the parent:

> My children, when I did truly weigh, rightly consider, and perfectly see the great care, labour, travaille, and continual study which parents take to enrich their children, some wearing their bodies with labour, some breaking their sleeps with care, some sparing from their own bellies and many hazarding their souls, some by bribery, some by simony, others by perjury, and a multitude by usury, some stealing on the sea, others begging by land portions from every poor man, not caring if the whole commonwealth should be impoverished, so their children enriched: for themselves they can be content with meat, drink and cloth, so that their children by their means may be made rich always abusing this portion of scripture: *He that provideth not for his own family is worse than an infidel*, ever seeking for the temporal things of this world and forgetting those things which be eternal.[20]

Leigh's message is somewhat contradictory. On the one hand she seems to disclose a powerful cultural understanding of the sacrifices that parents will make for their children and the subjugation of the self for the needs of the child; but at the same time she gently reprimands such earthly imperatives when true salvation can only be given by God. Yet even rehearsing the extent to which a parent will perjure or sacrifice themselves for their child

---

[18] *The Kindness of Strangers*, p. 38. Many of the texts and records on infanticide studied by both Dolan, *Dangerous Familiars*, and Travitsky, 'Child Murder' also focus on the deeply aberrant and 'unnatural' terms through which women who harm or kill their children are represented. See also John Bellamy, *Strange Inhuman Deaths: Murder in Tudor England* (Stroud: The History Press, 2005), who maintains that there is 'no sympathy expressed in print at least for a child in a tragic or traumatic situation... [therefore] clearly, there were few tears and thus no market for the suffering of children', p. 11.

[19] Frances E. Dolan, in her exploration of infanticide in the period, examines certain cases in which so powerful was the bond between mother and child that mothers could kill their children in an attempt to save them from further harm, *Dangerous Familiars*, p. 141.

[20] Dorothy Leigh, *The Mother's Blessing* (1616), pp. 1–3.

provides a greater understanding of the early modern child in context. Despite the zealous and punishing tones of many of these texts, the language of love is often in evidence. In a Christian humanist text about grief, *A Handkercher for parents wet eyes upon the death of children. A Consolatory Letter to a Friend*, the author, I.C., urges the grieving father to take comfort in the uncompromising inevitability of death while also acknowledging the profound and desperate sorrow of losing a child.[21] Although the relationship between parent and child is represented in often very different terms, the significance of that bond is never in doubt, as Richard Mulcaster suggests when he writes:

> In no other thing can one do more good than in respect to his children whether you consider the children persons, or the thing which is wished them. For in deed what be children in respect of their persons? Be they not the effects of God's performance in blessing? Or his commandment in increase? Be they not the assurance of a state which shall increase by sucession and not die in one brood? Be they not the parents natural purtract [portrait] their comfort in hope? For whom thye get all, for whom they fear nought? And can he which desire the good of this so great a blessing from heaven, so great a stay for the country, so great a comfort to parents devise how to pleasure them more in any other thing their care in provision.[22]

The language of 'care' as well as natural affection runs throughout Shakespeare's representations of children: complex and contested notions of 'nature' shape the dynamic between parent and child to represent a profound deviation from or assertion of the play's values. Natural, one of the most intricate terms in Shakespeare's lexicon, haunts the relationship between parent and child; at best an unshakeable marker of transcendent love and at worst a violation of human status itself, the language of 'nature' organizes the play-world's responses to forms of obligation.[23] When the ghost of Old Hamlet appears to his son, relating the circumstances of his murder, he pleads: 'If thou hast nature in thee, bear it not' (1.5.81), explicitly invoking the language of paternal duty to prick the sides of his son's

---

[21] I.C., *a handkercher for parents wet eyes, vpon the death of children. A Consolatory Letter to a Friend* (London: Printed by E.A. for Michael Sparkes, dwelling at the blue Bible in Greene Arbour, 1630).

[22] Mulcaster, *Positions* (1581), p. 287.

[23] Some of the most interesting work on the language of nature in Shakespeare's relationships focuses on the dynamic between the human and the animal and the contested ways in which the non-human world supports a model for human kinship as well as a point of departure, through which the human must assert its superiority; see Erica Fudge, *Brutal Reasoning, Animals, Rationality and Humanity in Early Modern England* (Ithaca, NY: Cornell University Press, 2006); Karen Raber, *Animal Bodies, Renaissance Culture* (Philadelphia: University of Pennsylvania Press, 2013); Charlotte Scott, *Shakespeare's Nature: from Cultivation to Culture* (Oxford: Oxford University Press, 2014).

intent. Hamlet is an interesting case in point, since the play makes it clear that the hero is thirty years old, while at the same time making his role as a son, although not a child, central to the dramatic scope of the narrative. As Keith Thomas wryly observes, children are 'ubiquitous' in the early modern period, but how are we to understand the representation of children as distinct, say, from sons and daughters, in literature?[24] Is each child unique to the story to which it belongs or do children bring with them a set of interpretative codes through which we recognize the values of their presence? Until the mid-sixteenth century children are rarely represented as themselves in literature: they are often talked about but not talked to; predominantly, they are illustrative of Christian arguments about obedience, duty, and innocence. Representational children tend to function symbolically, as moral examples of individual or collective failure. With the development of sixteenth-century theatre, however, children take on a powerfully visual role in the growth of early modern drama.

'WHAT ARE THEY CHILDREN? WHO MAINTAINS 'EM? HOW ARE THEY ESCOTTED?'

The question as to why children become so fundamental to the beginnings of public theatre is both complex and contradictory.[25] Early theatre records indicate that the use of children in drama evolved from the inherently performative nature of boys' humanist schooling. On the one hand, the rhetorical and oratorical imperatives of early modern education supported a pedagogical emphasis on the value of public speaking, on role playing, persuasion, debate, and eloquence. The classical models of dialogic debate demonstrated highly articulate examples through which children could explore the language of persuasion as well as performance.[26] Many choir schools further developed the performative range of their children through song and the long-held celebration of the pre-pubescent, soprano voice. Several of these children grew up performing both locally, in custom-made theatres for invited audiences, and privately, for elite or specialist events. Alongside the grammar and choir school traditions, however, there was

[24] Keith Thomas, 'Children in the Early Modern Period', in Gillian Avery and Julia Briggs (eds), *Children and their Books* (Oxford: Oxford University Press, 1989), p. 51. Oliver Ford Davis, *Shakespeare's Fathers and Daughters* (London: Bloomsbury, 2017).
[25] Edel Lamb, *Performing Childhood in the Early Modern Theatre: The Children's Playing Companies 1599–1613* (Basingstoke and New York: Palgrave Macmillan, 2009).
[26] Lynn Enterline, *Shakespeare's Schoolroom: Rhetoric, Discipline and Emotion* (Philadelphia: University of Pennsylvania Press, 2012). Enterline is especially interested in what she calls the 'theatricality of everyday life', in which imitation and punishment provide formative models of social development.

another more demotic tradition that celebrated the rise of the child in public performance. The medieval tradition of the boy bishop produced a ceremony, associated with the feast of Holy Innocents, whereby a boy was chosen to 'play' the bishop and parade through local communities with his selected children as members of the church, performing offices. Over the course of the sixteenth century the event became increasingly riotous and was finally abolished by Elizabeth I, having been previously stopped by her father, Henry VIII, but revived by Mary Tudor. The ceremony offers a resurrection of the child in response to Herod's Massacre of the Innocents after the birth of Christ. The symbolic identification of the child in the adult role, performing Christian offices, attempts to reclaim the allegorical figure of innocence while at the same time promoting the cultural and ideological power of organized misrule. The ceremony fell out of favour in the Elizabethan religious settlement not just because of its Catholic heritage but also because the boys' behaviour breached the boundaries of decorum reminding us of the deeply hierarchical structures of Elizabethan society.[27] Out of these traditions, however, developed a certain fascination, and familiarity, with the child in a dramatic role. The rise of the 'children's companies', throughout the sixteenth century, testifies to an enduring, if not all together transparent, enthralment to the young body on stage.[28] Recovering the cultural complexities of the child in performance is further hampered by a deep ambiguity as to how the child was perceived by the spectator. Much of the work in this area focuses on the types of plays that the children's companies performed, the audience's penchant for satirical comedy, the burlesque, and the 'self-consciously privileged transvestitism for the purpose of erotic titillation'.[29] The critical focus has often been on the physical presence of the body beneath the costume and theatre's powerful ability to simultaneously reference what it shows as well as what it conceals. Understanding the role that anti-theatricalists played in producing this critical culture, Evelyn Tribble explores the ways in which academic focus began to perceive children's companies as not only transgressive but also exploitative.[30] As she suggests, Alfred Harbage's description of the

---

[27] E. K. Chambers, *The Medieval Stage*, vol. 1 (Oxford: Clarendon Press, 1903), pp. 336–71; Harold Newcomb Hillebrand, *The Child Actors: A Chapter in Elizabethan Stage History* (New York: Russell & Russell, 1964), pp. 27–9.

[28] Michael Shapiro, *Children of the Revels: The Boy's Companies of Shakespeare's Time and their Plays* (New York: Columbia University Press, 1977). Michael Witmore, *Pretty Creatures: Children and Fiction in the English Renaissance* (Ithaca, NY: Cornell University Press, 2007).

[29] Susan Zimmerman, 'Disruptive Desire: Artifice and Indeterminacy in Jacobean Comedy', in Susan Zimmerman (ed.), *Erotic Politics: Desire on the Renaissance Stage* (London: Routledge, 1992), p. 39.

[30] Evelyn Tribble, 'Pretty and Apt: Boy Actors, Skill and Embodiment', in Valerie Traub (ed.), *The Oxford Handbook of Shakespeare and Embodiment* (Oxford: Oxford University Press, 2017), p. 628. See also Peter Stallybrass, 'Transvestism and the "Body Beneath": Speculating on the Boy Actor', in Zimmerman (ed.), *Erotic Politics*, pp. 64–83.

poor child player, 'little more than a chattle…huddled up in lodgings' and 'subjected to the miserable conditions of the children's company', has been somewhat revised by a more nuanced and diverse understanding of the role of the boy performer on the early modern stage.[31] Nevertheless, cultural anxiety about the exploitation or erotic potential of the child remains central to the current critical recovery of the past, and it may remain perennially opaque as to exactly what the early modern audiences wanted from their 'tender youths'. As Tribble says, understanding the diversity of attitudes to children in performance has allowed criticism to move away from specific models of exploitation and titillation to something that recognizes the significance of the role beyond the 'body beneath'. Within this context, the child actor can be sincere, sexualized, satirical, or vulnerable but there is no doubt that, especially within the children's companies, the diminutive or immature nature of the actor was a celebrated part of his role.[32]

One of the most intriguing and unresolved aspects of understanding children in the early modern period is undoubtedly perceptions of the children's companies. The most recent work in this area, Edel Lamb's *Performing Childhood in the Early Modern Theatre*, analyses how the children's companies produced certain discourses around both boy players and conceptions of childhood. Exploring the many strands that make up the children's acting companies, including managers, actors, shareholders, playwrights, and theatres, Lamb focuses on the institutional identity of performing children, and argues that 'the subjectivities of these players were shaped by their experiences of playing and being defined by these companies as children'.[33] According to Lamb, children were defined as such according to the varied interests and expectations of the children's companies which advertently or otherwise dramatically shaped the culture's perception of youth, as well as how institutional identities are formed in performance. Within this context, age, to a greater extent, was irrelevant, as many of the children's companies 'defined their players as children regardless of their biological age', focusing instead on 'a category of child player that is determined by a variety of factors within these theatrical institutions beyond that of physical age'.[34] What emerges from Lamb's study is a sense in which these companies, formative in the development of early modern theatre, drove a certain cultural perception of the child that was at once both symbolic as well as contrived.

[31] Alfred Harbage, *Shakespeare and the Rival Traditions* (New York: Macmillan, 1952), pp. 32–3.
[32] Bart Van Es, *Shakespeare and Company* (Oxford: Oxford University Press, 2013), pp. 205–6.
[33] Edel Lamb, *Performing Childhood in the Early Modern Theatre: The Children's Playing Companies, 1599–1613* (New York: Palgrave, 2009), p. 2.
[34] Ibid. p. 3.

Criticism has tended to address the problems of definition inherent in the term 'child' through a focus on puberty as the defining shift into adulthood. Mark Heberle, among others, has calculated the number of child parts in Shakespeare's drama on the basis of how the part is referred to ('boy', 'child') and the requirements of the role.[35] Within these terms we can assume the terminal for the child's part to be about 13 or 14, not only because this was the age at which boys were recruited to play women but also because it was the age at which children were understood to enter into a new phase of adolescence as well as be legally able to marry.[36] The heroine in *Romeo and Juliet* becomes an interesting case in point, both symbolically and dramaturgically, since the character's age, on the threshold of her fourteenth birthday, suspends her somewhere between being played by a boy child as a girl child or an adolescent boy as a woman. Unlike Ben Jonson, Thomas Middleton, and many other Elizabethan playwrights, Shakespeare did not write specifically for the children's playing companies that developed from the early sixteenth century onwards. Rosencrantz's sardonic comment that 'There is, sir, an eyrie of children, little eyases, that cry out on the top of question, and are most tyrannically clapped for 't. These are now the fashion, and so berattle the common stages' (*Hamlet*, 2.2.326–9) has usually been interpreted as an authorial dig at the popularity of the children's companies, and Shakespeare's reluctance to engage with them.[37] It may well be true that Shakespeare was annoyed with the success of the children's companies, especially Burbage's Children of the Chapel, but they were not direct competitors, since not only did the children's companies specialize in classical and satirical drama, but their successes were highly unstable. From the early sixteenth century the children's

[35] Heberle finds 'thirty-nine child characters in the canon', '"Innocent Prate': King John and Shakespeare's Children', in *Infant Tongues: The Voice of the Child in Literature* (Detroit: Wayne State University Press, 1994), p. 30; Mark Lawhorn finds 'forty-five, not counting the choristers mentioned in Henry VIII', Kate Chedgzoy, Susanne Greenlaugh, and Robert Shaughnessy (eds), *Shakespeare and Childhood* (Cambridge: Cambridge University Press, 2007), p. 233; Morriss Henry Partee, following Thomas Pendleton, claims that 'Of the roughly one thousand characters that Shakespeare creates, only about thirty are children', but he also acknowledges 'the enormous range of Shakespeare's references to childhood', *Childhood in Shakespeare's Plays* (New York: Peter Lang, 2006), pp. 1, 7.

[36] Laws on marriage largely focused on parental consent, which was a legal necessity. A statute of the 1550s made it a criminal offence for a girl under the age of 16 to marry without parental consent, Christopher W. Brooks, *Law, Politics and Society in Early Modern England* (Cambridge: Cambridge University Press, 2008), p. 380. In early modern France, on the other hand, an edict of 1556 set the legal age for marriage, without parental consent, at 30 for men and 25 for women, Richard Adair, *Courtship, Illegitimacy and Marriage in Early Modern England* (Manchester: Manchester University Press, 1996), p. 138.

[37] Anne Righter (Barton) considers this 'a striking and curious exception to Shakespeare's general practice', *Shakespeare and the Idea of the Play* (Harmondsworth: Penguin, 1967), p. 139.

companies had enjoyed considerable good fortune, developing their reputations through music and pageants.[38] As an offshoot of choir schools, the children, usually aged between 8 and 12 years old, were highly prized for their musical abilities, frequently entertaining in royal and noble households.[39] Trevor Lenman suggests that the boys held a fascination for audiences, especially Elizabeth, who seemed compelled by both their voices and their appearance. The desirability of these children has been evidenced by reports of young boys being abducted or forcibly removed from their parents in order to perform. Bart Van Es interprets this as somewhat standard practice for the boys' companies and claims that there was something inherently sexualized about the coterie audiences' experience of child players.[40] Lenman, however, notes that the accusations of abduction were in fact taken up by the Privy Council and by no means endorsed by the Crown.[41] Henry Clifton, father of the 13-year-old Thomas, who was 'with great force and violence' seized by Giles's men, filed a lawsuit against Giles, in which he described the outrageous implications of taking children out of school to perform in plays, 'for their own corrupt gain and lucre'. Clifton's greatest complaint was not only that these young boys were forcibly taken with 'great terror and hurt' but that they were not being employed to sing:

> Being children no way able or fit for singing, nor by any of the said confederates endeavoured to be taught to sing, but by them, the said confederates, abusively employed, as aforesaid, only in plays and interludes.[42]

Listing the names of various children who have been taken from their grammar schools, many of which were very highly regarded, including the school run by Elizabeth's former tutor, Richard Mulcaster, in order to

---

[38] Hillebrand notes the creation and use of 'experimental theatre[s]' for child actors within schools as early as 1538, *The Child Actors*, pp. 19–20. Shapiro, *Children of the Revels*.

[39] Mulcaster, in Germaine Warkentin (ed.), *The Queen's Majesty's Passage and Related Documents* (Tudor and Stuart Texts, Volume 4) (Toronto: Centre for Reformation and Renaissance Studies, 2004); see also Michael Witmore, *Pretty Creatures: Children and Fiction in The English Renaissance* (Ithaca, NY: Cornell University Press, 2007), pp. 62–3.

[40] See Bart Van Es's comments in an article for Oxford University's Magazine, <http://www.ox.ac.uk/news/2013-06-19-exploitation-elizabethan-child-actors-revealed>.

[41] Lenman writes, 'Glancing over the list of choir boys in 1574, we are reminded that one of them "being one of his principall plaiers" was abducted from Sebastian Westcott's menage in December 1575. This affair became a matter for immediate Privy Council action and a letter was sent to the Master of Revels instructing them to "examine such persons as Sebastian suspected and to procede with such as be founde faultie according to lawe"', 'The Children of Pauls, 1551–1582', in David Galloway (ed.), *The Elizabethan Theatre II* (London: Macmillan, 1970), p. 27. Cf. J. R. Dascent, *Acts of the Privy Council* (London, 1890–1907), ix, 156. Hillebrand, citing *Privy Council Registers, Elizabeth*, II, 408 (*The Child Actors*, p. 124).

[42] Glynne Wickham et al. (eds), *Theatre in Europe: A Documentary History: English Professional Theatre, 1530–1660* (Cambridge: Cambridge University Press, 2000), pp. 264, 265.

perform in plays, the heart of this complaint is both personal and ideological: the abduction of his own son and the violation of a child's education by 'the base trade of a mercenary interlude player'.[43] Such outrage recognizes, at least in part, a sense of childhood or difference, in which the child, albeit the privileged few, had access to an education and the development of certain skills commensurate with personal success. These documents record how the potential of the child player is moving beyond the chorister to the schoolboy, not specifically trained in singing, children with 'no manner of sight in song or skill in music', but able to perform through their grammar school education, 'acting parts in base plays and interludes'.[44] Henry Clifton clearly thinks very little of public theatre but what is not clear, however, is whether young boys were being taken from their schoolrooms in order to perform in plays because of their rhetorical training, or whether their age and physicality was the most desirable commodity they could offer. Perhaps it was both: but the detail with which Clifton records who was taken and from which school suggests that particular boys were targeted and this may well have been because they were especially powerful rhetoricians or convincing orators. Clifton's outrage at the children's abductions focuses on their loss of education, and the miserable plight of the player, rather than anxieties about exploitation. Many of these children grow up in the theatre and become adult players, their childhood spent in rehearsal, quite literally, for the adult world.[45] Going through these documents it is hard to discern what is at stake here: the idea of the child, innocent, vulnerable, dependent, unique; or the abuse of a value system which prizes humanist education over public entertainment.[46] The central concern of this book is to discover what makes children significant on Shakespeare's stage; how they are represented and in what ways Shakespeare reflects the culture in which he is writing and to what extent he re-imagines it.

How and why the child was valued on the Elizabethan stage remains highly ambiguous: Shakespeare's use of children, and his particular fascination with the relationship between children and parents, points to the dramatic power of the dynamic between affect and action. It is often, if not always, this intersection that proves the most compelling in Shakespeare's

---

[43] Ibid. 265.   [44] Ibid. 265–6.

[45] Edel Lamb perceives the children's companies as institutionalizing a view of children through performance that has less to do with age and more to do with the invention and re-invention of youth on the early modern stage. One the one hand the children's companies allowed children to transition into adulthood as a performance, on another hand they fetishized youth by continually re-inventing it through new roles, *The Performance of Childhood*, esp. chapter 4.

[46] Jane Eva Baxter, *The Archaeology of Childhood: Children, Gender, and Material Culture* (Oxford, New York, and Toronto: Alatamira Press, 2005), pp. 57–80. Jane Eva Baxter (ed.), *Children in Action: The Archaeological Papers of the American Anthropological Association*, No. 15 (2005).

drama. What happens, his works seems to ask, when you dramatize the affective bonds of both power and dependence? Much of the documentary evidence of the period appears to rehearse the same question. Elizabeth I issued various writs of impressment which allowed children to be forcibly engaged by choir masters when voluntary recruitments were low.[47] The child's unique status or stage in life made them highly valuable commodities for the Chapel Royal but it also fetishized the young body as a source of fascination rather than individuality. One of the most dominant and prevalent adjectives associated with child actors and parts is the term 'little': Ben Jonson's now famous epitaph on the child actor with the Children of the Chapel, Salomon Pavy, who died at the age of 14, in 1602, reads: 'Weep with me, all you that read | This little story.' This diminutive term is picked up throughout the period to identify child actors, irrespective of their age, and probably their size.[48]

At times, Shakespeare's use of children seems to directly coincide with some of the contemporary contexts through which they become visible. In an unusually satiric scene in *Love's Labour's Lost* involving a child actor Shakespeare exploits the terms of both size and sense. In an exchange between the lothario Armado and his page, Mote, Shakespeare appears to animate the comedy of the relationship between boy and man. Working through a loquacious conversation on the terms of melancholy, Mote refers to his master as 'my tough señor':

ARMADO: Why 'tough señor'? Why 'tough señor'?

MOTE: Why 'tender juvenal'? Why 'tender juvenal'?

ARMADO: I spoke it, tender juvenal, as a congruent epitheton appertaining to thy young days, which we may nominate 'tender'.

MOTE: And I, tough señor, as an appertinent title to your old time, which we may name 'tough'.

ARMADO: Pretty and apt.

MOTE: How mean you, sir? I 'pretty' and my saying 'apt'? Or I 'apt' and my saying 'pretty'?

ARMADO: Thou 'pretty', because little.

MOTE: Little pretty, because little.   (1.2.10–21)

[47] See, for example, Thomas Giles's Commission to impress Children, 1585; Nathanial Giles's commission to impress children, 1597; and the bill of complaint which records Henry Clifton's lawsuit against Nathanial Giles for the abduction of his son Thomas, 1601. Wickham et al. (eds), *Theatre in Europe*, pp. 262–7.

[48] Emma Smith, in *Shakespeare's First Folio: Four Centuries of an Iconic Book* (Oxford, Oxford University Press, 2016) records Sir Edward Dering's payment to two child actors in 1623, 'little Thompson there' and 'little Bourne, ye boy there', whom Smith identifies as Theophilus Bird. Both actors were in their mid-teens at this point, so the term 'little' suggests their role rather than their size, and Smith later records Dering referring to his own son in these terms.

The comedy here centres on the supple terms of size and age: the 'tough señor' is also the old senior, designated as such by the 'tender juvenal', the young juvenile. Playing on the difference between boy and master, senior and junior, tough and tender, the two characters exploit their love of learning and language to engage in a layered badinage about the differences between them. Here, the master's seniority is mocked, for he is no longer 'little', but also affirmed as in a position of power. The delight for both Mote and the audience is seeing that position of authority parodied in precisely the language through which it tries to assert itself. The playful way in which the terms 'señor' supply the multilingual references to seniority are also played out in a different key through the word 'pretty' and its proximity to 'little'. 'Pretty', especially if it is delivered in a mock Spanish accent, sounds very much like the French word, 'petit', also meaning little, so that the linguistic and comic emphasis of this scene is on Mote's size, equally pertinent to his name as meaning 'speck'. The classical contexts through which both characters move to parse their pretentious conversation about melancholy and the works of Juvenal are brilliantly undercut by the playful focus on the multilingual references to size. Mote, it seems, is little, pretty, and young: Armado is old, tough, and senior. Beyond the contexts of the schoolroom a more demotic conversation emerges between master and page in which size, and looks, matter. Here the child actor is celebrated as 'apt', 'pretty', and 'little' and a powerful match for the adult master, not in terms of status, but in stage presence.[49]

Despite the focus on the dynamic between child and master here, there is little that defines this theatrical space as childish. Quite the contrary, what makes Mote such a powerful stage presence is his ability to navigate the adult world with a curiosity and alacrity that permeates adult pomposity, but does not quite puncture it. At these moments there is no stable or unique concept of childhood or the child that operates at an ideological level, governing and focusing the cultural representation of the child.[50] There are, however, a great many narratives that inform, if not define, the reception of the child in the public imagination. Some of these are biblical and radiate from Herod's Massacre of the Innocents, in which the child, especially the male child, is understood to symbolize both purity and sacrifice: some of these narratives are contemporary, celebrating the

---

[49] Tribble discusses perceptions of boy actors in 'Pretty and Apt', pp. 628–40.

[50] That is not to say that being a child in the sixteenth and seventeenth century was anything other than brutal at times and a number of records show that children were treated at best indifferently and at worst appallingly; see Ivy Pinchbeck, *Children in English Society: From Tudor Times to the Eighteenth Century* (London: Routledge and Kegan Paul, 1969); R. A. Colon and P. A. Colon, *A History of Children: A Socio-cultural Survey Across Millennia* (Westport, Conn.: Greenwood Press, 2001).

child through his voice, his body, and his performative skill: others are familial, understanding the child to belong to a network of kinship in which love and futurity can be celebrated through the body as a creative force.[51] Not one of these narratives is stable or consistent: sometimes the child is valorized and celebrated, in Elizabethan progresses or morality tales; at others, the child is diminished, overlooked, and victimized. The role of the child in coronation ceremonies also testifies to the power of the symbolic body: often dressed as Truth, Faith, or Justice, children could represent qualities as distinct from the adult world.[52] Increasingly, however, we are constrained by problems of definition: the 'boy' actor could perform from the age of 7 to his early twenties; within that time, he could play a child, an adolescent male, or a female.[53] How we understand the term 'boy' or 'child' actor varies not only from play to play but from one historical moment to the next. Michael Shapiro has suggested that audience members gained particular pleasure from watching children perform adult roles, precisely because of the discrepancies between what the children performed, as adult characters, and what they knew, as children. According to Shapiro, playwrights like Marston, Jonson, and Chapman exploited opportunities to draw attention to the 'prepubescence of most, if not all, of the child actors'. For the most part, playwrights would amplify the bawdy elements of the text, including puns and double entendres, by having the youngest and smallest members of the companies perform these roles.[54] Shapiro, following a popular trend in mid-twentieth-century criticism,

---

[51] Since Chedgzoy, Greenlaugh, and Shaughnessy's important collection *Shakespeare and Childhood*, there has been a renewed interest in the child in Shakespeare studies which has produced some wonderful books, including Carol Chillington Rutter's *Shakespeare and Child's Play: Performing Lost Boys on Stage and Screen* (London and New York: Routledge, 2007); Marjorie Garber, *Coming of Age in Shakespeare* (London: Methuen, 1981), Morriss Henry Partee, *Childhood in Shakespeare's Plays* (New York and Oxford: Peter Lang, 2006); Deanne Williams, *Shakespeare and the Performance of Girlhood* (Basingstoke: Palgrave, 2015); Katie Knowles, *Shakespeare's Boys* (Basingstoke: Palgrave, 2015); Bruce W. Young, *Family Life in the Age of Shakespeare* (Westport, Conn.: Greenwood, 2009), Tom MacFaul, *Problem Fathers in Shakespeare and Renaissance Drama* (Cambridge: Cambridge University Press, 2012); as well as a number of books that are not specific to Shakespeare, including Elizabeth Goodenough and Mark Heberle (eds), *Infant Tongues: The Voice of the Child in Literature* (Detroit: Wayne State University Press, 1994); A. Gavin (ed.), *The Child in British Literature: Literary Constructions of Childhood* (Basingstoke: Palgrave, 2012); Naomi J. Millar and Namoi Yavneh, *Gender and Early Modern Constructions of Childhood* (Aldershot: Ashgate, 2011). Catherine Belsey, *Shakespeare and the Loss of Eden* (New Brunswick, NJ: Rutgers University Press, 1999), pp. 18–25.
[52] These figures were present at the coronation of Edward VI, who was also a child at the time, Hillebrand, *The Child Actors*, p. 30.
[53] David Kathman, 'How Old Were Shakespeare's Boy Actors?', *Shakespeare Survey*, 58 (2005), pp. 220–46; Marvin Rosenberg, 'The Myth of Shakespeare's Squeaking Boy Actor—or who Played Cleopatra?', *Shakespeare Bulletin*, 19 (2001), pp. 5–6.
[54] Shapiro, *Children of the Revels*, pp. 106–7.

does not understand this particular use of child actors to be 'smutty and depraved', since 'the belief in childhood innocence, on which such a judgment depends, would have been anachronistic in the period under discussion'.[55] However, he goes on to admit that 'self-referential discussions of actors, acting, plays, playhouses and stages...are far more common in plays acted by children's companies than in plays by adult companies'. The plays of the children's companies drew attention to the immaturity and youth of the child actors which suggests that these young bodies were of particular significance on the early modern stage. Unlike Shapiro, and many of the historians on whom he bases his discussion, I do not believe that the idea of childhood innocence was anachronistic: quite the contrary, the moral and emotional difference between the adult and the child is fundamental to the use of children on stage, both as children and in performing adult roles. Shakespeare's children never take part in ribaldry or deliver bawdy puns: sometimes they witness such comments or action, and sometimes they are drawn into it against their will, but the power of the child on Shakespeare's stage is that he or she stands in contrast to the adult world, excluded from its knowingness not a part of it. As Mistress Quickly remarks in *The Merry Wives of Windsor*, ''tis not good that children should know any wickedness. Old folks, you know, have discretion, as they say, and know the world' (2.2.115–17).

That Shakespeare did not write expressly for the children's companies should not be taken as a meaningful reflection of his interest in children on stage: quite the contrary; the plays of the children's companies, though formative in conceptions of youth, did not represent children as such, but young adolescent boys playing adults. Shakespeare created many parts for such figures in his female roles: but unlike many of his contemporaries, Marlowe and Jonson, for example, Shakespeare wrote parts for children, as children: young figures under the age of 14 who could not be played by an adolescent boy but demanded to be played by a child. During the 1590s the children's companies were disbanded due to their involvement in the Marprelate controversies and they never reached the full heights of their success again.[56] Although many of the companies regained favour and success at the beginning of the seventeenth century, their popularity waned and very few remained active after 1613. The demise of the children's companies almost directly coincides with Shakespeare's use of children on

[55] Ibid. 107. Shapiro cites Alfred Harbage's disgust at the use of children performing adult humour and refers to the highly influential work of Philippe Aries to support his claim that 'in belief childhood innocence' was anachronistic.

[56] W. Reavley Gair, *The Children of Paul's: A Story of a Theatre Company, 1553–1608* (Cambridge: Cambridge University Press, 1982), pp. 110–12. Katherine Butler, *Music in Elizabethan Court Politics* (Woodbridge: Boydell, 2015).

stage and it is my contention that he 'borrowed' child actors from The Children of the Chapel, Windsor, and St Paul's during their periods of non-performance. Shakespeare's greatest parts for children—Arthur in *King John*, the Princes in *Richard III*, Juliet in *Romeo and Juliet*, and the children of the late plays, or Romances, Mamillius, and Marina—would have all required a competent child actor, many of whom would have been available during this time, having worked with Burbage. The teenagers of the late plays, Miranda and Perdita, would probably have been played by an apprentice or boy player, rather than a child. Juliet is the most fascinating representation here since she is both child and teenager, and much of the play's emotional range depends on the actor successfully conveying the conflicting impulses of both. Shakespeare's text pointedly identifies Juliet as approaching her fourteenth birthday, a date she does not live to celebrate, and her character's age of 13 aligns her with the youngest of the boy players and therefore at the beginning of the spectrum of what the theatre companies advertise as 'children'.[57] In terms of this book's premise, Shakespeare's teenagers or adolescents are the most complex figures to analyse since they seem to occupy a unique space that is neither explicitly childish nor explicitly adult. Much of Shakespeare's greatest drama of childhood can be found in this murky wasteland between the worlds of the adult and child: none of these spaces is clear or easily navigable; rather they are fraught with injustice, disempowerment, partial information, and marginal authority, and the adult-child comes to represent a tragic strain in Shakespeare's music.

This book explores the agency and role of the child within the terms of the play-worlds they inhabit. Despite the rising interest in social history and the significance of the family in the early modern period, the majority of scholarly work in this area remains focused on the parent, rather than the child. Carol Rutter's *Child's Play* is an exception here, since she specifically engages with the performance of childhood, both early and modern, on Shakespeare's stage. But I want to shift the focus away from the performance of childhood to the individual figures of the child and to engage critically with the range and dramatic significance of children in Shakespeare's imagination. As we have come to recognize, Shakespeare's plays are full of children; young adults, adolescents, and infants, all inhabit his social and political worlds as powerful figures of conflict, tragedy, resolution, and hope.[58] In a period in which children have been excised from

[57] Kathman identifies the age range of apprentice boy players as between 13 and 21 years old; although some were enlisted as young as 11 it was not in fact legal to do so.

[58] Boswell records some of the complexities of definition: 'Scholarly discussions of chronological classification are not necessarily tied to social attitudes. Isiodore of Seville articulated a categorization that was followed, with variations, by much of the learned literature of the Middle Ages. According to him, up to 6 years constituted infancy, 7 to 13

the records, given no agency, rights, or special identity, why do they occupy such demonstrative roles in early modern theatre? The period that gave birth to public entertainment also created and sustained the performing child to an extent that would never be repeated in English theatrical history.

'SPEAK THOU, BOY: | PERHAPS THY CHILDISHNESS WILL MOVE HIM MORE | THAN CAN OUR REASONS'

The term 'child' appears over 200 times in the plays, and with a few notable exceptions, *Richard II*, for instance, it almost always refers to progeny.[59] Within this context Shakespeare seems most interested not only in the figure of the child itself but also in the relationship between parent and child and the potential drama or conflict that produces on stage. The most numerous uses of the word 'child' appear in *King John, Romeo and Juliet, Measure for Measure*, and *Richard III*, with *The Two Noble Kinsmen, King Lear*, and *Much Ado about Nothing* coming a close second. What all these plays have in common is a dramatic narrative that revolves around the child as a site of conflict. Intriguingly, however, what drives the significance of their stories is not the child as a small person—perhaps vulnerable or innocent, although this is certainly at stake in some of these plays—but the child as a marker of human success or failure, whether that is in the production of certain values or the preciousness of individual relationships. Sweeping across the range of instances of the child that these plays produce we find the child as a foetus (*Measure for Measure*); the child as a young boy or girl (*King John, Richard III*); the child as an adolescent (*Romeo and Juliet*); and the child as an emerging adult (*Much Ado, Two Noble Kinsmen*,

childhood, 14–27 adolescence, 28 to 48, youth, 49 to 76 maturity (*senectus*); and 77 to death, old age…' (*The Kindness of Strangers*, p. 30) Civil and religious laws evince a more complex and variegated picture. Among Romans, 'minority' extended from puberty, which occurred by statute from 14 to age 25. During this period freeborn 'minors' had legal capacity to act on their own, although even as adults Romans were not freed from paternal authority. Anglo-Saxon law considered males to be adults at 10, at least in terms of responsibility for their actions; the sixteenth-century Salic law made this distinction at 12. Contemporary ecclesiastical laws from the same parts of Europe, however, drew the line between child and adult somewhere between 15 and 20 and referred to 10-year-olds as 'young children', *The Kindness of Strangers*, pp. 31–2.

[59] Richard is unusual within this context because he uses the child as a metaphor for grief and for separation, 3.2.8; 4.1.149. In the poetry, however, the term is scarcely used by Shakespeare, once in *Venus*, six times in *Lucrece*, and eight times in the *Sonnets*, which, again, suggests Shakespeare's predominantly dramatic interest in the child as a site of conflict rather than as a poetic figure or trope.

and *Lear*). What becomes immediately clear from any brief assessment of Shakespeare's children is that it is not their age that makes them significant but the networks of love that they produce or confound on stage. This seems to be corroborated by the relative paucity of references to children in Shakespeare's poetry. Although the first 1–17 sonnets, the so-called procreation sonnets, are concerned with the fair youth reproducing his beauty in the fathering of a child, the poet's voice is not interested in the child itself but in the seduction of the young man through persuasion to reproduce. Similarly, the brief allusions to the child in sonnets 21, 37, 59, 124, and 143 are figurative markers of devotion or responsibility rather than young subjects. Bearing this in mind, we might assume that Shakespeare's dominant interest in the child is as an embodied figure of dramatic force and yet how that presents itself and what it means across the play-worlds changes throughout his works.

Observing the meaningful ways in which Shakespeare's children function as dramatic sources of conflicts produces certain patterns within the drama. The most abundant uses of the word 'child', and references to the figure of the child, occur firstly in the history plays and secondly in the comedies. Given what we are noticing about Shakespeare's children this is probably not surprising: the child produces dynastic struggles and images of historical responsibility as well as questions concerning allegiance, memory, obedience, and male authority. Within the narratives of chronicle history, the child emerges as a central register for the failure of the past as well as the responsibilities of the future: in the structure of comedy, which depends on cycles of disobedience and containment, the child becomes an instructive figure in the rehearsal of dominant institutional values. Where, in both genres, we might see the idea of the child as functioning symbolically, producing or representing a set of values as well as individual characteristics, in the tragedies the child appears much more idiosyncratically and powerfully determined by the parents (mostly fathers) who love them. Over the course of this book I explore the contexts and assumptions that drive Shakespeare's use of the child on stage and what makes them such vibrantly dramatic figures of collective and personal feeling.

My decision to organize the book along generic lines needs defending, if we consider genre to be at best arbitrary and at worst misleading. I consider genre to be neither of these things but instead a useful category of expectation that both defies and defends its borders. Genre serves a convenient purpose in allowing readers and audience members to anticipate certain conditions—love, death, marriage—they may not be exclusive but they serve as expedient pointers in the experience and unfolding of the story. Attending to genre as an organizing principle requires us to be aware of how we define its experience and whether we are guided by its formal or affective properties, or both.[60] According to Lawrence Danson such properties 'exist, then, in a kind of circularity between the general and the particular', or, as Alastair Fowler says, as belonging to 'tradition' but also 'a sequence of influence and imitation and inherited codes connecting works in the genre'.[61] Understanding genre in this way allows us to witness Shakespeare's children within the contexts of this circularity and connection—between the general traditions in which their story inheres and the particular effects that they produce: it is precisely this tension or dynamic that appears to engage Shakespeare's children and animate their place within the drama. Within this context I want to examine what shapes the representation of Shakespeare's children as spectres of historic responsibility (*Richard III*, for example) and the broken victims of parental failure (*Lear, Romeo and Juliet*); what makes them distinct on the stage (the child as opposed to the young woman, both played by boys), and how the symbolic networks of innocence, vulnerability, silence, and submission are reproduced or contested by Shakespeare.

Recent work on theatrical companies and early modern schooling has revealed a deeply layered culture of performance operating within the education systems, whether this is in the schoolroom or the guilds.[62] As I have already indicated, young boys and men could be brought up through a structure of learning and obligation in which they performed as choristers, boy players, apprentices, and adolescent actors.[63] Equally formative is the practice of playing that informed the study of rhetoric and the inherently theatrical space of the classroom which required students to rehearse, imitate, mimic, and memorize set speeches.[64] Within this culture, children learn to perform 'feeling', especially within the context of impassioned speeches, often 'achieving eloquence by giving a voice to the emotions of precisely those whom its rhetorical training was designed to exclude: women... and characters who could never aspire to gentility'.[65] Imitating

[60] Lawrence Danson, *Shakespeare's Dramatic Genres* (Oxford: Oxford University Press, 2000), pp. 3–4.

[61] Ibid. 4; Alastair Fowler, *Kinds of Literature* (Oxford: Clarendon Press, 1985), p. 42. David Scott Kastan, *Shakespeare and the Shapes of Time* (London: Macmillan, 1982) explores human conceptions of time in relation to genre, which is of particular relevance to Shakespeare's children in the history plays.

[62] For a detailed exploration of the inception and development of the children's playing companies, Hillebrand, *The Child Actors*, esp. pp. 9–89.

[63] David Kathman, 'How Old Were Shakespeare's Boy Actors?', pp. 220–46. David Kathman, 'Grocers, Goldsmiths and Drapers, Freemen and Apprentices in the Elizabethan Theater', *Shakespeare Quarterly*, 55.1 (Spring 2004), pp. 1–49.

[64] Lynn Enterline, *Shakespeare's Schoolroom: Rhetoric, Discipline and Emotion* (Philadelphia: University of Pennsylvania Press, 2011). Keith Thomas, 'Children in the Early Modern Period', pp. 63–5.

[65] *Shakespeare's Schoolroom*, p. 24.

and inhabiting another person's body or emotions is central to Shakespeare's drama and signposts some of the most important developments in early modern theatre. Lynn Enterline refers to the 'theater's ubiquitous presence in the classroom' in which children were taught to persuasively represent alternative arguments through the performance of rhetorical techniques and that 'the school's highly articulated hierarchy governed the repeated exercises that were to establish, within each boy, a set of approved gestures, tones, and facial expressions'.[66] Alongside the intellectually demanding regime of the classroom, recent studies of children's acting companies have tended to focus on the special interest that the young body afforded. Evelyn Tribble's current work on embodiment and acting suggests that boys' companies presented a certain physicality that was especially alluring, including 'a high level of proficiency and technical ability'.[67] In this way, both the schoolroom and the theatre exercised the child through verbal and physical skills centred on persuasion, lucidity, embodiment, virtuosity, and delivery. Within this regime, however, the idea of the child as unique may be lost, since the skill is in transcending the limits of the juvenile body rather than representing them. Shakespeare, however, evinces a special interest in childishness; in that stage of life which may be categorized as distinct from adulthood and through which the playwright explores some of his drama's most affective bonds.

Locating an established version of childishness in the early modern period has its own historical and conceptual complexities. As Michael Witmore has shown, the performative power of children, particularly in pageants and progresses, afforded them the role of visual spectacle that was simultaneously mechanistic and spiritual, ambiguous and arresting. The child's ability to represent adult concerns but without the adult's reasoning was a source of both intrigue and anxiety: 'child performers became a kind of living wonder, showing adults the free-floating power of music, spectacle and speech in a world where reason was not the originating force (or discriminating recipient) of highly affecting displays.'[68] Within such contexts the primary focus of the child remains its relationship to the adult world, and the extent and success of its participation, imitation, or affirmation of adult values. At what point, if any, do children acknowledge or exert their own agencies? Shakespeare's children are especially interesting in this regard since they are, more often than not, condemned by the adult worlds in which they live, but they also resist those adult worlds, challenge them, defy them, and question them in ways that do not always locate them as

---

[66] *Shakespeare's Schoolroom*, pp. 41, 40.
[67] *Early Modern Actors and Shakespeare's Theatre: Thinking with the Body* (London: Bloomsbury, 2017), p. 13.
[68] *Pretty Creatures*, p. 70.

childishly immature but as separate. Witmore's emphasis on the child as visually arresting but intellectually deficient does not always seems appropriate: one of the distinguishing features of Shakespeare's children is their perspicacity. In *Henry V*, for example, shortly after the King's rousing speech into the breach, a 'boy', fighting alongside Nim, Bardolph, and Pistol, is left alone on stage to reflect on his adult companions:

> As young as I am, I have observed these three swashers. I am boy to them all three, but all they three, though they should serve me, could not be man to me, for indeed three such antics do not amount to a man. For Bardolph, he is white-livered and red-faced—by the means whereof a faces it out, but fights not. For Pistol, he hath a killing tongue and a quiet sword—by the means whereof a breaks words, and keeps whole weapons. For Nim, he hath heard that men of few words are the best men, and therefore scorns to say his prayers, lest a should be thought a coward. But his few bad words are matched with as few good deeds—for a never broke any man's head but his own, and that was against a post, when he was drunk. They will steal anything and call it purchase...I must leave them, and seek some better service. Their villainy goes against my weak stomach and therefore I must cast it up.

(3.2.27–41; 49–51)

Here, in the midst of a contested war, Shakespeare places the child alone on stage to consider his position in relation to the adults around him. Using the term 'boy', to suggest his youth as well as his inferiority, Shakespeare produces a speech which offers a profound reflection on the inadequate value system that places status before ethics. As the boy attests, he is young and he is servile but he can see through the antics of his adult companions, and more than that, he judges them to be wrong. Exercising the kind of insight rarely attributed to children, this boy observes the moral failures of the adults around him. He, the child, can recognize the value of precepts, where Nim cannot; he, the boy, knows the difference between violence and courage, where Bardolph does not; and he, the inferior, understands integrity, where Pistol does not. The clear-sighted and poignant reflections that this speech affords places the child centre stage at a moment when war is at its most theatrically glorious. Yet, the underside to that glorious war is the likes of such dispossessed villains as Bardolph, Nim, and Pistol who have been disenfranchised and beggared by the process. The boy's recognition that he is more than these men, and yet made nothing by them, reflects on the play's wider critique of war where power and politics, not ethics and integrity, drive the narratives of success. The boy's earlier lament: 'Would I were in an alehouse in London. I would give all my fame for a pot of ale, and safety' (3.2.10–11) is deeply poignant after Henry's aria to those who would shed their blood with him and 'Cry,

"God for Harry! England, and Saint George!"' (3.1.34). The child speaks with truth and valour, honour even, in a way that the adults of this play cannot.[69] This is a trenchant example of Shakespeare's use of children: they critique the adult world yet are also products of it. There is no other early modern playwright so fascinated and absorbed by the perils and potentials of hypocrisy, paradox, and ambivalence and their manifestations through the eyes of the child.

In many ways, the impact of the child on Shakespeare's stage stems from their ability to remain distinct from the adult world while also aware that they are compelled, dreadfully and exhilaratingly, to become part of it. The terrible, but theatrically intense, paradox of Shakespeare's children is that they represent something unique to the narratives they inhabit but it is not sustainable: the children in Shakespeare's plays cannot survive as they are: they must die, grow up, or get married. This is the tragedy of childhood, it is always in the process of becoming history. Yet, if childhood is distinct, if the child is separate from the adult, rather than in preparation for it, the most powerful moments of drama occur at that instant of realization, when the child, as it were, 'is the father of the man'.[70]

In contemporary western cultures, we tend to privilege childhood as a discrete space while also recognizing the imperatives of socialization, or preparation for the adult world. For the early moderns, the boundaries between adult and child are more porous. While several early modern texts, legal, religious, or vocational, defined the shift into adulthood at around 14 or 15 years of age, many of them also recognized that the child remained in service to their parents until they died. Although girls could be betrothed at a very young age, especially in association with dynastic alliances, in practice they did not live independently or with their husbands until they were well into their twenties. The average age for marriage for women of this period was their late twenties and for men their mid-twenties. Similarly, young men and boys serving apprenticeships to masters of guilds or livery companies were bound for approximately six or seven years, from the age of 13 or 14 to their early twenties. Children sent out to work in service could go from as young as 7 years old and remain until their mid- to late teens.[71] To be a child in the early modern period was to be bound by a series of obligations—parental, social, economic, or professional—but in a highly hierarchical society children were understood

[69] Katie Knowles writes very well about the 'Boy' in *2 Henry IV, Shakespeare's Boys: A Cultural History* (Basingstoke: Palgrave Macmillan, 2014), pp. 112–19.
[70] William Wordsworth, 'My Heart Leaps up'.
[71] Anthony Fletcher, *Gender, Sex and Subordination, England 1500–1800* (New Haven and London: Yale University Press, 1995).

to be at the bottom of the social order and therefore dependent on a network of ties that reflected their inferiority.[72] Yet, as Boswell explains, only a minority of early modern adults ever reached the kind of economic or social independence that we associate with contemporary adulthood. Shakespeare's fascination with the child allows him to develop his prevailing interest in forms of obligation and affective relationships; whether through violence, politics, succession, desire, love, or revenge the child is an increasingly dominant figure of dramatic power precisely for the contested and tenuous position they occupy.

Although specific terms of childhood are somewhat indistinct in Shakespeare's drama, it often functions as an evocative reference point in the construction of relationships.[73] In *A Midsummer Night's Dream* and *The Merchant of Venice* it becomes a locus of friendship, in which the idea of a shared childhood defines a bond between characters that predates the life of the play-world. The history that the characters refer to, 'all school-days friendship, childhood innocence' (*Midsummer Night's Dream*, 3.2.202), demarcates a time that remains out of reach but powerfully formative in the representation of the relationships on stage. In the tragedies, the idea of childhood is invoked at moments of crisis to gesture towards a time, world, place where the bonds of kinship still hold. In *King Lear*, the 'child-changed' King invokes 'the offices of nature, the bond of childhood' (2.4.178) as an organized structure of obligation and belonging that exists a priori in a socialized world, whereas in *Romeo and Juliet*, the young hero represents childhood as a moment in time, a precious beginning that moves uncompromisingly forward. Recognizing their impending doom, Romeo tells Juliet, 'Now have I stained the childhood of our joy' (3.3.95). While the idea of childhood seems to be informed by remembering, it is usually accompanied by a sense of loss, longing, or regret, and signals back

---

[72] Anthony Fletcher, *Growing Up in England, The Experience of Childhood, 1600–1914* (New Haven: Yale University Press, 2008), Ilana Krausman Ben-Amos, *Adolescence and Youth in Early Modern England* (New Haven and London: Yale University Press, 1994). Linda Pollock, *Forgotten Children, Parent–Child Relations from 1500–1900* (Cambridge: Cambridge University Press, 1983). On the significance of hierarchies in early modern theatre see Stephen Orgel, *The Illusion of Power: Political Theatre in the English Renaissance* (Berkeley: University of California Press, 1975).

[73] Although there is little that represents the materiality of childhood on Shakespeare's stage—Mamillius's nurses and stories are the closest we come to its evocation on stage—the aesthetics of childhood are a frequent symbolic structure in performances, especially *The Winter's Tale*; cf. Carol Chillington Rutter, *Shakespeare and Child's Play* (London and New York: Routledge, 2007), pp. 96–150. Philip Greven recognizes a 'persistent theme of ambivalence towards infancy', which suggests that many evangelical parents expressed both a sense of love and affection for their infant children and a sense of distrust and fear as well, *The Protestant Temperament: Patterns of Childrearing, Religion, Experience, and the Self in Early America* (New York: Knopf, 1977), p. 28.

to something that the stage chooses not to represent. We see this at its most powerful in *The Winter's Tale* where shared memories—grief, loss, childhood, and the broken bonds of the past—form the edifice upon which the comedy must rise phoenix-like from the ashes of tragedy.

Conflict is central to all drama but Shakespeare is especially adept at generating the kinds of conflict that produce multiple experiences of the same phenomena. While there are a great many references to the child and children, though many fewer to childhood, how the plays talk about the state and how they represent it are often at variance. If there is an overriding atmosphere of childhood and children in Shakespeare it is one of loss and of the time that *was*, rather than *is* happening on stage. Beholden to the adult world, the child is invoked as a symbol of kinship, love, and duty; they are also an acute marker of destruction, pain, punishment, and retribution. To hurt, kill, or remove the child is to infringe upon or destroy the 'offices of nature', 'the bonds of childhood', or the 'joy' that they can represent. The semantic field of the child becomes a resonant marker for the play's value system as well as its moments of affective power. In this way, how Shakespeare's plays describe children and how they are represented are often strikingly different: at the most obvious level this might be because it is not the child who speaks of him- or herself but the adult remembering themselves as a child; while those children who speak as such on stage rarely exhibit anything idiosyncratically childish; rather, as the early modern schoolroom would support, they speak as interlopers in an adult world. But what makes children unique on Shakespeare's stage? The answer is almost always their attitude to the story they inhabit and the relationships they occupy rather than their age. Children, for Shakespeare, occupy a powerful space in the ways in which they erupt into the adult world: often disenfranchised, excluded, or oppressed, children belong to a counter-narrative in which the adult world is confronted, rarely successfully, by its own failings. How we understand and define the children in Shakespeare's drama is largely dependent upon the relationships they inhabit and the affective landscapes they control.

The voice of the child on Shakespeare's stage is predominately defined by status, where the presence and role of the parent condemns the character to a certain position within the play. These are often the most enthralling representations of the child, since Shakespeare is keenly invested in the drama of emotion rather than institutional structures of age. Focusing on the drama of feeling I have divided the book into four sections which correspond to genre, rather than biological stages. Beginning with the history plays I consider the role of the child in talking about the past. The figure of the child has often become a powerful image of political failure and social responsibility and Shakespeare's history plays are critically invested in how the child functions in this way. As victims of adult action, the child comes to represent an acute space of loss, powerlessness, and grief: but it is not the child who suffers the anguish of history but the adult, tormented by the spectre of failure, responsibility, and wrongdoing; the dead children of the past become torments to an eternal present. In the tragedies, however, the children emerge as independent of the shackles of history, like Romeo and Juliet, crawling towards a version of free will in which they have the apparatus to make their own deaths, if not their own lives. The comedies tell a different story of childhood, however, in which the majority of young people are on the threshold of marriage and attempting to relinquish their childlike status of dependence in order to become parents themselves. Here, childhood is something that preceded the play: a formative memory or experience, it shapes the characters' journeys away from their young selves and into the adult world.

Although the Histories, Tragedies, and Comedies represent very different stages of the child's life, from toddler to teenager, they share a profound interest in the difference, for better or worse, between the adult and the child. The late plays, or Romances, however, which correspond to the plays written between 1611 and 1614, seem to mark a clear shift in their preoccupation with the figure of the child. I end the book with a focus on some of these plays because they represent the culmination of Shakespeare's theatrical investment in the child.

To be a child in Shakespeare's plays is to take part in a theatrical world in which all roles or identities are assumed. The child performs their role according to the relative dynamics in which they are put. As with Shakespeare's adults, men or women, there is no comprehensive view of children, neither is there one of old age nor teenagers; rather the child establishes his or her childishness in relation to the networks in which they exist.[74] Thus to be a child in Shakespeare is to be in a constant state of performance and nowhere is this more transparent nor more tragic than in the history plays. One of the central questions addressed in this book is what makes a child childish? The answer is modulated throughout Shakespeare's drama as each play is in search of its own representation of the child that is both unique to that play but also recognizable within the larger frameworks of Elizabethan and Jacobean drama. The individual

---

[74] Following Thomas Pendleton, Partee identifies 'of the roughly one thousand characters that Shakespeare creates, only about thirty are children, and only thirteen of these have fairly significant roles', *Childhood in Shakespeare's Plays*, p. 7. Heberle notes thirty-nine child characters in Shakespeare, 'including the boy actor merely functioning as a servant, messenger or performer', *Infant Tongues*, p. 30. Mark Lawhorn provides an annotated list of the children in Shakespeare's plays, which numbers forty-five, *Shakespeare and Childhood*, pp. 233–48.

play-world's representation of their child or children depends on to whom they are speaking, what role they have within the play's moral or narrative arc, and how they, as children, shape or impose upon the other characters in the play. Apart from serving men or messengers children are the only characters in Shakespeare's drama that can reside, or even preside, on stage and remain silent without losing the impact of their role. Indeed, one of Shakespeare's most powerful and also most pathetic children, King Henry VI, is silent for a good deal of the first part of the tetralogy and of few words for much of the second part. Only in Part 3 does Henry perform longer speeches and take a dominant vocal role in the drama. Only one other demographic in Shakespeare performs silence so effectively and that is, of course, women. It is perhaps no coincidence, then, that the same bodies who play children may well have played women. Essential, silent, abused, valorized, and vilified women and children shape a good deal of the emotional and moral density of Shakespeare's drama. Here I will look at the various stages of childhood that Shakespeare presents, and the dramatic lives that children inhabit, from the mewling infant to the truculent teenager; growing up in Shakespeare's drama is a life-threatening, and life-changing, business.

2

'Never such Innocence'

Mourning Children in the History Plays

Halfway through Shakespeare's *Richard III*, and at the zenith of Richard's murderous appetite for kingship, he malevolently reflects on the young prince's precociousness: 'So wise so young, they say, do never live long' (3.1.79). 'What say you, uncle?' (3.1.80), enquires the young prince, apparently unable to hear: 'Without character fame lives long,' Richard replies disingenuously. This is a unique moment in Shakespeare's drama because it is the only instance when a character breaks through another's aside. It is particularly significant that the character is that of a child. The electric atmosphere between Richard and the young princes is entirely dependent on the differences between the adult and the child worlds. This difference is maintained by the instability of words, to slip from a fixed sense and offer up the murky world of interpretation. Relishing his duplicitous position, Richard admits: 'Thus like the formal Vice Iniquity, | I moralize two meanings in one word' (3.1.82–3). Critics have frequently noted that Shakespeare does not present a necessarily recognizable version of childishness in which the child can be linguistically and imaginatively distinguished from the adult but here he points to one of the most vertiginous moments in any child's life, which is the failure to understand the adult and the adult's wilful manipulation of the child's ignorance. The play does not make clear the extent to which the prince did actually hear his uncle, and whether he attempts to reveal his knowingness, or whether he is convinced by Richard's false repetition, and was genuinely confused by what he heard. This ambiguity is key to the space in which Shakespeare locates the complexity of the child's relation to the adult world. Left alone in a world of implication, the prince's attempt to insert himself into his uncle's aside registers the force of adult language to withstand the attempts of the child.[1] Our interpretation of this moment greatly contributes to

---

[1] See also my essay, 'Incapable and Shallow Innocents: Mourning Shakespeare's Children in *Richard III* and *The Winter's Tale*', in Richard Preiss and Deanne Williams (eds),

how we perceive the young princes in *Richard III*: whether the boys come across here as precocious and knowing little people or tragically powerless instruments of adult machinations informs the play's larger commitment to its tragic structures.

As much of Shakespeare's drama testifies, to be innocent or ignorant is both a blessing and a curse. But this pivotal scene with the young princes is entirely determined by the extent to which the boys may speak as well as the degree to which the boys may know. Richard's relish in recognizing that he may 'moralize two meanings in one word' refers to the adult's distinct powers of cognition: he, the grown-up, understands how meaning can operate at different levels and how the child, predominantly literal, is excluded from that knowledge. One of the most powerful ways in which Shakespeare represents children is not in their idiomatic terms of innocence or play but in their deafening exclusion from the rites of language.[2] To understand double-meanings, to read body language or inference and gesture, is to be initiated into the multifaceted world of adult communication. The dangerousness of the prince's ignorance is amplified by his response to Richard's false repetition of the aside. Returning to their conversation about the Tower, where the children are forced to 'repose', the young prince wonders, 'Did Julius Caesar build that place?' What follows is a powerfully ironic conversation about history, posterity, and forms of record. The young prince speaks through the language of the schoolroom, sententious, repetitious, and rudimentary; he reflects:

> Death makes no conquest of this conqueror,
> For now he lives in fame, though not in life…
> An if I live until I be a man,
> I'll win our ancient right in France again,
> Or die a soldier as I lived a king.   (3.1.87–8, 91–3)

Richard's following aside takes great relish in the irony of these words, not only in the boy's ill-fated optimism that he will live to be a king but also in the kind of proverbial wisdom that such children were being taught. When Richard responds: 'Short summers lightly have a forward spring,' he again manipulates proverbial wisdom for its proleptic effects. The precocious (forward) young boy will have a short summer, as it were, and die before he can become king. Turning the generic language of the schoolroom to

Childhood, Education and the Stage in Early Modern England (Cambridge: Cambridge University Press, 2017).

    [2] Garber, *Coming of Age*, pp. 80–110, Opie and Opie, *The Language and Lore of School Children*, pp. 21–36; Ilana Krausman Ben-Amos, *Adolescence and Youth in Early Modern England* (New Haven and London: Yale University Press, 1994), esp. pp. 28–34.

his unique advantage Richard highlights the distance between youth and experience and between lore and life.

The drama of this distance is predominantly animated by the image of the child: a figure of all our previous selves, vulnerable through inexperience and potent through potential. As if to develop this point further, Shakespeare has his young princes reflect on adult meaning and intention. When the younger prince arrives into the scene he recalls a comment made by Richard,

> O my lord,
> You said that idle weeds are fast in growth;
> The Prince my brother hath outgrown me far...
> And therefore is he idle?

RICHARD DUKE OF GLOUCESTER

> O my fair cousin, I must not say so.   (3.1.102–4, 105–6)

Once again highlighting the relationship between words and meaning, the prince confronts his uncle with a literal interpretation of his remarks. One of the great pleasures of watching or listening to children is observing the ways in which they can, without guile, dismantle the structures that adults put in place to control them. One of these structures is of course knowledge: the implication here is that Richard knows more than the young prince and therefore, when questioned on the validity of his comments, he should seemingly stick by them. Instead, of course, Richard makes an exception, revokes his original meaning, and flatters the prince as a king. Richard is playing a long game here and his ability to unsettle as well as educate the children is alarming. The children, however, either intensely naive or instinctively astute, attempt to push the point. The disjuncture between the adult and child worlds becomes increasingly ominous as the two boys, apparently secure of the representational stability of words, enter deeper into Richard's world. When the young York asks for his uncle's dagger, something Richard will give 'With all my heart', his elder brother enquires: 'A beggar, brother?' to which the young boy responds:

> Of my kind uncle that I know will give,
> And being but a toy, which is no grief to give.   (3.1.113–14)

Within these brief lines Shakespeare compresses two defining elements of the adult/child relationship. The first is decorum: the prince gently reprimands his younger brother for asking an adult to give him something before it may or may not be offered; the second is the disjunction between fantasy and reality, or make-believe and lived experience. The young prince is suspended on the edge of the adult world; presumptuous and fearless he sees instruments of violence as toys and toys as trifles that can be given away. For this child, like many others, all weapons are toys and all toys are animated by the imagination. The elder prince's admonishment here gestures towards a knowingness that is amplified in Richard's portentous gift of the dagger, with all his heart. The point, I think, of this elaborate and carefully constructed scene is to dramatize both the pathos and the power of childhood. To live, as adults do, in a world in which all meaning is subject to interpretation and distortion and there are no toys, only objects of work or weaponry, is to be experienced; to be exempt from that world as a child is to be free, but only for so long and up to a certain point. Shakespeare's princes may be ignorant of their uncle's intentions (although this is debatable) but they are not carefree. This scene like so many of Shakespeare's representations of children explores the agony of innocence and the dreadful legacy of experience. Recognizing his brother as an irritation to Richard, the prince asks, 'Uncle, your grace knows how to bear with him.' To which the young York replies:

> You mean to bear me, not to bear with me.
> Uncle, my brother mocks both you and me.
> Because that I am little, like an ape,
> He thinks that you should bear me on your shoulders.   (3.1.128–31)

The extent to which this retort reveals the young boy as either highly astute or pathetically ingenuous depends on performance but Shakespeare allows for the possibility of both. Most children, depending on their exposure, will accommodate forms of disability until they are instructed to do otherwise. It is not entirely clear at whose expense the joke is—the little boy as an ape or the hunchback uncle as a fool. Yet, for all of Richard's malice within this play, the one thing he is not is a fool. The power of this moment, as Buckingham is so quick to comment on, is the compelling space between the adult and the child:

> With what a sharp, provided wit he reasons!
> To mitigate the scorn he gives his uncle
> He prettily and aptly taunts himself.
> So cunning and so young is wonderful.   (3.1.132–5)

The child, who can remain ignorant of the duality of language while at the same time using it so proficiently and to his advantage, is 'wonderful'. But the wonder that Buckingham feels is dependent on the young York's vulnerability. He can admire such 'cunning' in a child where he would despise it in an adult. The young princes emerge from this scene as precocious and pathetic, as brilliantly adept and terrifyingly vulnerable. Taking the young boys to the limits of both their power and their understanding, Shakespeare exploits one of the most important characteristics of the child, which is their trust of an adult. In order to effectively characterize the young princes as children Shakespeare promotes the dangerous distance between language and meaning. Richard's asides, double entendres, and puns allow him the space of interiority where what he means can be only partially or complexly reflected in what he says. Children have no such theatrical interiority precisely because they adhere to a system of signs in which language is both fixed and assertive. One of the most defining and often charming aspects of the child is their inability to self-censor. Socialization, paradoxically, teaches the child that not everything they think can or should be said out loud. Only when the child realizes that they must keep quiet, lie, or obfuscate does the possibility of an interior self emerge. Shakespeare's understanding of the child as transparent becomes even more dramatically powerful when they are in the company of adults.

The dynamic between two or more characters that differentiate in their cooperation with forms of representation is exceptionally rich for Shakespeare who exploits it not only through the figure of the child but through cross-dressing, letters, and other forms of sensory manipulation. Putting your characters and your audience in different positions of comprehension allows Shakespeare to examine and develop a variety of techniques, including irony, narrative, characterization, and identification. Children are a key element in this development because, unlike other character types (women, Jews, Moors, for example), they are ethically uncomplicated. Rarely do we see a child in a position of moral culpability (the exception here might be the 'Boy' who procures Tyrell for the murder of the young princes, 4.2.35–6); rather they must become who they are in front of us, on stage or in the eyes of the play-world. The dramatic potential that Shakespeare creates in presenting his children as untainted by language as a system of manipulation is endlessly enriched by the threat, and knowledge, that these young people will be corrupted. The adult world of interpretation is always snapping at the heels of the young bodies and Shakespeare exploits this with varying degrees of subtlety across the history plays.

'AY, IS IT NOT A LANGUAGE I SPEAK?'

Child characters are unique in Shakespeare's drama because they are represented as not fully, or even partially, equipped with the language of equivocation. Shakespeare's young children (the princes, Arthur, Prince Henry, Mamillius, young Rutland, young Talbot, for example) do not have the agency or experience to recognize inflection, implication, or obfuscation; those children on the cusp of adulthood (Romeo, Juliet,

Miranda, Mariana, Perdita, Ophelia) are painfully, often tragically, initiated into the adult world of words where meaning becomes contingent, contextual, and conflicted. Distinguishing children in this way—as only partially aware of the world of words—explains the degree to which children are expected to remain silent. The Victorian adage that 'Children should be seen and not heard', for example, has an extensive pre-history in the linguistic separation of the child from the adult world.[3] Buckingham's observation that 'this little prating York | Was... incensed by his subtle mother' (3.1.150–1) recognizes the child's chatter as an idle echo of the parent. He speaks as a child (prating) but he is informed by the intrigues of the adult (subtle mother). Richard, however, refuses to see the young York as a powerless engine of his mother, instead he is a

> parlous boy
> Bold, quick, ingenious, forward, capable.
> He is all the mother's, from top to toe.   (3.1.153–5)

Perhaps in justification of the atrocities he will sanction or perhaps because Richard himself denies the individuation of the child ('I had no father, I am like no father', *3 Henry VI*, 5.6.780) he denudes young York of his childlike status and renders him a mini version of his mother.[4] In the moment that Richard describes the boy as 'capable' he makes him an adult: as one adept at comprehension and understanding the young boy is no longer protected by his childlike status, and, as if to make this unequivocal, Richard compares him to his mother, 'from top to toe'. In direct contrast to the Duchess of York's earlier rendition of her grandchildren as 'incapable and shallow innocents' (2.2.18), the degree to which children are defined as 'capable' represents their ability to understand, and take part in, the adult world. Representing the child in these terms tells us more about perceptions of children per se than the individual characters. In contrast to the young princes, Clarence's children, distinguished only as 'girl' and 'boy', are represented as symbolic receptacles of adult fears and emotions. In the scene with their grandmother, the old Duchess of York, we witness the pitiful portraits of two ignorant and unknowing people who can only respond to, rather than communicate with, their adult company. Calling them 'incapable and shallow innocents', the Duchess remarks on Richard's machinations, 'O that deceit should steal such gentle shapes, | And with a virtuous visor hide foul guile' (2.2.26–7). The

---

[3] See Gillian Avery, 'The Voice of the Child', in Goodenough and Heberle (eds), *Infant Tongues*, pp. 16–27.

[4] The Queen also refers to him as 'a parlous boy', 2.4.35. Here, however, the emphasis seems to be on mischievous rather than dangerous. See Bethany Packard, 'Richard III's Baby Teeth', *Renaissance Drama*, 41 (2013), pp. 107–29.

children's inability to comprehend 'deceit' defines them as 'incapable', and the pun on 'steal' suggests that Richard robs them of everything: their father, their innocence, and, finally, their lives. Defining children in this way helps the play-world to establish its tragic range. While the portrayal of Clarence's children is no doubt pathetic, the children do not move beyond their roles as reactionary ciphers for the old Duchess and Queen. What this scene does establish, however, is the foundation upon which the idea of the child is built. Bereft of their father, of information about his death, of empathy, and of clarity, the children wail in choric tones a generic grief that resonates with the women as only a version of their much more profound adult loss.[5] The Duchess of York's loss is greater, so she tells us, not because she loves more but because she understands more:

> Was never mother had a dearer loss.
> Alas, I am the mother of these moans.
> Their woes are parcelled, mine are general.   (2.2.78–80)

This scene, in which women and children compete for the depth of their grief, verges on the absurd in its crude rendition of loss but the baseline from which we view these children is important. Generic figures of gendered youth, they are depersonalized but they record in their lamentations a version of dependence and immaturity that denotes the frailty of children. They are informed and directed by adults and therefore they live only within the remit of the adult's vision. Clarence's children exist as no more than shadows of imagined children. The young princes, however, attempt to break out of this amorphous image of youth and compete for a voice in the adult world. Redefined as 'parlous' or 'capable', Richard shifts the young bodies into the adult world and makes their transition to murder victim easier to accommodate: 'I wish the bastards dead, | And I would have it suddenly performed' (4.2.18–19). Delegitimizing the children supports Richard's progress to rendering them 'deep enemies' (4.2.71). Startlingly, however, when they are killed they return to versions of the symbolic child again—a vestige and vision of innocence and purity that no adult can describe without violating the very terms of its perfection.

It is perhaps no surprise that grief trails the representations of so many of Shakespeare's children. Part of what defines the child in this drama, and perhaps in any intuitive response to children, is a sense of potential that is haunted by loss: whether that is the loss of time, or what might have been, of what could have been, the figure of the child comes to represent the infinite possibilities of hope in a fallen world. A dead child is a grief so

---

[5] See Ann Blake's excellent essay 'Children and Suffering in Shakespeare's Plays', *The Yearbook of English Studies*, 23 (1993), pp. 293–304.

resonant, so shattering that we need not claim a relationship to that child to feel it. As even the most hardened murderers will testify, it cuts to the very core of who we are:

> The tyrannous and bloody deed is done,
> The most arch-act of piteous massacre
> That ever yet this land was guilty of.
> Dighton and Forrest, whom I did suborn
> To do this ruthless piece of butchery—
> Although they were fleshed villains, bloody dogs—
> Melting with tenderness and kind compassion,
> Wept like to children in their death's sad stories.
> 'Lo, thus,' quoth Dighton, 'lay those tender babes.'
> 'Thus, thus,' quoth Forrest, 'girdling one another
> Within their innocent, alabaster arms.
> Their lips were four red roses on a stalk
> Which in their summer beauty kissed each other.
> A book of prayers on their pillow lay,
> Which once,' quoth Forrest, 'almost changed my mind'.   (4.3.1–15)

As has often been noted this extraordinarily mawkish picture of the two dead princes is somewhat at odds with the detailed exchanges presented in the previous scenes. Not only have the young boys become 'babes' again but their desperate attempts to take part in the adult world of language has been entirely erased. Precocity and capability have been replaced by a tableau of reformed Christian ideals: love, faith, and charity reside in the description of the young boys. The alabaster arms, lips like roses, kissing in their full bloom, encircling each other, and framed by a prayer book supports an iconic image not specifically of children but of innocence and beauty. The images here focus our minds on the fantasy of what could have been. Petrarchan images of beauty alongside articles of Christian faith as well as a focus on kinship and unity memorialize the children as figures of arrested perfection. Tyrell's response, like his report of Forrest and Dighton, is less concerned with the representation of the young prince and his brother and more committed to the concept of the child. Harking back to Herod's Massacre of the Innocents, this deed, like all acts of infanticide, registers a profound, irreconcilable, breach in the moral fabric of human life. To kill a child is to break the bonds that define our humanity: as Euripides says, even the worst of mortals love children. Elaborating on the responses of the 'fleshed villains', Tyrell reiterates their reaction:

> 'We smothered
> The most replenished sweet work of nature
> That from the prime creation e'er she framed.'

Thus both are gone with conscience and remorse.
They could not speak.   (4.3.17–21)

The description here of the 'sweet work of nature' is one of the most articulate representations of the idea of the child in the Christian imagination. Central to this concept, however abstract, is a sense of abundance (replenished) and origin: the child is the first and last vestige of human potential; we cherish the child only so far as we believe in goodness, purity, and redemption. Even these 'bloody dogs', Dighton and Forrest, understand that all hope begins with the child. Tyrell's opaque reference to the men being '*gone* with conscience and remorse' suggests that they are stupefied by the implications of their own act. One of the most fascinating aspects of this speech is the extent to which Shakespeare brings the children and the murderers together. Earlier in the speech Tyrell observes how the men 'Melting with tenderness and kind compassion, | Wept like two children in their deaths' sad stories' (7–8). Who these analogous children are is not clear: does he refer to children in general who will weep at the story of the boys' deaths? Or does he mean that the princes wept at the prospect of their own deaths? Either way the adult murderers are compared to weeping children, vulnerable, and bereft of any form of power except tears. Weeping registers one of the few avenues of emotional expression for the child and yet it also signals a kind of purgation. In his *Positions* (1581), Richard Mulcaster understands that crying, like laughing, is an exercise that children must be taught in order to control, through release, their passions:

> IF laughing had no more wherfore to be enrouled in the catalogue of exercises, then weeping hath, they might both be crossed out. And yet as they be passions, that tende in some pointes, to the purging of some partes, so some may thinke it, a verie strange conceit, to laugh for exercise, or to weepe for wantonnesse. For as laugh one may with a heartie good will, so weep none can but against their will, to whom it is allotted in the nature of an exercise.[6]

The crucial distinction here is that you can cheerfully perform laughing but nobody wants to cry, so that even in the rehearsal of the action the emotion is present. In this way, weeping becomes an authentic emotion, even driven by performance it produces the sadness on which it traditionally attends. The conflation of the murderers with the child—'like to children'—recognizes the value of weeping, both in the 'nature of the exercise' but also in the moral compass of the emotion. The children in this speech become symbolic images of civility, meekness, and Christianity.

[6] *Positions*, p. 63.

The description of their sleeping bodies reflects an idealized image of the textbook child. In *The Civilitie of Childhood*, Erasmus suggests how children should go to sleep:

> Lie not upon thy belly, not upon thy back, but first thou shall lie on the right side, laying the armes a crosse, laying thy right hand vpon the left shoulder, and thy left hād vppon thy right shoulder. Of the thought that one shoulde haue in bed or euer he slepe. Before thou slepe thou shouldest rede some exquisite thynge and worthy of memory, and if therevpon slepe doe take thee, whan thou awakest, serche what that was.[7]

Describing the children in this way, circling each other in their arms, with a prayer book on their pillow, confirms to the audience, and to the murderers, that the profanity of this deed lies not just in the individual lives that have been extinguished but in the idealized image of childhood promoted by intellectuals such as Erasmus. Richard's commands have killed more than the princes; they have destroyed the very foundations of obedience and faith upon which his society should rest.

When Tyrell comments that the murderers are 'gone' he also notes their silence: 'They could not speak.' These men become gargoyles of sin— silently screaming through the profundity of their 'arch deed'; they have done that which cannot be spoken of, or ever reiterated. Shakespeare, of course, exploits the irony that children are most typically represented and understood to be silent. That the men should return to this state is Dante-esque in its circular presentation of sin and suffering. But the silence of the child is more complex than that of the stupefied murderers.

'WOE TO THE LAND THAT'S GOVERNED BY A CHILD'

Shakespeare's use of silence is variously complex: sometimes, like Brecht's Mother Courage, it can be used as a violently inaudible protest (Cordelia); other times it registers a terrible chasm of disenfranchisement (Isabella); and at other times it is a brutal enforcement and denigration of individual humanity (Lavinia).[8] All such silences are, of course, liable to interpretation

---

[7] Erasmus, *The Ciuilitie of Childehode, with the discipline and institucion of Children, distributed in small and compēdious Chapiters, and translated oute of French into Englysh*, by Thomas Paynell. Anno. Do. 1560, sig. 107.

[8] The majority of the work in this area tends to focus on women and silence: Jill Levenson, 'What the Silence Said: Still Points in King Lear', in Clifford Leech (ed.), *Shakespeare 1971: Proceedings of the World Shakespeare Congress* (Vancouver: University of Toronto Press, 1972), pp. 215–29; Philip C. McGuire, *Speechless Dialect: Shakespeare's Open Silences* (Berkeley: University of California Press, 1985); Cynthia Marshall, *Last Things and*

and part of their dramatic power lies in the multiplicity of possible meanings. For children, however, silence is more of an expectation than a response. Shakespeare's child king, Henry VI, is more than silent for the first half of the play; he is absent. Entering in act three, scene 1, when he is historically 5 years old, having become king at nine months, he speaks briefly, referring to his 'tender years' (65). Almost all the characters of the first part refer to Henry's youthfulness, either directly calling him a 'child' or highlighting his naivety, need for protection, and vulnerability. In this play, and indeed all three parts of *Henry VI*, Shakespeare seems less concerned to portray Henry historically accurately as a child and more interested in the dramatic potential of a young boy/man standing at the centre of political in-fighting and civil dissension. Henry does not speak as a child, whatever that may mean historically, but he stands as a child— diminutive, perhaps, but devoted to his faith and his education and reeling from the adult complexities of discord, intrigues, and sexuality. Beyond the references to his youth, however, it is difficult to gauge how Shakespeare envisaged the youthfulness of the king. If a child actor played Henry then it would significantly affect the ways in which we understand the chronicle histories as well as the first tetralogy. The lament at the end of *Henry V* in which the chorus anticipates Henry VI's failure as a king makes much more sense if we see that king as a child. Given the dating of the play, 1592, which coincides with the disbanding of the children's companies, it is very likely that a young boy, from perhaps Children of the Chapel or Children of St Paul's, played the child king. Shakespeare's children struggle to achieve any agency within the drama and positioning a child at the centre of 'mighty men' (*Henry V*, Epilogue) leaves the young Henry little ability to succeed. Understood in this way, the loss of France is more boldly critiqued through the 'many' 'who had the managing' of it than the child who lost it. This is not to suggest that the play tacitly endorses absolutism but the fact that a child stands at the centre of these plays, less in representation and more symbolically, certainly highlights the profound problems of power that accompany an infant king. Perhaps Shakespeare goes even further to baulk at a tradition in which hereditary titles endorse and enable poor governance. *Richard III* acknowledges this openly through a conversation between three citizens; rehearsing his proverbial wisdom the third citizen exclaims, 'Woe to the land that's governed by a child' (2.3.11). The citizens develop their discussion though the example of Henry VI,

Last Plays: Shakespearean Eschatology (Carbondale: Southern Illinois University Press, 1991); Harvey Rovine, *Silence in Shakespeare: Drama, Power and Gender* (Ann Arbor: UMI Research Press, 1987).

'crowned at Paris but at nine months old' (17), but the distinction they make between Henry and the young Edward is important; for Henry

> This land was famously enriched
> With politic grave counsel, then the King
> Had virtuous uncles to protect his grace.   (2.3.19–21)

Ironically, of course, it is the same man who will bring both children to their deaths, Richard, Duke of Gloucester, and later King. The conversation between the citizens very briefly explores two perspectives on child rule—one, that the child will grow up and become a good king, and two, that he will survive in that role only if he is protected by the virtuous. Both opinions acknowledge, tacitly, the immediate inadequacy of a child king: 'Better it were they all came by the father | Or the father there was none at all' (23–4). The anxiety of child rule pervades Shakespeare's *Henry VI* plays but it centres on Henry's naivety and inexperience rather than any specifically, or idiosyncratically, childish traits. He is not, unlike the princes in *Richard III* or Arthur in *King John*, shown to respond 'childishly' to events, he does not 'prattle' or 'weep' and he attempts to imitate the language of adulthood in his discussions with his elders. Perhaps, more unsettlingly, Henry's 'tender years' are suggested or implied by, on the one hand, his susceptibility to the machinations of those around him who use his youth to their own advantage, especially Suffolk; and, on the other, those who try and protect him, particularly Humphrey, Duke of Gloucester. The plays present the idea of the child through two distinct perspectives: Richard sees children as pestiferous and often invokes the child in a pernicious analogy, as when he tells Winchester that he is so loathsome, 'As very infants prattle of thy pride' (*1 Henry VI*, 3.1.16); later in the trilogy, Margaret, bored by her young husband's devotion to prayer and books, dismisses him as a 'pupil' whose 'loves | Are brazen images of canonized saints' (*2 Henry VI*, 1.3.50, 58–9). Her lengthy complaint about her husband centres on his desire for learning and asceticsm rather than her, and represents the young man/boy as sexually uninterested. Shakespeare's subtle portrait of Henry's youth focuses on his desire to separate himself from the rites of adulthood, while simultaneously acknowledging them: 'Believe me lords, my tender years can tell | Civil dissension is a viperous worm | That gnaws the bowels of the commonwealth' (3.1.72–4) We know he is 'bookish' and has 'church-like humours' (*2 Henry VI*, 1.2.244), as we also observe the moments when he is apparently unable to cope with the demands placed on a child king. Forced to manage the row that breaks out between Vernon and Basset, shortly after his coronation, he begs:

> O, think upon the conquest of my father,
> My tender years, and let us not forgo

> That for a trifle that was bought with blood.
> Let me be umpire in this doubtful strife.   (4.1.148–50)

Henry is distinctly uncomfortable with kingship—unlike his father and his uncles, he shrinks from the idea of power. He is profoundly unambitious and he seems to follow, rather pathetically, the advice of those, both good and bad, around him. Yet if there is one aspect of adulthood and childhood that haunts the trilogy it is a masculine notion of sexuality or perhaps a sexual notion of masculinity.

In Part 1 the young John Talbot enters as a child but almost instantly transforms any comprehensive notion of what that status should mean. He has not seen his father for seven years and yet is compelled to join him in his fight against the French and he pledges such allegiance to the death. The effect of the exchange between him and his father is—like much of this play—dependent on the extent to which the young boy is played as a boy, by a child actor. The reunion between father and son is cast as a tutoring 'in the stratagems of war' so that if Talbot should die his son may carry on his name and his prowess (4.5.1–5). Making a strange volte-face, Talbot decides the stars are foreboding and John must leave instantly. These short scenes between the characters provide a dense counterpoint to the bookish, devotional Henry who, unlike John, is cowed by the spectre of his father's prowess and seeks only to invoke him as a gesture of vain hope rather than as a role model. At no point does Henry try to become his father in the ways John, like an eager puppy, bounces at his father's feet:

> Stay, go, do what you will: the like do I,
> For live I will not if my father die.   (*1 Henry VI*, 4.5.50–1)

One of the many striking aspects of the brief scenes between long lost father and son is that they are written in rhyming couplets. This produces a synchronicity between the characters that prevents John from being distinguished as a child with a childish subjectivity. His sing-song responses to his father make the two characters appear as one, blindly and doggedly intent on battle. His father, having almost instantly been set upon by the French, amplifies this in the next scene where we see John rescued. Briefly the child's vulnerability is recognized as his father pulls him from the attack but the glorification of war, from both characters, merges into a lyrical lust for bloodshed. Rehearsing how close his son came to death, and lingering over emblems of penetration and blood, Talbot exclaims:

> The ireful Bastard Orleans, that drew blood
> From thee, my boy, and had the maidenhood
> Of thy first fight, I soon encountered,
> And interchanging blows, I quickly shed
> Some of his bastard blood.   (4.6.16–20)

The analogy of a woman losing her virginity endorses bloodshed as a rite of passage from childhood to adulthood.[9] The relationship between war and penetration is amplified by the Bastard's reference to John's 'puny sword' and, perhaps for the first time, acknowledges John's status a child. To be 'puny' is to be a junior, usually in relation to an older teacher or instructor: hence, John's 'puny sword' is less about size and more about his inferiority, his youthfulness, and his inexperience. More shocking perhaps, is the description of Talbot as 'the most bloody nurser of his harms' (4.7.46). Here is the great destroyer of childhood: the carer turned abuser. As a whole, the trilogy presents a devastating drama of the abuse of childhood: from the infant Henry with the 'sceptre in his childish fist' (*2 Henry VI*, 1.1.244) to the death of 'sweet Ned', Henry's son, killed and then looted in front of his mother. Despite her passionate lamentations at the death of her own son, Margaret is no stranger to cruelty, having paraded the death of young Rutland before his father with a blood-soaked handkerchief in Part 3 (1.4.156–61). The children in *Henry VI* are exclusively characterized through the adults who, at different points, animate, uplift, and destroy them. Unlike the princes in *Richard III* or Arthur in *King John* the children in *Henry VI*, including the king himself, exist only to react to the world around them. Their passivity is at once heart-breaking and also symbolic—for these 'little abstracts' are destined by their forefathers to carry the burdens of the adult world without adult comprehension. Richard relishes this disjunction when he tells the young prince:

> Sweet prince, the untainted virtue of your years
> Hath not yet dived into the world's deceit;
> No more can you distinguish of a man
> Than of his outward show, which God he knows
> Seldom or never jumpeth with the heart.   (*Richard III*, 3.1.7–11)

Richard, of course, takes particular pleasure in such a statement, as he himself is the testimony to its truth. The little prince is wary of his uncle, to be sure, but he is powerless to do anything except discuss the history and architecture of his place of imprisonment. The destruction of childhood is written deep into the fabric of these plays but they also resist any clear sense of what childhood means to these young people. Partly, of course, all of the children here are defined by their fathers insofar as they belong to a hereditary system of expectation or they impose that system upon themselves. The child exists, as Talbot declares of his own son, as an extension of the father and therefore all children who take part in the adult world are also victims of it. The paradox of portraying childhood is that,

---

[9] This point is noted by Rutter, *Shakespeare and Child's Play*, p. 13; and Katie Knowles, 'Shakespeare's Terrible Infants', in Gavin (ed.), *The Child in British Literature*.

in order for it to be effective dramatically, it needs to remain distinct from the adult world, but it can only be represented through the adult terms in which it is understood. Two of the most powerful aspects of the adult world relentlessly haunt Shakespeare's children: one is sexuality and the other is death. In some instances they accompany each other, and almost always through the adult's perceptions or descriptions. Such 'coming of age' moments are rarely relished by Shakespeare; instead they mark, often catastrophic, turning points. For the young John Talbot his initiation into war is his road to imminent death; for the young Henry his initiation into sex is the beginning of his downfall.

'THE AMOROUS MONSTER': SEX, POWER, AND POLITICS

Suffolk's politically and sexually motivated wooing of Margaret to be the young King's wife is a deeply disturbing moment in the play. Henry declares himself too young, not only for marriage, but also for sex:

> Marriage, uncle?
> Alas, my years are young,
> And fitter is my study and my books
> Than wanton dalliance with a paramour. (*1 Henry VI*, 5.1.21–3)

Irrespective of production choices, Shakespeare makes it very clear that the king is a child: more comfortable with what he knows, the schoolroom or prayer, devotion or learning, than with female sexuality. Even more revealing is the young boy's description of sex or marriage—the 'wanton dalliance with a paramour'—which could have come straight out of *Venus and Adonis*. Such language is at once pompous and naive but beautifully exposes the struggle of the child in an adult world. The trilogy, and especially Parts 1 and 2, show Henry in a constant state of reaction—trying to respond to and live up to the expectations of the adult world. Elaborating on Margaret's beauty and dowry, 'the lady's virtuous gifts', Humphrey, Duke of Gloucester, attempts to impress upon the king the value of such a choice. Henry, however, registers no interest in her beauty but responds dutifully and ceremonially with a 'jewel, pledge of my affection' (47). Having a boy actor in this role makes scenes like this electrifying—not only for the ways in which they dramatize the loss of innocence but also as a subtle critique of power. Shakespeare, like many of his contemporaries, does not represent an idea of childhood which we can confidently identify as having been lost or compromised here: instead, and perhaps more powerfully, he shows a young boy in a position of power, surrounded by adults who are variously trying to use that power for his own protection or their own advancement. What resonates through this play is not a conception that Henry could have been, or indeed is, a child in any modern sense of the world; but rather that he is bound by duty and expectation to belong to the adult world without adult understanding. It is this blinding inequality and disenfranchisement that makes Shakespeare's children such powerful spectres on the early modern stage.

The pain and potency of Shakespeare's child king is that he is nothing more than a vessel of history, sacrificed by age and chance to 'sad stories of the death of kings' (*Richard II*). Shakespeare uses these moments to engage with the destructive power of adults, rather than the fragility of the child. He will develop this more profoundly in *The Winter's Tale*, but here, the idea of the child slips into the adult world and becomes imperceptibly lost amid sex, power, and politics. When Suffolk, seduced by Margaret's beauty, who is referred to as a 'sweet child' (5.5.104), declares his intention to woo her for the king he puts it in these terms:

> An earl I am, and Suffolk am I called
> Be not offended nature's miracle,
> Thou art allotted to be ta'en by me.
> So doth the swan his downy cygnets save,
> Keeping them prisoner underneath his wings. (5.5.9–13)

Describing her destiny as one in which she is 'ta'en' by him, as a swan rescues their cygnets, Suffolk puts himself in the image of a parental, maternal even, figure who is protecting their child. Using the image of the swan, Suffolk tries to convince Margaret that what may seem like imprisonment is actually protection. As modern readers we are highly attuned to the horrific synthesis of the abuser/carer but here I think Shakespeare is more invested in mapping the trajectories of adult manipulation rather than identifying Suffolk as a paedophile. The conversation that develops between Margaret and Suffolk on this point is dominated by asides from both characters, each one demonstrating to the audience their naivety (Margaret) or their scheming (Suffolk). Once again the power of this scene lies in the inequality between the two characters: occupying different spaces of cognition and understanding, Shakespeare places Margaret and Suffolk within a theatrical tension dependent upon her inexperience. Where ignorance or literalism may be comic in some of Shakespeare's young characters (the clown in *The Winter's Tale*, for example), in children it is devastating, precisely for the opportunities for exploitation it affords.

Shakespeare's renditions of childishness are subtle and inherently dramatic: the plays assert the power of the child through the dynamics of the playing space. How we perceive or understand Shakespeare's children depends upon the relative networks of authority in which they are placed. Silent, partially aware or uninformed, and at the mercy of their elders the young figure becomes enmeshed in the politics of the playing space. Placing the child in a position of weakness in relation to the adult, either literally in the position they occupy on the stage, or figuratively in the information they have access to, exposes the powerful ways in which Shakespeare explores the distance between adult and child.[10] Many of the most compelling representations of the child emerge through forms of indecorum or inappropriateness: where the adult learns to self-censure, play the game, as it were, the child does not and behaves as they have been instructed to, which is to speak the truth. Shakespeare's portraits of the young princes in *Richard III* depend on this dynamic where we observe the 'prating York' fail to guard himself against his perfidious uncle and speak whatever appears to come into his mind. His elder brother, the prince, is more cautious but still reverts to charmingly childish utterances, as when he calls the tardy Hastings a 'slug' (*Richard III*, 3.1.23). In *1 Henry VI*, however, the scene between Margaret and Suffolk is very subtly drawn. Suffolk's desire for Margaret overwhelms him, especially in the context of his own marriage; attempting to manage his feelings for this young person he makes frequent asides, speaks elliptically, and becomes lost in reveries of passion and anxiety. Margaret's response to him is not that of an experienced woman, who is used to men finding her powerfully attractive, but as a child who takes everything they see at face value:

SUFFOLK [aside]:   Fond man, remember that thou hast a wife;
    Then how can Margaret be thy paramour?
MARGARET [aside]:   I were best to leave him for he will not hear.
SUFFOLK [aside]:   There all is marred; there lies a cooling card.
MARGARET [aside]:   He talks at random; sure the man is mad...
SUFFOLK [aside]:   I'll win this Lady Margaret. For whom?
    Why, for my king—tush that's a wooden thing.
MARGARET [aside]:   He talks of wood. It is some carpenter.

(5.5.37–41, 44–6)

[10] While production choices can highlight the myriad and complex renditions of the childhood that Shakespeare's plays imply, there are also a number of textual details that establish this dynamic. Most famously, perhaps, Cordelia's supplication to her desperate father, as both characters kneel to each other in an attempt to retrieve the bond between them, revealing the devastating turmoil of parental and child relations (5.3). Where, in *Lear*, the text reveals the physical response of the character, in *Titus Andronicus*, Young Lucius makes his childishness known in relation to not understanding his aunt, Lavinia (4.1).

We see a man, who is married, attempting to procure a young woman for the young king, with the intention of sleeping with her himself. Margaret sees a man talking to himself and unable to hear her. The disjunction between these two perceptions would be amusing if the stakes were not so high: Suffolk's desire for, and ultimate affair with, Margaret has devastating consequences for both her and Henry. Margaret's vulnerability in this scene is repeatedly marked by the moments in which she *almost* hears Suffolk's real intentions:

> SUFFOLK: I'll undertake to make thee Henry's queen,
>   To put a golden sceptre in thy hand,
>   And set a precious crown upon thy head,
>   If thou wilt condescend to be my—
> MARGARET: What?
> SUFFOLK: His love.   (5.5.73–7)

As we noticed in *Richard III*, Shakespeare's children have an apparently unique ability to listen: as the young prince broke through Richard's aside Margaret picks up on Suffolk's slip-of-the-tongue. Powerfully perspicacious, the young people in Shakespeare hear and see a great deal that they can neither affect nor comprehend. Like Henry, Margaret is not ready for marriage; she sees it as 'bondage' and 'base servility' (68, 69) but also like Henry she is at the mercy of her elders: 'An if my father please, I am content' (83). As Part 1 draws to its end, the childish world begins to slip from both Henry and Margaret. Speaking to Suffolk, Henry admits:

> My tender youth was never yet attaint
> With any passion of inflaming love,
> I cannot tell; but this I am assured:
> I feel such sharp dissension in my breast,
> Such fierce alarums both of hope and fear,
> As I am sick with working of my thoughts.   (5.7.81–6)

Returning to this 'tender youth', Henry acknowledges he has never felt desire but he does feel fear. Historically Henry was in fact 23 and Margaret 15 years old at the time of their marriage but Shakespeare takes care to emphasize the youthfulness, and especially the naivety, of the king.[11] The play ends as Henry is forced to grow up: discord and dissension, desire and duty demand his attention and he is inexperienced and incapable.

---

[11] For a discussion of conventional ages of marriage see Krausman Ben-Amos, *Adolescence and Youth*. Although monarchs were often 'married' young this was a purely legal arrangement. See also Williams' chapter on the Princess Isabella, wife of Richard II, who was historically 9 years old at her marriage, *The Performance of Girlhood*, pp. 52–71.

Recognizing the impossible position in which he now stands, he begs of Humphrey:

> If you do censure me by what you were,
> Not what you are, I know it will excuse
> This sudden execution of my will.   (5.7.97–9)

Henry appeals to a universal understanding of the child, in which inexperience excuses error. This is the moment Henry grows up: positioning himself in this way affords him insight into who he is precisely at the moment it becomes who he *was*. The first act of Part 2 continues to refer to Henry as a child but shifts the emphasis away from youthfulness and more towards his character. The most formative transition occurs when Henry is urged, forced even, to relinquish the protection of Humphrey, Duke of Gloucester: 'the king is old enough himself | To give his censure' (1.3.120–1). Margaret's patronizing observation marks, for the audience at least, the realization that Henry may be legally 'old enough' but he is not experienced enough to see the danger of those closest to him. The extent to which we understand Henry as a child is defined by the reactions of the play-world. Despite Margaret's self-seeking insistence that he should dismiss the role of Protector we continue to observe Henry's inability to function as a leader. As those around him talk cryptically about discord, ambition, and plots, Henry not only seems oblivious but also takes constant refuge in religious platitudes. When he makes the statement, 'Henry will to himself | Protector be' (2.3.21) we feel a distinct sense of unease. Margaret, however, translates this moment into Henry growing up, referring to him as a 'king of years'. The faintly farcical, and deeply pathetic, attempt at growing up is almost instantly undermined when the king is required to preside over a 'combat' between master and servant, the latter having accused the former of treasonous remarks. In this highly unusual scenario, where the servant would have been completely inexperienced in fighting, the master is portrayed as drunk. The king may have grown up, as far as Margaret and others are concerned, but representing him presiding over such a parody of justice makes fools of all of those concerned. Henry's complete inability to manage his role is represented as an extension of his childishness. It is almost as though the role of king has arrested his development. The metaphor of the child haunts the rest of the play, registering, in various different keys, a sense of loss, grief, or separation. One of the most profound analogies comes from Henry, mourning the betrayal and loss of Humphrey, whom he compares to a calf being taken to slaughter, bound and beaten by the butcher, 'As the dam runs lowing up and down, | Looking the way her harmless young one went' (*2 Henry VI*, 3.1.214–15).

Perhaps like many children in Shakespeare this is the moment when Henry does grow up: when he loses the parental or protective figure. Recasting the roles between them, Henry is the mother and Humphrey the child: the heart-breaking analogy registers not only Henry's instinctive, deeply rooted, distress but also his powerlessness against the amorphous figure of the 'butcher'. Growing up, for Henry, and in this context, means recognizing that the world is unjust, unfair, and remorseless: 'Who's a traitor? Gloucester, he is none.' (*2 Henry VI*, 3.1.222). Such a betrayal, represented in parental terms, initiates Henry into the sophisticated and adult world of injustice: and he, who 'hold[s] the sceptre in his childish fist' (1.1.244), has become part of it. As if to finally and painfully mark Henry's severance with his childish self, Margaret reflects on Henry's poor judgement, which has put him at the mercy of Humphrey, 'as the mournful crocodile'

> With sorrow snares relenting passengers,
> Or as the snake rolled in a flow'ring bank
> With shining chequered slough doth sting a child
> That for the beauty thinks it excellent.   (*2 Henry VI*, 3.1.226–30)

Despite being 'a king of years', Henry remains 'a child' to his wife, who uses the term pejoratively to denote his gullibility and lack of judgement. Towards the end of the play, Henry concedes the impossibility of the child king:

> Was ever King that joyed an earthly throne
> And could command no more content that I?
> No sooner was I crept out of my cradle
> But I was made a king at nine months old.
> Was never subject longed to be a king
> As I do long and wish to be a subject.   (4.8.1–6)

Henry's lament focuses less on his childishness and more on his monarchy. In a series of plays that obsessively dramatize the longing for power, the schemes and plots of ambitious aristocrats, and the problems of good government, the man/child who holds the crown longest in Shakespeare's entire history cycle longs and wishes it were not so. The reluctant King, with his 'bookish rule' and 'church-like humours', is crowned as he learns to crawl.[12] For Henry VI, history is an endurance test, where the dream of living life as a 'subject' is also to live the life of a child, in abeyance to someone else but free of the pernicious implications of power. Henry's

---

[12] Ironically, of course, in Part 3, Henry holds tightly to the power he seems to despise here, to the extent that 'first shall war unpeople this my realm' before he relinquishes his crown, *3 Henry VI*, 1.1.125–31.

lament, however, is complicated by those who inhabit his world both as subjects and as children. The histories, and certainly the trilogy of *Henry VI* plays, refuse to present any consistent notion of the child, or even of childhood: every child in these plays is forced, willingly or otherwise, into the adult world as quickly and as efficiently as possible. For the most part that transition results in death: children become testaments to a frailty, optimism, or justice that the play-world cannot withstand. Such intense cynicism spreads like a stain through these plays and reaches its crescendo in the death of young Rutland in Part 3.

The naive, politically unaware Henry of the previous plays has been replaced by a wryer, more assertive man who can command, albeit briefly, the 'factious Duke of York' to 'kneel for grace and mercy at my feet. | I am thy sovereign' (*3 Henry VI*, 1.1.74–6) Henry may be 'old enough now' (113) but the weakness of the child has become the scourge of the adult: 'Base, fearful and despairing Henry'; 'faint-heated and degenerate king, | In whose cold blood no spark of honour bides' (1.1.179, 184–5). Henry's fearfulness and inability to anticipate the consequences of his actions defined much of his childish self but now, as an adult, these qualities are less forgivable, as is his inability to accept any kind of responsibility.[13] Having characterized many of these qualities as childlike, Shakespeare has Henry assimilate them into adult life and the transition into manhood appears muddy and contested. What makes Henry an adult other than his age? Very little, the play seems to say and it does so through a reintroduction of a central child role. Henry's son, Prince Edward, is introduced towards the end of this first scene, in which Henry has agreed to pass the crown to Edward, Duke of York, after his death rather than to his own son. The disinherited Edward gently confronts his father and then leaves to battle his rights with his ferocious mother alongside him. The contrast between King and child is striking: partly for the strange reversal of history in which the young child hopes to be king, rather than has it thrust upon him, but more compellingly, for the roles that the two characters assume. Henry is infuriatingly weak, self-serving, and cowardly while Prince Edward is terse, absolute, and single-minded: 'When I return with victory from the field, | I'll see your grace. Till then, I'll follow her' (*3 Henry VI*, 1.1.262–3). Here the child becomes the father to the man. The play's understanding and representation of the child belongs to a chronicle of power in which the child reacts or is reacted to. Henry's inheritance of the crown as an infant arrests his development and translates his adulthood

---

[13] Referring to his loss of France in the early years of kingship, Henry asserts: 'The Lord Protector lost it, and not I. | When I was crowned I was but nine months old' (*3 Henry VI*, 1.1.111–12). Almost all of France was lost to Henry by the time he was 32 years old.

into one of staggering passivity, 'simple Henry' (1.2.59). In contrast, the young Prince Edward and the young Rutland try, however futilely, to resist their destiny.

'THE THOUGHT OF THEM . . .'

The scene that follows, in which Clifford murders young Rutland in revenge for his father's death, is brief and bloody and leaves little room for characterization, pity, or emotion. It is shocking for its insensible violence but the act is generic, rather than individual. The tutor's plea, 'Ah, Clifford, murder not this innocent child | Lest thou be hated of both God and man' (1.3.8–9) recognizes the moral resonance of infanticide. Yet even within this short scene, less than fifty-five lines, there are flashes of childishness that make the tutor's words ring out across the stage. The most resonant example of Rutland's youth is not his open engagement with his murderer (to be powerfully developed in *King John*), his admission that he is 'too mean a subject for thy wrath', or his gentle, reasonable words but the silent, short moment in which he pretends to be dead:

> How now—is he dead already?
> Or is it fear that makes him close his eyes?
> I'll open them.   (1.3.10–12)

Clifford's horrible observation takes us straight to the world of the child, where to close your eyes prevents you from seeing, but also, crucially, so the child thinks, from being seen. Shakespeare takes us to the heart of a child's mind, briefly, brilliantly, and beautifully, before he has him killed. There is no more acute observation of the mind of the child than this moment in this play.

Pleading for his life, Rutland reminds Clifford that he is a father and his son may 'be as miserably slain as I' (1.4.43) if this cycle of revenge continues. Rutland is a devastating example of the biblical injunction that the sins of the father may be visited on the child.[14] As he exclaims there is no 'cause' to kill him, to which Clifford replies: 'No cause? Thy father slew my father, therefore die' (47). Rutland's brief life is just one part of the play's wider chronicle of factionalism and revenge. The murder of children seems inescapable in this play where they are destroyed and flaunted as

---

[14] The Bible is somewhat conflicted on this point: Exodus records the judgement of 'visiting the iniquity of the fathers upon children, and upon children's children', 34:7; while Deuteronomy 24:16 states: 'The fathers shall not be put to death for the children, neither shall the children be put to death for the fathers, every man shall be put to death for his own sin.' Many early modern texts on parenting, taking the Bible as their cue, debate this point.

dramatic emblems of affect, each character attempting to take the other to the limits of their own endurance. Proffering a napkin soaked in his son's blood, to see 'if thine eyes can water', Margaret attempts to take York to the absolute limit of his endurance. Margaret's speeches here are some of the most shocking in all of Shakespeare: her horrifying exposition of Rutland's death and the delight she takes in trying to 'make thee mad' is matched only by Webster in *The Duchess of Malfi*, where the heroine's apparently murdered children are paraded in front of her by her homicidal brother.[15] The long speech, delivered by a boy actor, in which she sets York on a mole hill with a paper crown on his head and the blood of his dead son in his hand, is quite extraordinary in its power to shock. The point of the child here is to devastate the father: but unlike his son, who closed his eyes in fear, hoping the monster would disappear, York withstands Margaret's assault, only to reflect:

> How couldst thou drain the life-blood of the child
> To bid the father wipe his eyes withal,
> And yet be seen to bear a woman's face?   (1.4.139–41)

Indeed: we share York's horror and register, like him, the shock that a woman, a mother, could behave in this way: she makes even Lady Macbeth seem maternal. The full horror of the Queen comes to reside in her attitude to the murdered child, not the act itself (it was, of course, Clifford who killed him):

> That face of his the hungry cannibals
> Would not have touched, would not have stained with blood—
> But you are more inhuman, more inexorable,
> O, ten times more than tigers of Hyrcania.   (1.4.153–6)

When Margaret responds by stabbing York it seems as nothing compared to the inhumanity of her behaviour in this scene. There is no doubt that Shakespeare fully understands the resonance of infanticide and that we share York's feelings towards this woman but the power of this moment remains wedded to the emotional range of the audience, not to the representation of the child. That fleeting and extraordinary glimpse into the closed eyes of the frightened Rutland takes us all somewhere, however instinctive or inexplicable that place may be, and Shakespeare builds, imperceptibly, on the imaginative capacity of children to penetrate the dramatic worlds of his audience.

Yet Part 3 of *Henry VI* takes this dynamic even further as it not only dramatizes the impact of the child's death on the father, but the father's

---

[15] 4.1.

death on the son. In one of the play's most devastating critiques of war a nameless solider brings on the body of the man he has just killed, with the intention of looting it, only to discover it is, in fact, his father:

> And I, who at his hands received my life,
> Have by my hands of life bereaved him.
> Pardon me, God, I knew not what I did;
> And pardon, father, for I knew not thee.   (2.5.67–70)[16]

Watched over by King Henry, a second soldier brings on the body of a dead man to discover that it is, in fact, his son: 'how butcherly, | Erroneous, mutinous, and unnatural, | This deadly quarrel daily doth beget' (2.5.89–91). Henry stands on, echoing laments of grief, for war, for loss, for 'these rueful deeds'. As the soldier scoops up his dead child, 'these arms of mine shall be thy winding sheet', the young Prince Edward flies onto the stage, pursued in battle by Warwick. This tableau of grief, played out through the unintentional killing of fathers by sons and sons by fathers, registers a profound chaos at the centre of the play's chronicle. The amplified language of the 'unnatural' supports a wider breakdown in the play's representation of human order. Adumbrating the apocalyptic visions of *King Lear*, 'Humanity must perforce prey on itself \ Like monsters of the deep' (4.2.48–9), the play's destruction of familial bonds becomes the point at which all hope fails. When Margaret witnesses the death of her son, 'sweet Ned', she, too, reverts to the language of butchery, cannibalism, and the unnatural:

> Butchers and villain! Bloody cannibals!
> How sweet a plant have you untimely cropped!
> You have no children, butchers; if you had
> The thought of them would have stirred up remorse.   (5.5.60–4)

The irony here is not lost on the audience who watched in horror as she tormented York with the blood of his murdered son but even she, the tiger-woman, invokes empathy and imagination as the bastions of human hope. 'The thought of them', children, that is, pervades all three parts of *Henry VI*. Watching Henry 'hold the sceptre in his childish fist' to willingly disinheriting his own son to maintain the crown in his lifetime we witness a very arrested form of development that fragments the child into dramatic moments of reflection and crisis. Although they people the stage at critical moments within the trilogy, it is *the thought of them*, more than their bodily presence, that shapes Shakespeare's art. These children are the victims of circumstance, war, and adult emotion, including anger, revenge,

---

[16] The resonance here comes from Luke 23:35, when Jesus, at his crucifixion, declares: 'Father, forgive them, for they know not what they do.'

desire, and punishment. They are not fully realized characters—even Henry himself never moves beyond the 'bookish' boy with 'church-like humours'—but triggers for the individual play-worlds to explore its humanity. Thinking on the soldiers who variously discover that they have killed their own father or son and the devastating costs of war seems a long way from *Henry V's* rhetoric of heroic familial bloodshed. But these moments—the young boy holding a sceptre, or a sword, the terrified Rutland with his eyes closed before his murderer, or the howling cries of a bereaved parent seem to affirm Warwick's observation in *Henry IV*: 'There is a history in all men's lives': and it is often the history of children that shape such men.

'THIS LITTLE ABSTRACT . . . '

Shakespeare's *King John* stands apart from the rest of Shakespeare's history plays, not simply because it represents a period long before the wars of the roses, and the subsequent Tudor reigns, but also because it presents history as opaque, whimsical, and ambivalent. Unlike the plays of the first and second tetralogies, *King John* does not appeal to any larger providential plan, it puts little faith in God or monarch, and the ethical and political boundaries become so porous it is very difficult to determine what is precisely at stake in this play: Catholicism? Heredity entitlement? Feudalism? Or the moral outrage at the death of a young boy? As critics have frequently observed the narrative of the play centres on the life and death of young Arthur.[17] Shakespeare departs from his source, typically Holinshed's *Chronicles*, to keep Arthur as a young boy throughout the play's action and to make his potential claim to the throne, alliance with France, and subsequent death the dramatic locus of John's reign. Most significantly, as Heberle observes, 'Shakespeare is responsible for making Arthur a child. Historically, the prince was sixteen when he died in 1203, and Holinshed notes that he helped lead the army that captured John's mother in Anjou in 1202, an exploit dramatized in scene three of *The Troublesome Reign*.'[18] This is an important point since it helps us realize that, unlike other playwrights, Arthur's childishness was central to Shakespeare's dramatic vision.[19]

[17] Mark Heberle observes that 'Shakespeare has altered his sources drastically so that the work's dramatic structure and political theme depend crucially upon two child characters, the royal princes Arthur and Henry', *Infant Tongues*, p. 30, cf. p. 33. Cf. Peter Saccio, *Shakespeare's English Kings* (London: Oxford University Press, 1977), p. 202.

[18] *Infant Tongues*, p. 34.

[19] The authorship and status of *The Troublesome Reign of King John* is contested. Over the years it has been variously attributed to eight different playwrights, including Peele, Marlowe, and Shakespeare himself. Little is known for sure about the play other than that

Most of the first and second tetralogies are taken up with the conflicts of civil dissension and challenges to the throne. Although *King John* is similarly preoccupied with these issues it strikes a very different note from Shakespeare's other history plays. One of the most remarkable elements of this play is the way in which it presents religious as well as dynastic divisions. The moral landscape of the play is very confused: we reject John for his treatment of Arthur, his bad government, and rapacious self-interest; yet we, and especially an Elizabethan audience, find it difficult to ally ourselves with France or indeed with the Catholicism that both King Philip and Pandulph represent. There is no doubt that the waters of morality are very murky in this play: King Philip defends Arthur's claim to the throne, only to change his 'vantage' when John marries his daughter to Philip's son; Pandulph, the 'holy legate of the pope', demands that John curbs his authority over the church, only to be commanded to report back to the pope that:

> From the mouth of England
> And thus much more, that no Italian priest
> Shall tithe or til in our dominions;
> But as we, under God, are supreme head,
> So under Him that great supremacy,
> Where we do reign, we will alone uphold
> Without th' assistance of a mortal hand.   (3.1.78–84)

Protestant ears would have pricked up at John's speech, which echoes closely the language of Henry VIII's 1534 Act of Supremacy. John's rejection of the pope and his strategic alliance with France make him an apparently ideal model for English monarchy, and one distinctly at odds with a historically accurate portrait of the late twelfth-century king.[20] Shakespeare's focus on Arthur—not only as the son of John's elder brother and therefore the rightful heir but as the moral centre of the play— renegotiates the significance of John's history. For a child actor, Arthur is Shakespeare's most intense part: the role demands long speeches, including the only soliloquy delivered by a child in Shakespeare's drama, as well as being present on stage, without speaking, for large periods of time.[21]

---

it was published anonymously in two parts in 1591. For a comprehensive discussion of the history and status of this play see Ramon Jimenez, *The Oxfordian*, 12 (2010).

[20] The historical King John was in fact supported by Pope Innocent in his attempts to quell civil dissension and war with France. Shakespeare is, of course, more indebted historically to Holinshed and the *Troublesome Reign* but his representation of John as an antagonist to the pope, and his self-serving reasons for being so, is highly resonant for a contemporary audience.

[21] As noted in the introduction, the Boy in *Henry V* delivers a speech alone on stage but despite the dramatic resonance of this moment he remains a nameless character with little agency within the play.

This role requires a certain range from an actor, who is on stage for the majority of the play. The scene in which Arthur is nearly blinded by Hubert but goes on to develop a compelling and pathetic attachment to his gaoler is without doubt the most demanding, but the play is full of long scenes where Arthur is either present but entirely silent (3.1) or present and par-tially silent (2.1). In many of these scenes Arthur is relentlessly discussed; talked about rather than to and referred to only as 'the child' or the 'oppressed boy'. Such scenes make intense demands on the young boy who plays Arthur, for his very presence defines the dynamics as well as the impacts of the scene.[22] It is tempting to speculate that Shakespeare used an experienced child actor, one of the Children of the Chapel or St Paul's, perhaps, to play Arthur's part. There are only sporadic records of individ-ual children, largely those who belonged to choir schools, and no specific names that we can attach to the role of Arthur, but the timing of the play and the significance of the part make it perfectly plausible. The Children of Paul's had enjoyed particular success in the late 1580s but they did not appear at court again until 1600.[23]

We can all recognize that childhood and childishness are culturally contingent categories and are always in the process of being redefined. In Shakespeare's plays children become children only insofar as those around then treat them as such. Shakespeare rarely writes a child's part through childish idioms, but that does not exclude the possibility that such child-ishness exists for the early moderns as it does for us. One of the most penetrating critiques of the abuse of childhood emerges through the appropriation of such idioms. As Arthur is relentlessly discussed as well as ignored by those attempting to determine his future, King Philip demands that John rightfully restore Arthur to the crown, which he refuses. At this point, Eleanor, his grandmother and John's mother, beckons him over in an apparently loving or protective gesture and exclaims: 'Come to thy grandam, child' (2.1.159), to which the furious Constance replies:

> Do, child, go to it grandam, child;
> Give grandam kingdom and it grandam will
> Give it a plum, a cherry, and a fig:
> There's a good grandam.   (2.1.160–3)

[22] Heberle notes that the actor playing Arthur must be relatively small or light, as he is carried off stage by Hubert alone, p. 34. Cf. Martin Holmes, *Shakespeare and Burbage* (Bognor Regis: Phillimore and Co., 1978), pp. 140–1.
[23] Hillebrand is circumspect as to why the Children of St Paul's should have suffered so heavily as to have been completely 'dissolved' due to their connections with the Marprelate controversies. He does acknowledge, however, that there are no records of the company having performed between 6 January 1590 and 1 January 1603, *The Child Actors*, pp. 143–50.

This exquisite parody of infantile language is a pernicious indictment of Eleanor's failure to protect her grandson's rights. Reproducing the adult version of childish language, Constance suggests that Eleanor fails to recognize Arthur's role in the adult world. This is one of Shakespeare's very brief glimpses into conceptions of childhood as being linguistically distinct from adulthood. Constance's barbed comments to her mother-in-law elicit a horrified response from Arthur:

> Good my mother, peace!
> I would that I were low laid in my grave:
> For I am not worth this coil that's made for me.   (2.1.163–5)

Arthur not only speaks for the first time here in this scene but he also cries, 'poor boy, he weeps' (166). As the women squabble over his treatment, using him to bat their ambitions and quarrels about the stage, we see a pitiful example of the fragility of childhood in contest with the adult world. As the young Rutland kept his eyes shut against the murderous Clifford, so Arthur wishes he were dead, away from the world that surrounds him. Many of these plays register the powerful moments at which children declare their wish to be taken away from the world in which they live. Teetering on the verge of the adult world, let in enough to see its fears and ambitions but not enough to have agency, the children of the history plays often wish they were dead, elsewhere, or someone else. This heartbreaking vignette into the powerlessness of the child erupts in the electric tension between Constance's mockery and Arthur's tears: her's is a parody of the child's world, his is the only expression available to him. The two women then erupt into a series of accusations, each one blaming the other for the child's distress. Like the victim of a bitter divorce, the child becomes the vehicle for adult punishment, variously victimized, stigmatized, and silenced by the adult accusations that surround him. Developing Arthur's vulnerability from these moments into something much more sophisticated in terms of characterization allows Shakespeare to move beyond the child as a reflexive echo of adult injustice (Clarence's children in *Richard III*, for example) into something profoundly moving and deeply rewarding.

Some of the most intense drama of the histories emerges from the child as a victim of circumstance. In a play-world replete with adult dissension, national conflict, and partisan politics Arthur's remarks, observations, and reflections reveal a hankering for ordinariness. He is not the prating or parlous boy of *Richard III* or the pious, bookish Henry or even the tenacious young Rutland but a 'green boy' who feels he is 'not worth this coil'. Arthur's relationship to the rest of the play-world is the most striking element of his characterization. In Arthur's detachment we see shadows of

Hamlet; in his vulnerability and reticence we see reflections of Cordelia; and in his staggering faith in adults we see traces of Mamillius. Arthur is one of Shakespeare's greatest children and in his treatment and development we can see the rehearsal of many of the themes and traits that would come to dominate the tragedies, and most particularly *King Lear*. Grief, loss, parenting, innocence, torture, and integrity define the networks through which Arthur moves and this is especially compelling when we imagine the presence of a young child on stage.

Even those within the play-world, however, are keen to capitalize on the physical impression of Arthur. As the divisions between John and the French develop, King Philip points to the boy and declares:

> Look here upon thy brother Geoffrey's face;
> These eyes, these brows, were moulded out of his:
> This little abstract doth contain that large
> Which died in Geoffrey: and the hand of time
> Shall draw this brief into as huge a volume.   (2.1.99–103)

Here the significance of the child is that he is an image of his father, a version of Geoffrey; a child in which we recognize the man. Focusing on the diminutive term 'little' which attends so many of the references to children and boy actors, Arthur's physical presence dominates this moment. The language here is fascinating, especially for the play on the various meanings of 'abstract': as an idea, a brief description, or an image, the word 'abstract' produces a range of meanings which collide around the young boy's face to suggest, crucially, that he represents something else.[24] The child is a representation of another and not the thing itself. Only time will bring the child into his own 'volume'. As a 'brief', the child is an abbreviation of adulthood, again a version of something or someone that can only be developed or properly revealed in time. The terms of Philip's appeal reveal a fascinating insight into the relations between child and adult. What is of most significance here to the French King is that the little boy looks like his father and that image defends hereditary rule as legitimate. Despite entering at the beginning of the act, Arthur has yet to speak on stage: but all eyes are on this boy as he stands, silently, in defence of John's deposition. Arthur's bodily presence supports the drama of this moment: seeing the young boy pushed forward with the weight of history on his head as he is forced into the adult world of power and politics

---

[24] Katie Knowles is right to point out the textual implications of this metaphor: see 'This Little Abstract: Inscribing History upon the Child in Shakespeare's King John', *Orality and Literacy (Esharp)*, 10. We see other uses of abstract in this way, especially in Hamlet when the players are described as 'brief abstracts and chronicles' and later when Hamlet forces his mother to look into her soul.

amplifies the impossible, tragic, position of the child. Understanding the physical presence of the actor helps us to engage with the representation of the child in this play.

Having already explored the place of the child actor in Chapter 1 we can begin to appreciate how the representation of children became increasingly important in the development of public drama and the experience of theatre for an early modern audience.[25] Historians have shown that child actors pre-dated adult actors not only in their popularity and success but also in their development of acting as a form of both education and entertainment.[26] Seeing children perform was a commonplace of early modern life: whether in the public theatres, inns of court, pageants, and royal progresses the diminutive figure was publicly displayed.

Although the majority of child actors were young boys, usually developing their roles through choiring, some girls performed in public festivals and progresses.[27] Yet when did children play children? In other words, children may have been a mainstay of early modern drama but they were almost always playing adults in adult stories. Although royal progresses and pageants tended to use children to represent allegorical figures or abstract ideas, most of the drama in which children acted was centred on biblical or mythological stories, developing in the late sixteenth century into the fully fledged commissioned drama for the professional boys' companies.[28] Although audiences may be accustomed to seeing a young child in performance they were rarely characterized as such. This, of course, has huge implications for the ways in which Shakespeare writes his children

[25] Bart Van Es, *Shakespeare in Company* (Oxford: Oxford University Press, 2013); Lucy Munro, *Children of the Queen's Revels: A Jacobean Theatre Repertory* (Cambridge: Cambridge University Press, 2005); Rosalind Knutson, *Playing Companies and Commerce in Shakespeare's Time* (Cambridge: Cambridge University Press, 2001); Siobhan Keenan, *Acting Companies and their Plays in Shakespeare's London* (London: Bloomsbury, 2014); Andrew Gurr, *The Shakespeare Company, 1594–1642* (Cambridge: Cambridge University Press, 2004).

[26] See Hillebrand, *The Child Actors*, pp. 27–30. E. K. Chambers, *The Elizabethan Stage* (Oxford: Oxford University Press, 1923); E. K Chambers, *The Mediaeval Stage* (Oxford: Oxford University Press, 1903); Shapiro, *Children of the Revels*.

[27] 'When the queen was received at Norwhich in 1575, there was arranged a stage whereon stood "eyght small women chyldren spinning worsted yarne, and at the other side as many knittynge of worsted yarne; and in the midst of the stage stood a pretie boy richly apparelled, which represented the Commonwealth of the city"', John Nichols, *Progresses and Processions of Elizabeth* (London, 1823), p. 144. Cf. Hillebrand, *The Child Actors*, p. 32.

[28] See Alice Hunt on the coronation progresses and their relationship to the development of early modern drama, *The Drama of Coronation: Medieval Ceremony in Early Modern England* (Cambridge: Cambridge University Press, 2007). Siobhan Keenan writes that 'The boys companies appear to have enjoyed considerable success during their second phase of public performing [first decade of the sixteenth century] not only briefly rivalling adult companies in reputation but securing plays from most of the leading playwrights (including Ben Jonson, John Marston and Thomas Middleton)', *Acting Companies and their Plays in Shakespeare's London*, p. 14.

on stage and for the ways in which we perceive those small bodies. To some extent these insights give us a greater appreciation of the role of representation in the development of theatre. Early modern audiences would have no problems, we imagine, with seeing men play women when they have grown up with a culture of representation in which children play adults. Hillebrand claims that 'I can see no vital respect in which the obvious limitations of the young actors were reflected in their plays.'[29] Yet much of the popularity of the children's companies seems to have emanated from their performance of bawdy, comic, and satirical drama which Hillebrand describes as 'directly favour[ing] the talent of the children'. Unlike Shapiro who suggests that there was something titillating about seeing children play comic bawdy parts, Hillebrand understands that the success of the children's companies lies in their grammar school training and their ability to perform plays drawn from the classics. Even within that tradition, however, Hillebrand notes that 'There was nothing in the average play of the period which transcended the abilities of a boy of twelve.'[30] Hillebrand's point is that children were capable of performing in almost any play of this period, and celebrated for it.

When Philip points to this 'little abstract' and Arthur is put centre stage we realize the impact of his little shape. He says nothing until he breaks into the quarrel between Eleanor and Constance, begging them to stop. As the stage is peopled by kings and officials, the little child stands silently at the centre of the adult world. How we see Arthur is exclusively defined by how the adult world presents him, as well as his separation from it. He is everything and nothing: the centre of the play-world and yet small, silent, and apart from it. This is not to suggest, however, that Shakespeare relies exclusively on the spoken word for character or effect: we know how powerfully he develops physical presence throughout his drama and none more devastatingly than in the figure of Lavinia. Mutilated and raped she remains on stage, tongueless and handless, as a powerful reminder of the body in action.[31] But where Lavinia's dramatic presence is supported by shock and trauma, Arthur's is defined by his longing to be anywhere else but there. His exclamation, like young Rutland's before his murder, that he is 'not worth the coil', registers the child's intense distress at the adult world.[32] Just as Philip described the boy as a 'little abstract' so Arthur sees himself as unimportant in the maelstrom of grown ups that surround him.

---

[29] *The Child Actors*, p. 258.
[30] Shapiro, *Children of the Revels*, p. 106; Hillebrand, *The Child Actors*, p. 261.
[31] See Rutter, *Child's Play*, pp. 35–88. Charlotte Scott, *Shakespeare and the Idea of the Book* (Oxford: Oxford University Press, 2007), pp. 27–56.
[32] Cf. Rutland's exclamation: 'I am too mean a subject for thy wrath: | Be thou revenged on men, and let me live' (1.3.396–7).

Distinguishing themselves in this way allows the children to remain outside of the comprehension of the adult world. No child in the history plays can fully engage with the adult world, despite their best efforts, and their remove is both a blessing and their curse. Even the precocious Princes in *Richard III* are, ultimately, defined by their innocence and ignorance, unable as they are to accommodate the dissimulation of the adult world.

Arthur's failure to engage with his claim to the throne makes him a distinct voice within the play. In contrast, his mother, far more ambitious for him than he is for himself, reveals the precariousness of his status as a child:

> If thou, that bid'st me be content, wert grim,
> Ugly, and slanderous to thy mother's womb,
> Full of unpleasing blots and sightless stains,
> Lame, foolish, crooked, swart, prodigious,
> Patch'd with foul moles and eye-offending marks,
> I would not care, I then would be content,
> For then I should not love thee: no, nor thou
> Become thy great birth, nor deserve a crown.   (2.2.43–50)

Maternal love, according to Constance, is dependent upon both appearance and potential. With obvious echoes of *Richard III*, Constance defends her ambitions for Arthur on the basis of that he is 'fair' and full of 'nature's gifts'. In this way, Arthur is once again denuded of any unique identity: he is the child loved only because of how he looks and who his father was. The terrifying fragility of the parental bond is powerfully explored throughout Shakespeare's drama but where we notice its breakdown we also observe its ideal.[33]

The scene which depicts the developing relationship between Hubert and Arthur is the dramatic locus of the play. Hubert has been enlisted by John to murder 'yon young boy', during a conversation in which neither men can actually name the deed, instead referring cryptically to 'a grave' (3.2.75–80). The scene begins with Hubert calling the 'little prince' to him, to which Arthur responds by noticing that his gaoler is 'sad'. A conversation then ensues between the little boy and his would-be murderer

---

[33] See Tom MacFaul, *Problem Fathers in Shakespeare and Renaissance Drama* (Cambridge: Cambridge University Press, 2012). Early modern literature is again divided on the nature of instinctive parental love: where many Christian texts note parental love to be dependent on the behaviour of the child, many other texts, and indeed the drama, represent an overwhelming belief in the unconditional nature of parental love. Bruce Young, '*King Lear* and the Calamity of Fatherhood', in Thomas Moisan and Douglas Bruster (eds), *In the Company of Shakespeare: Essays on English Renaissance Literature in Honor of G. Blakemore Evans* (Madison, NJ: Fairleigh Dickinson University Press, 2002), p. 47; Deborah Shuger, *Habits of Thought in the English Renaissance: Religion, Politics and the Dominant Culture* (Toronto: University of Toronto Press, 1997), esp. pp. 220–30.

about their state of mind, Arthur reflecting on his own egoism in thinking only of his feelings rather than others. It is a remarkable scene for the audacious way in which Shakespeare has the child dominate the stage. The electric power of this scene emanates from a single statement by Arthur:

> Is it my fault that I was Geoffrey's son?
> No, indeed, is't not; and I would to heaven
> I were your son, so you would love me, Hubert.   (4.1.22–4)

Arthur, like any child, wants to be loved by their parent. Such humility strikes a deep chord not only in Hubert, who recognizes that this 'innocent prate' 'will awake my mercy' (25–6), but also with the audience who recall Constance's conditional devotion to the boy who should 'become... [his] great birth' (2.2.50). Amid the powerful in-fighting, political machinations, and factionalism of the play-world, Arthur's desire to be loved transforms him into a universal voice of childhood. He is no 'little prince' here but a young boy in search of safety and care. The relationship that then unfolds between the characters in this scene is quite remarkable in its brave exploration of human dynamics. Arthur, the fatherless child, becomes the carer to the man commissioned to murder him:

> Are you sick, Hubert? You look pale to-day.
> In sooth, I would you were a little sick,
> That I might sit all night and watch with you:
> I warrant I love you more than you do me.   (4.1.28–31)

In a fascinatingly perverse turn of events, Arthur finds his identity not as the 'little prince', the 'oppressed' or 'green' boy, the 'sweet child', or the 'pretty' boy but as a protective and loving son to a surrogate father. Shakespeare's exploration of love, or care, and of an instinctive familial dynamic is strikingly at odds with the world in which the child lives. But the gesture here towards a different world overturns the dramatic range of the play. *King John* becomes less about a flawed king's attempts to maintain power and more about the voice of the child in adult history. Arthur's attempt to change that history and to speak out against the world around him manifests here in his reproduction of a parental relationship. In a chilling moment of revelation, Hubert shows Arthur the paper on which the instructions for his torture are written. This is Hubert's first sign of weakness to the child as he attempts to show he is not responsible for the injunction. Arthur's response is emotionally very sophisticated but also compellingly instinctive—he sees Hubert's role as a betrayal of their relationship:

> Have you the heart? When your head did but ache,
> I knit my handkercher about your brows,
> The best I had, a princess wrought it me,

And I did never ask it you again;
And with my hand at midnight held your head,
And, like the watchful minutes to the hour,
Still and anon cheer'd up the heavy time,
Saying, 'what lack you?' and 'Where lies your grief?'
Or 'What good love may I perform for you?'   (4.1.41–9)

Shakespeare interweaves both the naive and the sophisticated in Arthur's response. The little asides about the handkerchief, which was embroidered for him by a princess, reveal the childish pride in tokens of friendship and the desire to keep hold of one's gifts! Shakespeare takes care here to create a history for Arthur, outside of the adult politics of the rest of the play, in which he and Hubert have a past. Arthur's disbelief that the man he took care of could hurt him is reflected in a powerful belief that good will outweigh evil:

Ah, none but in this iron age would do it!
The iron itself, though heat red-hot,
Approaching near these eyes, would drink my tears
And quench this fiery indignation
Even in the matter of mine innocence.   (4.1.60–4)

Arthur's extensive articulation of the horror of Hubert's commission persistently forces the audience to engage with infanticide. That the boy should have to face the anticipation of his own torture as well as its execution is emphasized by Shakespeare through the reiteration of disbelief—how could anyone, let alone a father figure, carry out such a deed: 'And if an angel should have come to me | And told me Hubert should put out mine eyes, | I would not have believ'd him, —no tongue | But Hubert's' (68–70). Shakespeare anatomizes the betrayal of a child from both the personal, individual, point of view, that of Arthur; and the universal, conceptual view that sees infanticide as the greatest of human crimes: 'The foul corruption of a sweet child's death' (4.2.81). Arthur's dependence on Hubert becomes increasingly tragic as we see him negotiate desperate forms of relief:

Nay, hear me, Hubert, drive these men away,
And I will sit as quiet as a lamb;
I will not stir, nor winch, nor speak a word,
Nor look upon the iron angerly:
Thrust but these men away, and I'll forgive you
Whatever torment you do put me to.   (4.1.78–83)

Even the executioners, 'these men', are relieved to be sent away from such a deed. In contrast to the deaths of the Princes in *Richard III*, narrated rather than shown, this scene is remarkable for its detailed presentation of the boy's fear, the bond between gaoler and prisoner, and the powerful descriptions of love and betrayal.[34] Shakespeare confronts infanticide head on and forces his audience to engage emotionally and visually with the possibility of child murder. The scene progresses through a dominant interest in the relationship between Hubert and Arthur. The emotional range of this scene is intensely drawn as Arthur desperately looks for the person he loves in the man who is compelled to torture him. Observing signs of hope—Hubert fails to heat the iron pokers—Arthur declares: 'O, now you look like Hubert! All this while | You were disguis'd' (4.1.125–6). This is the turning point for Arthur, in true Aristotelian fashion, the anagnorisis, or recognition.[35] Arthur's identification of the Hubert he knows is also his recognition that he will be safe, albeit briefly. Hubert will protect him, 'And pretty child, sleep doubtless and secure, | That Hubert, for the wealth of all the world, | Will not offend thee' (4.1.129–31). This entire scene is structured around the presence of Arthur, who has for the majority of the play remained silent: here his eloquence and physicality, his mixture of humility and outrage, vulnerability and defiance, make him one of the most powerfully affecting child characters that Shakespeare would write.[36] Whoever played Arthur in Pembroke's Men would have also probably played female roles in Shakespeare's repertoire and there is no doubt that this role was a gift to any boy actor with ambition.[37]

In its treatment of familial betrayal, grief, torture, failure, and mistakes *King John* traces many of the concerns that Shakespeare would develop in *King Lear*. One of the most powerful devices that Shakespeare exploits in his tragedies is, of course, dramatic irony. After the scene in which Hubert pledges to protect rather than torture the young boy, the play is almost exclusively taken up with the implications of Arthur's apparent, and then realized, death. The painstaking conversations between John and Hubert in which Hubert pretends to have killed Arthur and John bitterly regrets having ordered him to do so are fraught with dramatic irony: we know Arthur is alive and yet Hubert keeps his promise to withhold this

[34] Although precise dates of composition are not known for *King John*, the first printed text belonging to the 1623 folio, it was probably written around or before 1598 with *Richard III* having been written towards the beginning of the 1590s.

[35] Aristotle, *Poetics*, XI.2.

[36] Some critics have suggested that Shakespeare composed Arthur after the death of his own son, Hamnet, and that his loss inflected the boy's part. See G. B. Harrison, 'Shakespeare's Topical Significances', *TLS* (1930), p. 939. Edgar I. Fripp, *Shakespeare, Man and Artist* (Oxford: Oxford University Press, 1938), p. 435; W. Robertson Davies, *Shakespeare's Boy Actors* (New York: Russell and Russell, 1964).

[37] Heberle also makes the point that the boy playing Arthur probably also played Prince Henry, who closes the play with a 'boyish eloquence ... together with this final tableau of adult subjects pledging him their allegiance presents the most positive valorisation of the child in Shakespeare's histories and tragedies', *Infant Tongues*, pp. 39, 38.

information from the king. The king is deeply remorseful for an act that has not actually happened; the populace is in outrage at the rumours of Arthur's death, while Arthur, reprieved, attempts to escape from his prison, even as Hubert is about to release him, having admitted to a hugely relieved King John that he is in fact alive. Everything, of course, goes wrong: Arthur falls accidentally to his death, while trying to escape, Hubert is held responsible, despite being the only character who tried to protect the boy, and the terrible moral implications of infanticide remain in place—despite the accidental nature of the boy's death. The hideous emphasis on accident, chance, and misjudgement is equalled only by *King Lear* and the failure of Edmund's envoy to prevent Cordelia's death. Even the promise of having your eyes gouged out is fulfilled in *King Lear,* which comes to represent the most appalling and terrifying consequences of failed parental love. In *King John*, however, the death of Arthur takes hold of the public imagination and generates a tragic symphony of despair:

> Young Arthur's death is common in their mouths:
> And when they talk of him, they shake their heads
> And whisper one another in the ear;
> And he that speaks doth gripe the hearer's wrist,
> Whilst he that hears makes fearful action,
> With wrinkled brows, with nods, with rolling eyes.   (4.2.187–92)

This Bosch-like image of grimacing subjects, rolling their eyes and grasping each other's wrists, seems to spread the news of Arthur's death like an infection. The physical responses generate a powerful sense of movement in the play-world. In contrast to the static beauty of the dead Princes in *Richard III*, which resulted in the speechlessness of their murderers, Arthur's death compels the body into action, animating grief through words, movement, gesture, and expression. When Arthur falls to his death as he tries to escape, even as Hubert is coming to release him, he is found by the Bastard and Salisbury who interpret the accident as murder, and catastrophic in its moral implications:

> It is the shameful work of Hubert's hand,
> The practice and the purpose of the king:
> From whose obedience I forbid my soul,
> Kneeling before this ruin of sweet life,
> And breathing to this breathless excellence
> The incense of a vow, a holy vow,
> Never to taste the pleasures of the world,
> Never to be infected with delight
> Nor conversant with ease and idleness,
> Til I have set a glory to this hand,
> By giving it the worship of revenge.   (4.3.62–72)

Salisbury's reaction to the child's death conflates both religious and philosophical attitudes to infanticide. Relinquishing his soul's allegiance to the King defies authority and places him in contrast to Herod's Massacre of the Innocents; committing himself to a 'holy vow' of abstinence gestures towards the ascetic or monastic orders whose faith transcends earthly experiences; while worshipping revenge puts Salisbury squarely outside Christianity and in the hands of individual anarchists, who believe, like Francis Bacon, that 'revenge is a kind of wild justice', but justice nevertheless.[38] The language and tone of the various responses to Arthur's death amplify the profound implications of child murder. The religious language of worship, glory, unification, and commitment bind the onlookers in a catechism of horror. In an unusual moment of joint speaking, the Earl of Pembroke and Lord Bigot exclaim: 'Our souls religiously confirm thy words' (73). Like Salisbury, they emphasize their soul's allegiance to Arthur and what his death represents for them. Mediating their response through the idea of the soul identifies the whole-hearted extent to which the men morally distinguish themselves from King John and all he represents. In this way, the child's death establishes a powerful point of characterization for the other members of the play-world. In an otherwise historically and ethically murky play, Arthur's death provides the only moment of moral clarity. Even then, of course, the narrative is not entirely straightforward: neither Hubert nor John is in fact directly responsible for the boy's death, although both attempted it in either thought or action. The play only manages to force some kind of clarity at this crisis point, and Arthur's death defines not only how we and the other characters feel about John's reign, but also how we feel about history itself.

As the dead bodies of many of the children in these history plays testify, they are victims of birth, place, or accident. None of these children has any agency over their future or their bodies and even the young King Henry becomes a pawn in a series of political and personal games that he is simply ill equipped to play. What is especially fascinating here, however, is the extent to which Shakespeare creates the child character in order to expose the unjust vagaries of history, and the men (and occasionally women) who make it so. On the one hand, we can trace a deterministic view of history in which the figure of the child becomes a symbolic image of political failure choreographed by the fantasy of predestination. On the other, the children of the history plays offer opportunities for transformation, and for engaging in the ways in which the future can be changed through

---

[38] *The Complete Works of Francis Bacon*, ed. Brian Vickers (Oxford: Oxford University Press, 2008), p. 347. John Kerrigan, *Shakespeare's Binding Language* (Oxford: Oxford University Press, 2016), pp. 67–90.

a recognition of the value of the child within the narrative of history as progressive. Many of these plays explore the idea of history itself as a fiction, a false record, and an oppressive paratext in which dominant powers produce an organized response to the past. Within this version of history the child is an opportunity—almost always a lost one—in which the past could have been changed, as well as the future. In this way, the figure of the child comes to haunt history as a moment of potential wherein the time was in contention. As Queen Elizabeth says to Richard:

> The parents live, whose children thou hast butcher'd,
> Old wither'd plants, to wail it with their age.
> Swear not by time to come; for that thou hast
> Misused ere used, by time misused o'erpast.   (*Richard III*, 4.4)

Creating such morally and emotionally complex narratives through the figure of the child allows Shakespeare to address questions of divine order and free will but also, perhaps most importantly, of historical responsibility. For the Elizabethans, and indeed for us, history's use of the child forces us to confront our past as well as our legacy. Think of the piles of children's shoes outside Nazi concentration camps: think of the girls abducted by Boko Haram in Nigeria; think of the image of the 3-year-old Syrian boy washed up on the shores of Greece; all of these images tell us about our history; our failures as well as our allegiances. Shakespeare's children tell a similar story of failure, alliance, violence, and political negligence but they also remind us of who we are and how we understand, respond, and attempt to change that history even as it is unfolding.

3

The End of the Beginning

Shakespeare's Tragic Children

'He used to be a child: he has become adult. That is a difference of quality. For the child is irrational, the adult rational.'[1] Seneca's observation was commonplace for many Elizabethans, who understood the child as inferior, in all faculties, to the adult. Such inferiority was represented, institutionally, through forms of submission and obedience. The transition from irrational to rational, or child to adult, is largely determined by the acquisition of knowledge through which certain processes of socialization take place. Within the terms of knowledge and experience the 'rational' faculties allow humans to interact successfully with each other. All forms of socialization, whether dialogic or hierarchical, are determined by a relationship in which the adult is superior to the child. Where, in the histories, however, we perceive this dynamic through the child as a victim of circumstance, condemned by their relative frailty to suffer the slings and arrows of outrageous fortune, in the tragedies we begin to see a more instrumental view of the young person. For many of Shakespeare's tragedies the child is at the centre of the drama and they begin to take control of their world. This chapter will explore the forms of control that Shakespeare's tragic children take and how this comes to redefine the perimeters of his tragedies as well as our perceptions of children.

In what follows I examine the children of *Romeo and Juliet*, *Titus Andronicus*, and *King Lear*, showing how they evolve from victims to agents of tragedy. Each play explores forms of socialization through which the child is understood to develop. Strategies of socialization, in which children are prepared for the adult world, depend on a number of key assumptions. One of them is that childhood is a discrete stage of human development and can be adequately identified by age or status; another key assumption is that the adult is a fully developed role model

---

[1] *De Ira*, 2.20, 2–5. Cf. Thomas Wiedemann, *Adults and Children in the Roman Empire* (Abingdon: Routledge, 1989), esp. pp. 5–48.

through which the child can learn positive behaviour. All of Shakespeare's tragedies complicate this model of development through socialization, not least of all through unpicking the two major assumptions upon which they depend. The children of Shakespeare's tragedies vary in age from infants (Aaron and Tamora's newborn baby) to their twenties and thirties (Lear's daughters): what makes them a child, albeit only briefly in the play-world, is their relationship to the parent. As anthropologists have long recognized, childhood is not a universal condition; it is culturally specific and always in a process of categorization. The Elizabethans also understood childhood to be a somewhat elastic term which could refer to any stage of development between birth and marriage.[2] The plays under discussion in this chapter appear keenly interested in the relationship between children and parents. Locating the child as an ethical category, in which there are expectations of duty, obedience, innocence, and truth, is central to the drama of destruction that these plays narrate. The child, whatever their age, occupies a unique position in the parental imagination. The plays under discussion here demonstrate the extraordinary power that the child represents in opposition to the adult worlds.

When, in *Romeo and Juliet*, the friar refers to 'unbruised youth with unstuffed brain' he suggests a relative version of youthfulness in which the young person is defined by what they are not. In contrast, the adult tacitly emerges as both bruised and full of cares, a dichotomy that the plays continually return to.[3] For the audience, however, the friar's comment is both portentous and ironic. Having just witnessed the powerfully charged scene in which the young lovers declare their feelings for each other, as well as the impossibilities of their situation, we do not necessarily agree with the friar. The brains of these two young people are stuffed with worries, and

---

[2] Daniel Tutelville in *St Paul's Threefold Cord* (1635) writes that boys and girls achieve "ripeness of age" at 14 and 12 respectively and can then put themselves into a monastery, (p. 172). Krausman Ben-Amos notes, however, the variant views on childhood and adolescence as informed by social and economic standing as well as geographical difference: 'The Countess of Warwick recalled in her autobiography that her brother, who married in his late teens, "being then judged to be too young to live with his wife", was sent shortly after the ceremony to France, while his wife was brought to their house. Her own son who was married about the age of 19, was likewise sent abroad while his new wife was taken to live with the Countess of Warwick,' *Adolescence and Youth*, p. 32.

[3] Henry IV makes a similar observation through contrasting himself with the shipboy who can sleep despite the rough weather while he, the king, is full of anxiety. This is as much about status as age but the choice of the child amplifies the distinction, *2 Henry IV*:

> Canst thou, O partial sleep, give thy repose
> To the wet sea-boy in an hour so rude;
> And in the calmest and most stillest night,
> With all appliances and means to boot,
> Deny it to a king? Then, happy low, lie down!
> Uneasy lies the head that wears a crown.   (3.1. 26–31)

they will be fatally bruised before they reach adulthood. The idea of youthfulness that the play-world creates—against the realities of the lovers' experience—is central to Shakespeare's conception of the child. *Romeo and Juliet* dramatizes the death of childhood, not simply in the destruction of the young couple themselves but long before that in the play's refusal to allow youthfulness either frailty or freedom. Juliet is pushed by those around her between the adult and infant worlds, between the bonds of the nurse who relishes the memories of the toddler Juliet and the adult world of marriage and sexual maturity. Both maternal figures, the nurse and Lady Capulet, insist that Juliet is both a child and an adult, dependent and independent. Recalling her husband's comments on the young Juliet, the nurse remembers:

> 'Yea', quoth he, 'dost thou fall on thy face?
> Thou wilt fall backward when thou has more wit,
> Wilt thou not, Jule?' And by my holidam,
> The pretty wretch left crying and said 'Ay'.   (1.3.43–6)

The conflation of the child who has fallen over with the woman who will be supine in sexual intercourse is a comic reflection on the brevity of childhood. Here the 'merry' husband of the nurse reflects on the difference between the child and the adult Juliet; falling first on her face and then on her back, the trajectory from toddler to twenty-something seems fraught with tears for this child. The departing child, crying 'Ay'—registers that she is both subject (I) and consenting (yes) to such a future, although she weeps as she does so. The play-world admits youth in order to comment on its relation to adulthood: like the friar, the nurse's husband understands youth as a rehearsal for adulthood. The proximity between the child and the adult is what drives the tragedy of *Romeo and Juliet*, at both a narrative and symbolic level. The narrative depends on the parental feuds that drive the lovers together and apart: it also depends on the tension produced by the characters who fail to understand the agency of the child.

One of the most powerful accounts that this play produces is that of autonomous youth. Condemned by mistiming, misunderstanding, and breakdowns in communication, the tragedy of the lovers focuses on their failure to gain control of their own lives, rather than their untimely deaths. We do not so much lament the loss of their youth but their place in a world which refused to take youth seriously. Almost nobody listens to Romeo or Juliet: Mercutio mocks his friend's desires; the friar thinks Romeo capricious and superficial; Lady Capulet perceives her daughter too young for marriage only to insist on a union with Paris, despite Juliet's reluctance; and Capulet threatens to disown his recalcitrant daughter, who swears she is 'too young to marry' (3.5.186). Only the nurse, the keeper of

Juliet's childhood and childish self, attempts to engage with the character's transition into womanhood.[4] But this play makes few concessions to the childish: youth is a stage of being not a concept and, paradoxically, those who relish it most ferociously are the young couple themselves. Their deaths are not a transition into adulthood, as many have argued, but a fulfilment of the childhood they were both denied.[5] Death is the space, the time, the nursery, and the liberty that the play-world refused them: the 'old Freetown', perhaps, of justice.[6] Childhood means very little in this play, indeed across Shakespeare's drama it is an idea 'more honoured in the breach than in the observance', but in *Romeo and Juliet* it is the absence that fills up the room; the 'thing' that the lovers are denied both in hindsight and in the action of the drama: 'Speak briefly, can you like of Paris's love?' (1.3.98).

BRIEF LIVES

In this section I want to address why Romeo and Juliet are considered youthful, how that impacts on their narrative, and the ways in which the other characters speak to and about them. Shakespeare is very specific about Juliet's age: she is 13, two years younger than her source character, and she does not live to see her fourteenth birthday. Romeo's age is less defined, and he certainly appears more experienced than Juliet, but the play suggests they are contemporaries, give or take a few years.[7] The play's representations of youth take various different forms: the couple present themselves to the audience as reckless, passionate, and fearless which corresponds to a particular idea of youthfulness; the parents of the lovers treat their children as young when it benefits them, and expect them to grow up when it does not. Like many of Shakespeare's tragedies, the play is concerned with networks of control and how forms of insubordination may emerge as socially necessary rather than destructive. The power of youth, so brilliantly portrayed in the febrile and unstable relationships of Verona, is mobilized across various extreme states of feeling; love, like war, conflict, fear, or anxiety, supports the play's combative environment and allows it to become host to the drama of youth. Many of the early modern texts that

---

[4] See Jennifer Higginbotham, *The Girlhood of Shakespeare's Sisters* (Edinburgh: Edinburgh University Press, 2013), pp. 26–7; Williams, *Shakespeare and the Performance of Girlhood*, pp. 43–51.

[5] Julia Kristeva is especially interesting on this point, 'Adolescence', *The Psychoanalytic Review*, 94 (October 2007), pp. 715–25.

[6] See 1.1.97.

[7] David Farley-Hills perceives a marked shift in the representation of Juliet in the second quarto, see 'The Bad Quarto of Romeo and Juliet', *Shakespeare Survey*, 49 (1996), pp. 27–43.

address parenting focus on youth, the stage between the child and the adult, as the most formative, but also the most threatening. While Ralph Blower considers young children to be easily moulded by their parents, 'for that the minde in Infants is like a table booke wherein nothing is written, and like a tender twig which may be bowed euery way', an anonymous text entitled *A President for Parents* (1571) is expressly concerned with the potential 'offences' of youth. Establishing that young men need to be watched more carefully than children, the author goes on to explain:

> Yong men ought more narowly be loked to than *children*, [who] be small and curable, perpetrated perhappes through the negligence of gouernors, and committed by disobedience? But the trespasses and offences of yongmen, are oftentimes great, horrible, and the transgressions of yong men miserable, as intemperate gluttonie, and rauening of the bellie, the expilation and robbing of their fathers goodes, cardes, diceplay, banketting, the lawless love of virgins and women the pollutings of... marriages.[8]

Most of the anxiety that inheres in such conceptions of youth focuses on forms of insubordination and attempts to reiterate the necessity of the will of the father over that of the child or youth. Freedom to choose your own spouse is a consistent point through which many of these texts rehearse forms of authority, as John Stockwood's *A Bartholomew's Fairing for Parents* makes clear: 'That children may not make their own choice in marrying: I prove after this manner, no child may take upon him the dutie and office of his father.'[9] In this way, the idea of the child remains focused less on age and more on obedience. Doing what your parents tell you is a dominant rite of passage in many of the tragedies, but Shakespeare does not present us with uncomplicated pictures of familial order. Quite the contrary, disobedience becomes a necessary development in the formation of his social values.

The role of Elizabethan doctrines of obedience in the formation of a nation state has been well documented and tends to focus on the privileging of power relations.[10] The relationship between parent and child is central to such discourses and frequently emerges in the analogy that a

---

[8] *A President for Parentes, Teaching the vertuous training vp of Children and wholesome information of yongmen. Written in greke by the prudent and wise Phylosopher Choeroneus Plutarchus, Translated and partly augmented by Ed. Grant: very profitable to be read of all those that desire to be Parents of vertuous children.* ANNO. 1571, sig. 111.

[9] John Stockwood, *A Bartholomew's Fairing for Parents* (1589), p. 34.

[10] Louis Montrose, 'Spenser and the Political Imaginary', *ELH* 69 (2002); 'Professing the Renaissance; The Poetics and Politics of Culture', in H. A. Veeser (ed.), *The New Historicism* (New York and London: Routledge, 1989), pp. 15–36. David O'Hara, 'Political Obedience and the State: Elizabethan News Pamphlets and Rebellion in Ireland', *Media History*, 21.2 (2015); Wallace T. Macaffrey, *The Shaping of the Elizabethan Regime: Elizabethan Politics, 1558–1572* (Princeton: Princeton University Press, 1968).

father is to his child, what a monarch is to his/her subject. Stockwood is again typical when he asserts:

> For the rule of the parentes ouer theyr *children*, ought to resemble the gouernment of good princes towards their subiects, that is to say, it must be milde, gentle, and easie to be borne, for as they, so like wise parents so far as concerneth them and lieth in theyr abilitie to performe, they must carrie such an euen and vpright hand in their gouernement.[11]

Stockwood's relatively genial tone does not compromise his commitment to absolutist forms of authority, which are similarly picked up in the conflation of children and servants.[12] Within these terms the child becomes a subject to both state and father, but, ultimately, of course, to God. While there are many Elizabethan texts that are specifically directed at children, a great number of early modern books use the figure of the child to establish the relationship between human subject and God.[13] Addressing all human subjects as children within the context of their service to Christianity reproduces the figure of the child as both submissive and in need of instruction.[14] All of these texts focus on obedience as the dominant value in the relationship between father and child which can be rehearsed in a variety of ways. *Romeo and Juliet*, like *King Lear*, establishes the parental relationship within the contexts of conformity. In both tragedies, the children assert themselves against the wishes of their parents, or more specifically father in *King Lear*, to both their release and their destruction. Yet what is specific to *Romeo and Juliet* is an Elizabethan culture of youth, in which passion prevails as both intemperance and energy, vitality and destruction.

The emphasis on the couple's age has been amplified in the twentieth century with two film versions casting teenagers in the roles. Franco Zeffirelli's 1968 film used actors who were 17 and 15 years old and Baz Luhrmann's more recent film (1996) used Leonardo di Caprio and Clare

---

[11] Stockwood, *A Bartholomews Fairing*, p. 80.

[12] Hugh Rhodes, for example, in his *The book of nurture for men servants and children* (1560), explicitly treats children and servants as vassals of the house and master, understanding that correction and discipline are essential to all forms of authority.

[13] Some examples of these texts include: Henry Middleton, *Certain short questions and answers (for children about godly and Christian matters)* (1580); John Oakes, *A short Interpretation of the Lord's Prayer* (1627); John Carpenter , *Contemplations for the Institution of Children in the Christian Religion* (1601).

[14] Henry Petowe, *THE COVNTREY AGVE. OR, LONDON her Welcome home, to her tyer'd retired Children* (1625); Leonard Wright, *The Pilgrimage to Paradise. Compiled for the direction, comfort, and resolution of Gods poore distressed children, in passing through this irkesome wildernesse of temptation and tryall* (1591); *A CELESTIALL Looking-glasse: To behold the beauty of Heauen. Directed vnto all the Elect Children of God, very briefly composed, and authentically penned, that it may be effectually gained* (1621).

Danes who were 22 and 17 respectively. Stage performance history has revealed a more conservative attitude to casting the lovers as especially young: two iconic actresses to take the female lead, for example, were older; Ellen Terry was 35 when she played Juliet to Henry Irving's Romeo at the Lyceum in 1882, and Leslie Howard, as Romeo, was 42 playing the role in a 1936 film version directed by George Cokor. Zeffirelli's stage production in 1960, however, began to shift the casting of the lovers into a distinctly more youthful realm: Judi Dench was 26 when she played Juliet and John Stride only 24 as Romeo. The extent to which we understand the lovers as youthful has become even more developed in recent critical history, partly through adaptations which allow directors to trim long speeches and adapt the script to the actor and partly through a greater cultural acceptance of sexually confident teenagers. Zeffirelli's film was perhaps the boldest in this respect by casting Olivia Hussey, who was below the legal age of consent at the time, and yet all the reviews of the film focused on the actors as exceptionally thoughtful and effective choices. There is no doubt that Zeffirelli paved the way for a deeper appreciation of the youthfulness of the lovers. In this way acting experience or a well-rehearsed ability to speak Shakespeare's verse was not the most important element in performing the drama. What almost all critics admired in both Zeffirelli and Luhrmann was the risks they took in putting relatively inexperienced actors in these roles and how the camera emphasized their close-up reactions, fragility, and wonder rather than the long shots of beautifully spoken verse that we have come to associate with the direction of Branagh or Olivier.[15]

We have no direct performance records for the play until William Davenant's production in 1662. However, on the basis of the title page of the first quarto (1597), which insists that it 'hath been often (with great applause) plaid publiquely, by the right Honourable the L. Hunsdon his servants', we can assume that the play was performed at the Theatre, with Richard Burbage in the title male role and an accomplished young boy playing Juliet. Burbage would have been around 20 years old at this time and the boy playing Juliet would probably have been around 12 or 13, about the same age as the character, and the age that many boys were recruited as apprentices to guilds to train alongside adult actors. As social historians have demonstrated youth can last a relatively long time for the Elizabethans and there is no doubt that Shakespeare intended his title

---

[15] For a detailed discussion of the performance histories of the play see Russell Jackson, *Romeo and Juliet: Shakespeare at Stratford Series* (London: Arden, 2003); David Bevington, *This Wide and Universal Theatre: Shakespeare in Performance Then and Now* (Chicago: University of Chicago Press, 2009); Russell Jackson (ed.), *The Cambridge Companion to Shakespeare on Film* (Cambridge: Cambridge University Press, 2007).

characters to appear young; but what that means within the play-world remains complex.[16] The central questions here are why is their youth relevant to the play and how does Shakespeare exploit or explore this idea of youthfulness?

Individually Romeo and Juliet represent different ideas of youth: Romeo, like Jacques's teenager in his seven ages speech, appears as the lover 'sighing like a furnace, with a woeful ballad made to his mistress' eyebrow'. Characterized by his love first for Rosalind and then for Juliet, Romeo's youthfulness becomes defined by his desire. Before we meet Romeo, Montague introduces his son through the pains of love:

> Many a morning hath he there been seen,
> With tears augmenting the fresh morning's dew,
> Adding to clouds more clouds with his deep sighs...
> Away from light steals home my heavy son,
> And private in his chamber pens himself,
> Shuts up his windows, locks fair daylight out,
> And makes himself an artificial night.   (1.1.127–9, 133–6)

Equally powerful, perhaps, is the Galenic understanding of youth as fiery tempered and intemperate which resonates through Romeo's associations with Mercutio and Tybalt, as well as the play's overarching narrative of feudal hostility and teenage rebellion. Galen understood the human body to be governed by four types or humours, which not only indicated your temperament but also your life stage.[17] Widely adopted by the Elizabethans, Galenic medicine understood babies to be governed by the blood, which was associated with spring, passion, air, and childhood, whereas youth was governed by 'the red choler, which was also associated with hotness and dryness, with the summer season, and with fire'.[18] The play is dominated by the 'heat' of red choler, both metaphorically and literally: the narrative takes place in the run-up to Lammas day, a harvest festival of the first day of August, and therefore the hottest time of the year, while the male characters, both Capulets and Montagues, define themselves as passionate, angry, energetic, and intemperate.[19] The climate and atmosphere of the play

[16] Krausman Ben-Amos, *Adolescence and Youth*; see also Hugh Cunningham, *Children and Childhood in Western Society since 1500* (London: Longman, 1995); Colin Heywood, *A History of Childhood: Children and Childhood in the West from Medieval to Modern Times* (Cambridge: Blackwell, 2001).

[17] See Gail Kern Paster, *Humoring the Body: Emotions and the Shakespearean Stage* (Chicago: University of Chicago Press, 2004).

[18] Krausman Ben-Amos, *Adolescence and Youth*, p. 16.

[19] Lammas day is no longer celebrated as such on the liturgical calendar, but the Christian calendar continues to celebrate 'harvest festival', which is a version of Lammas. The nurse refers to the festival at 1.3.15.

is entirely Galenic in its commitment to the humour of adolescence. And yet, compellingly, the heroes attempt to distinguish themselves from the intense narrative of youth in which they are trapped. Juliet is the most consistently infantilized character within the play and yet this conception of childishness is neither complete nor comprehensive. The nurse provides the most pervasive references to Juliet's childishness, which she largely construes in hindsight, remembering her as a baby, recalling seminal stages of development, like weaning and walking, and reminiscing about the innocence and ignorance of her early years. The nurse's relationship to Juliet represents them both through a sense of shared history and, unlike any other character in the play, positions Juliet firmly within the memory of her childish self.

'THE CHILDHOOD OF OUR JOY'

Juliet carries two great burdens within the play; one is her name and the other is her status as a child. Juliet is more defined than any other character by the parental networks within the play. We learn that Juliet was breast-fed by the nurse because she lost her own daughter, whom, she suggests, Juliet both replaces and fails to replace, since her presence is another child's absence. We also learn that Juliet is an only child and carries the full weight of parental expectation. Thinking on the possibility of Juliet's marriage to Paris causes both the nurse and Lady Capulet to reflect on the child Juliet. A minor squabble between the two women as to Juliet's exact age reveals the nurse to be the better keeper of the child's history:

> Come Lammas Eve at night shall she be fourteen.
> Susan and she—God rest all Christian souls—
> Were of an age. Well, Susan is with God;
> She was too good for me. But as I said,
> On Lammas Eve at night shall she be fourteen,
> That shall she, marry, I remember it well.
> Tis since the earthquake now eleven years,
> And she was weaned—I never shall forget it—
> Of all the days of the year upon that day;
> For then I had laid wormwood to my dug,
> Sitting in the sun under the dovehouse wall.
> My lord and you were then at Mantua—   (1.3.19–30)

The detail through which the nurse remembers the moment of weaning focuses our attention on Juliet's immaturity: to have been weaned from the breast only eleven years ago makes her seem still very young but it also points to the first stage of separation that Juliet is forced to endure, pre-empting the second in her potential marriage to Paris. The nurse's reference to her own dead daughter, an exact contemporary of Juliet, not only highlights the maternal bond that the woman feels for her charge but it also provides us with a specific context as to why the nurse could breast-feed.[20] The nurse's speech, with its visual precision ('under the dovehouse wall') and its factual observations ('My lord and you were then in Mantua') as well as its formative place in her memory ('I never shall forget it') supports an imaginative framework for the history of Juliet. Despite the traumatic nature of this event for Juliet, the memory seems to have become far more important to the nurse than it has to the child:

> But as I said,
> When it did taste the wormwood on the nipple
> Of my dug and felt it bitter, pretty fool,
> To see it tetchy and fall out with the dug!...
> And since that time it is eleven years
> For then she could stand high-lone—nay, by th'rood,
> She could have run and waddled all about.   (1.3.31–4, 37–9)

The series of reflections, prompted by the mention of Juliet's marriage, reveal the formative events of Juliet's infancy which highlight her youth as well as its inevitable transition into adulthood. Focusing on the role of wet-nursing supports a greater bond between the nurse and Juliet than she might have with her mother. Although it was customary for aristocratic women, or those of the 'higher and richer sort', as Elizabeth Clinton calls them, to enlist a wet-nurse, most texts on this subject recognize the formative role that breast-feeding plays in establishing a bond between child and carer. The profundity of this bond is ordained by God but driven by instinct, 'for by His secret operation, the mothers affection is so knit by natures law to her tender babe, as she findes no power to deny to suckle it.'[21] The nurse's memory of weaning Juliet, as 'tetchy and fall[ing] out with the dug', replays the strength of this bond and the maternal networks through which Juliet is presented. Tracing the seminal steps of

---

[20] See Beatrice Groves for a discussion of breast-feeding, 'The Morality of Milk: Shakespeare and the Ethics of Nursing', in Patrick Gray and John D. Cox (eds), *Shakespeare and Renaissance Ethics* (Cambridge: Cambridge University Press, 2014), pp. 139–58. Elizabeth W. Marvick, 'Nature versus Nurture: Patterns and Trends in Seventeenth-Century French Child-Rearing', in Lloyd deMause (ed.), *The History of Childhood: The Evolution of Parent–Child Relationships as a Factor in History* (London: Souvenir Press, 1976), pp. 259–301. For contemporary references see Thomas Elyot, *The Governor* (London, 1531), fo. 18; James Wolveridge, *Speculum Matricis* (1671); Cf. Audrey Eccles, *Obstetrics and Gynaecology in Tudor and Stuart England* (Kent, Oh.: Kent State University Press, 1982), p. 98.

[21] Elizabeth Clinton Lincoln, *The Countess of Lincoln's Nurserie* (1622), p. 8.

development, the nurse remembers that when Juliet learnt to run, she fell
and 'broke her brow'.

> And then my husband—God be with his soul,
> A was a merry man—took up the child.
> 'Yea', quoth he, 'dost thou fall on thy face?
> Thou wilt fall backward when thou hast more wit,
> Wilt thou not, Jule?' And by my holidam,
> The pretty wretch left crying and said 'Ay'.
> To see now how a jest will come about!   (1.3.40–7)

The tender way in which the nurse maps her recollections, both amused and
wistful, is produced by glimpses into the idioms of that bond—referred to
as 'Jule', the little girl, called briefly by another name, is animated by
the memories of the dead. There is something distinctly poignant about
the remembrance of the living child through the dead husband and the
moments in which those perspectives come together in tears as well as
laughter. The child Juliet will always remain attendant on the adolescent
Juliet of the play's action because of the tight hold that the nurse's memory
has on those formative years. Lady Capulet is bored and irritated by the
nurse's memories of her daughter and yet we hear that only she is now the
keeper of Juliet's past. The nurse's husband is dead and what remains of
Juliet's childhood are these glimpses into the developmental milestones
when every doting parent recalls the huge changes in their child's life. But
these memories are not protected by the boundaries of childhood, where,
like Polixenes and Leontes, innocence was exchanged for innocence; instead
these memories are animated by the present where the young girl offered in
marriage is also the infant who fell over and lay on her back: 'To see now
how a jest will come about!' The power and pertinence of the nurse's
speeches here reside in her ability to suspend Juliet's childhood above the
stage, as a spectral image of what she has lost, both nurse and child, but also
as an image of what is to come. The crying child who says 'Ay' to the joke
she does not understand becomes a powerful metaphor for what is left of
Juliet's short life.

   Within the context of the nurse's memories, Juliet's gentle insistence
that she is too young to marry becomes more profound. As both her
mother and her nurse prepare her for a marriage she does not want, Juliet's
response registers obedience rather than agreement: 'But no more deep
will I indart mine eye | Than your consent gives strength to make it fly'
(1.3.100–1). The contrast to Romeo is marked: where he is groaning from
love and languishing in his chamber, she has yet to feel such an emotion
or consider its fulfilment. Despite Lady Capulet's unlikely insistence that
'younger than you | Here in Verona, ladies of esteem, | Are made already

mothers' (1.3.71–3) the average age for marriage in early modern England was mid- to late twenties.[22] If we consider the transition from youth to adulthood as marked by autonomy and responsibility marriage functions as a useful marker for the consideration of the length or space of childhood.[23] Much of the youthful energy of the play emanates from the high proportion of single, or unmarried, characters. The predominantly male world of Verona is upheld by the sexual energies of Mercutio, Benvolio, Tybalt, Paris, and even Samson and Gregory, who, as well as Romeo and Juliet, all stand in contrast to the elders of the play—the parents of the heroes and the widow nurse. Within these terms the play-world is dichotomized by the contrast between adolescence and adulthood. Marriage, the 'honour' that Juliet 'dreamt not of', becomes the gateway into the adult world and yet it cannot function successfully as such.[24] Undertaking an illicit marriage that defies both ceremony and authority, and appearing to be dead before she can take part in an ordained version of the event, Juliet travesties the concept of marriage as a socially functioning institution. If marriage operates as the entrance into the adult world of the play then the lovers baulk at that boundary, resistant it seems to the false 'honour' of conformity. Rewriting marriage as a private rite of their individual desires, Romeo and Juliet legitimize their union through individual agency which will give them the right to die, if not to live. Mercutio's cynical reflections on desire reproduce marital sex as an act of conformity, rather than pleasure. The spectre of Queen Mab preparing women for sex and pregnancy: 'This is the hag, when maids lie on their backs, | That presses them and learns them first to bear, | Making them women of good carriage' (1.4.90–2) rehearses the loss of youth in marriage whereby the maid becomes the hag, once she's learnt to lie still.[25] Here the adult world of institutional orthodoxy becomes fraught with the toxic resistance of youth.

[22] I say unlikely because if she had married and given birth at Juliet's age she would be 28 in the play, but she is frequently referred to as 'old'. Twenty-eight was, in fact, the average age that many men of this period married, and women at about 26.

[23] Alan MacFarlane, *Marriage and Love in England: Modes of Reproduction 1300–1840* (Oxford: Basil Blackwell, 1986); Peter Laslett, *Household and Family in Pastime* (Cambridge: Cambridge University Press, 1972). Studies in the archaeology of childhood have also revealed the ways in which play is conventionally organized around gender, so that children prepare for their domestic roles through role play and games; see Baxter, *The Archaeology of Childhood*.

[24] According to Helen Berry and Elizabeth Foyster, 'marriage defined the achievement of social adulthood in early modern England', *The Family in Early Modern England* (Cambridge: Cambridge University Press, 2007), p. 108.

[25] See Patricia Crawford for a compelling discussion of perceptions of sexuality in this period, not least of all the emphasis on a 'good' and fulfilling sex life within marriage, which she describes as 'the only site of lawful sexual activity', *Blood, Bodies and Families in Early Modern England* (London: Routledge, 2014), ch. 2.

Just before the scene in which the lovers meet, the Chorus reasserts the dynamic between youth and age in fatal terms: 'Now old desire doth in his death-bed lie, | And young affection gapes to be his heir.' Beyond the whims of Romeo's desires the Chorus reminds us of the tension between youth and age that the play presents. To understand the representation of youth in this play, and the extent to which it is meaningful in Shakespeare's development of Juliet, we must attend to the various means by which the play puts together an archaeology of childhood. In other words, how do we distinguish the adolescent from the adult world? Beyond the nurse's memories the most formative distinction is created through space and the ways in which the lovers negotiate the world around them. Having no space to call their own—neither the indoors of the domestic sphere nor the outdoors of masculine control—the lovers create their own hinterland, somewhere between the two.[26] The dark night and the space their voices occupy somewhere between the ground on which Romeo stands and the window through which Juliet leans provides a unique place for the lovers to explore their childish selves amid adult imperatives. The long scene in which the lovers meet is an exceptional synthesis of intemperance and self-reflection. Nowhere does Shakespeare capture the tension between optimism and anxiety more beautifully than here. Both characters run ahead with their desire then hold themselves back; passionately express themselves and then attempt to be more restrained. That they are capable of both intemperance and control positions them beautifully on the border between the intrepid child and the cautious adult. The adults in this play-world suggest that marriage is a form of socialization, perhaps the final developmental stage through which the child must pass in order to become a responsible and capable member of the adult world. Part of that socialization is to learn decorum, self-control, and responsibility, which is precisely what Romeo and Juliet try to do in this scene. Both characters speak in asides, self-censoring: Romeo tells himself he is 'too bold' (57); while Juliet begs him not to think she is 'too quickly won' (138). As the lovers find each other they also lose their childish selves, and Juliet most powerfully so.

The defining moment for her is not when she disobeys her parents but when she withholds herself from the nurse: 'Go, counsellor; | Thou and my bosom henceforth shall be twain' (3.5.239–40). This severance from the nurse marks the final stage in the narrative of Juliet's childhood—as she was weaned, she walked, she ran, and now, finally, she stops communicating. The crying toddler that said 'Ay' to the nurse's husband when he asked if

---

[26] For a discussion of the relationships between early modern space and identity see Lorna Hutson, *The Usurer's Daughter* (London: Routledge, 1994), pp. 20–9.

she would 'fall backward when thou hast more wit' now says 'I' when she shuts herself off from everyone: 'My dismal scene I needs must act alone' (4.3.19). She is and has become the agent of her own destiny. Much like the nurse's husband's comment, the end of childhood is both merry and sad. The joy that the lovers' express in their devotion to each other is quickly tempered by the destruction that their desire has begun. After the murder of Tybalt, Romeo fears Juliet's reaction: 'How is it with her? | Doth not she think me an old murderer, | Now I have stained the childhood of our joy?' (3.3.92–4). The act of murder has aged Romeo as it has also destroyed their childhoods, as well as the infancy of their love. The play on childhood is emphatic here—conflating the early stages of their love with their own youths, Romeo knows that Tybalt's death has altered their trajectory forever, as well as their innocence. He is now 'old' and their 'childhood' is over. Yet as the couple attempt to redefine themselves as distinct from their parents, to break free of the name they were given at birth, they become powerfully and irrevocably returned to the status of children. When the nurse finds Juliet, apparently fast asleep, before her intended marriage to Paris, her response is to infantilize her: 'Why lamb, why lady! Fie, you slug-a-bed' (4.4.28). The tender way in which the nurse tries to wake her is translated into appalled grief by her parents who believe her to be dead: 'O me, O me, my child, my only life' (43). Capulet responds: 'O child, o child, my soul and wit my child! | Dead art thou, alack, my child is dead; | And with my child my joys are buried' (4.4.88–90). What resonates through these last scenes is grief, and most profoundly for the individuals as children: when Montague sees his son he exclaims, 'What manners is in this, | To press before thy father to a grave' (5.3.214). The loss that this play laments, finally, is the loss of the child, not as an idea of innocence or freedom, but to the contrary, as an individual relationship and a breakdown of human order. As Montague exclaims, no child should die before their parent. The play never commits to what it means to be a child, there is no overarching or defined sense of childhood, only the individual stories or moments that the characters relate. The past that the nurse creates for Juliet offers an intense moment of connection between the infant and adolescent self, which, the nurse suggests, is inextricably entwined. Through the nurse's memory we perceive that infancy and childhood is not a discrete space but a rehearsal for adulthood. Adulthood looms in this play as both a punishment and a reward, defined as it is by marriage and sexuality. Alongside the memories of Juliet's toddler self, the play produces a virile energy through the characterization of the young men. Despite the spectre of adulthood, however, and the imposing energies of fulfilled and unfulfilled sexualities, no young person in this play lives to marry, or even to grow up.

'AS GOOD TO DIE AND GO, AS DIE AND STAY'

Yet marriage and growing up are not always so obviously connected. Where in the comedies (discussed in Chapter 4) the path to marriage is apparently represented as a process of socialization, in which the child adapts to an institutional framework based on gendered norms, in the tragedies marriage is often much more tenuous, fragile, and even temporary. If marriage can take the child away from their parent, the death or rejection of a spouse can return them to their childish self. The most devastating example of this is in *Titus Andronicus*, where we see Lavinia married to Bassianus, then widowed through his murder, and herself mutilated and raped. Her ordeals return her to the house of her father where she becomes, once again, his dependant. Mute, helpless, and isolated she returns to the family network for life, and, ultimately, death. The play is dominated by the child: from Aaron's newborn baby, to Young Lucius, Lavinia, and the adolescent sons of Tamora, Chiron and Demetrius, the idea of the child pervades the drama.[27] Fascinatingly, however, despite the vast number of children alluded to in this play it shows absolutely no interest in the concept of childhood. Perhaps more in line with *Romeo and Juliet* in this way, *Titus Andronicus* defines its children by the parental bond, and not as a discrete or individuated space of growing up. What it means to be a parent in *Titus Andronicus*, however, is always under construction.

The play opens with a triumphal procession in honour of Titus, who has returned victorious from a war with the Goths. About seventy lines into this scene a stage direction alerts us to the entrance of Titus, Tamora, and Aaron, as well as, between them, seven 'sons', alongside a coffin, which is set down on stage.[28] In this coffin are the remains of some 'five-and-twenty valiant sons', for whom Titus will demand the sacrifice of the 'eldest son of this distressed queen' (1.1.106). Already a prisoner herself, the 'distressed queen', Tamora, makes an impassioned plea for her son's life:

> Victorious Titus, rue the tears I shed,
> A mother's tears in passion for her son!
> And if thy sons were ever dear to thee,
> O think my son to be as dear to me.   (1.1.108–11)

---

[27] Julie Taymor's film version, *Titus Andronicus* (1999), opens with a child sitting at his breakfast table, playing soldiers, with a paper bag over his head. Covering his toy figures in tomato sauce and battling with them, the child is transported through an explosion and rescue into the bleak, ceremonial world of the play, where he remains.

[28] The quarto includes 'two of Titus's Sons...then two other Sons...and then the Queen of the Goths and her [three] sons'. The Folio omits Alarbus and mentions only two of Tamora's sons. See Bate's introduction, p. 103 and note p. 132.

Tamora appeals to Titus, in empathy, as one parent to another: her argument, although emotional, makes the point that 'Sweet mercy is nobility's true badge' (122), to which Titus responds that the ghosts of those slain in war 'Religiously they ask a sacrifice. | To this your son is marked, and die he must' (127–8).[29] Titus's response reveals the moment at which the cataclysmic events of the play seem fixed: Titus will sacrifice Tamora's son and she will, in revenge, encourage the rape and mutilation of his daughter; and he, Titus, will take revenge on Tamora through the murder and forced cannibalism of her remaining sons. The brutal cycle of revenge is focused on the child as the means to inflict pain on the parent. Within this cycle the 'child', be they infant or teenager, has no dispensation for their status and the play offers only rare glimpses into versions of childhood. Central to our understanding of *Titus*, then, is not a vision of childhood, or even the individual role of the children themselves, but the impact of the child on the parent. I shall end this chapter with a discussion of *King Lear*, wherein I hope to show how fundamental the parent/child relationship has become to the success of Shakespeare's tragedies, but here in *Titus* we see it emerging as an experimental narrative in the execution of both conflict and emotion. There is no greater testimony to the power of Shakespeare's investment in the performative body than in his characterization of Lavinia. Following her rape and mutilation, the entire drama depends, not on her verbal laments or expositions on suffering, but on the inchoate bond between father and child that pushes Titus to the limits of his comprehension.

Lavinia, silent, from act 2, scene 2, following her ordeal, remains central to the action of the play, not only within the narrative of revenge, but as the focal relationship through which Titus determines his action. Returned to her father's house, dependent and mute, Lavinia becomes a dominant visual motif for forms of dependency as well as love. The entire emotional landscape of the play is dominated by the familial dynamics of the Andronici, and Shakespeare, challenged to inspire allegiance to Lavinia without the power of speech, organizes excruciatingly intense moments of domestic and familial unity that transcend the imperial Roman context of the play. The first and most surprising of these moments is in act 3 scene 2, when the Andronici sit down to a meal together. This scene, sometimes known as the mad or fly-killing scene, did not appear in the 1594 quarto of the play, only in the 1623 folio text.[30] Whether it was performed

---

[29] This pattern is repeated by Tamora, who denies Lavinia 'mercy' when she begs the Empress to intervene and prevent Chiron and Demetrius from raping her (2.2172–83).

[30] The *New Oxford Shakespeare*, ed. Gary Taylor, Terri Bourus, and John Jowett (Oxford: Oxford University Press, 2016), attributes this scene not to Shakespeare but to Thomas Middleton.

in the 1590s or added later is a matter of speculation but the scene is important for the devastating ways in which it focuses on the family. Titus opens the scene directing his daughter, Lavinia, his nephew, young Lucius, and his brother, Marcus, to sit at a table and to eat. Titus makes no attempt to offer this meal as a source of pleasure or hospitality, only survival:

> So, so, now sit, and look you eat no more
> Than will preserve just so much strength in us
> As will revenge these bitter woes of ours.   (3.2.1–3)

Lavinia has no hands to offer food to her mutilated mouth and Titus has only one hand left, having had the other severed on the false pretence of saving the life of one of his sons. On sitting down to eat with a young child and a defaced daughter, Titus begins to rail on the misery of their situation, that they are bereft of the means to 'passionate our tenfold grief' or end their lives. Gently reprimanded by his brother, Titus collects himself and says: 'Come, let's fall to, and gentle girl, eat this' (3.2.34). The suggestion is that Titus attempts to feed his daughter, and then offer her a drink, at which point Lavinia appears to gesticulate:

> Here is no drink! Hark, Marcus, what she says:
> I can interpret all her martyred signs—
> She says she drinks no other drinks but tears
> Brewed with sorrow, mashed upon her cheeks.   (3.2.35–8)[31]

The intimate detail of this scene is astonishing. Shakespeare will never again write a scene in which a family sit down to eat together, let alone a family who have been mutilated. Watching a father attempt to feed his tongueless and handless daughter is a terrifying synthesis of tenderness and brutality. Like a helpless infant, Lavinia relies on her father for sustenance yet she also denies the life-giving support that food offers. The power of her own abjection, her physical endurance, and the paradoxes of hospitality, where agency is both given and taken away, drive the drama of this scene.[32] Instead we learn of her from her father who watches her signs with the devotion of 'begging hermits in their holy prayers'. As Titus focuses on his daughter's misery, the young Lucius tries to distract him and suggest he makes his 'aunt merry with some pleasing tale' at which Marcus observes: 'Alas, the tender boy in passion moved | Doth weep to see his grandsire's heaviness' (3.2.48–9). Every moment in this short scene is directed towards and about the family dynamic: each person attempts to help or engage

---

[31] The possible interpretations of this line indicate either that the cup is empty or that Lavinia refuses the drink offered.

[32] See Derrida's essay *Of Hospitality, Anne Dufourmantelle Invites Jacques Derrida to respond* (Stanford, Calif.: Stanford University Press, 2000).

with another member of the group and the atmosphere is electric with tension, horror, and compassion.

Quite suddenly, the dynamic is changed by the abrupt movement of Marcus striking a dish with a knife. He is, he explains, attempting to kill a fly, which had entered the room. This swift, violent movement resonates with Titus as another example of the brutality in which they are mired and he asks Marcus: 'How if that fly had a father and a mother?' (3.261). Titus's horror at Marcus's action reveals itself through the logic of family love: what if, he suggests, the parents who now had to suffer its loss loved that fly? The question is absurd but it is also entirely reasonable within the narrative of the play. Tamora asked the same question of Titus when she begged him not to sacrifice her son: what if that was your son? The meaning of empathy, to which Titus now appeals, resonates throughout the drama since such a condition did not make sense to Titus until he had experienced the loss of a child outside of the imperial contexts of Roman warfare.[33] The conflation of Roman ceremonies which justify the sacrificing of soldiers does not permit the landscape of familial feeling: only when Titus experiences pain outside of that context does empathy become possible. The play has often been understood as a critique of humanist valorization of the Roman past and this is at its most visible through the figure of the child.[34]

The death of a fly, so insignificant in relation to the devastating human loss within the play, prompts a revelation about the dynamic between cause and effect. The implication is that Titus is irrational in attributing human qualities and networks to an insect and Marcus, apparently playing along with Titus, justifies his actions in similar terms: 'Pardon me, sir, it was a black ill-favoured fly, | Like to the empress' Moor. Therefore I killed him' (3.2.67–8).[35] Titus fully accepts this justification and embraces the idea of representation in which he, too, can strike at the fly 'That comes in likeness of a coal-black Moor' (79). Titus's move from protection to denigration retains the significance of the fly as an object of feeling. Where Titus wanted to protect he now wants to kill and the compelling and tumultuous movements from love to violence continue to bind the

---

[33] See MacFaul, *Problem Fathers in Shakespeare and Renaissance Drama*, esp. pp. 55–6.

[34] About Rome, see T. J. B. Spencer's 'Shakespeare and the Elizabethan Romans', *Shakespeare Survey*, 10 (1957), pp. 27–38; G. K. Hunter, 'The Sources and Meanings in Titus Andronicus', in J. C. Gray (ed.), *The Mirror up to Shakespeare* (Toronto: Toronto University Press, 1983), pp. 171–88; Heather James, *The Fatal Cleopatra: Imitation, Gender and Cultural Criticism in Shakespeare's Translations of Empire* (Berkeley: University of California Press, 1991).

[35] The fly was commonly associated with unfettered sexual appetites. I have discussed this scene in detail in 'Still Life? Anthropocentrism and the Fly in *Titus Andronicus* and *Volpone*', *Shakespeare Survey*, 62 (2011).

characters in this scene. Marcus, too, looks pityingly on his brother as someone in whom 'Grief has so wrought on him | He takes false shadows for true substances' (3.2.80–1). The startling brilliance of this scene lies in its layering of emotions, one upon the other. We stare in horror at a young mutilated woman being fed by her father, a little boy trying to distract his grief-worn grandfather, and a grown man killing a fly as a symbolic act of human revenge. What binds these images and events together is the love of one human for another, and never more overwhelmingly than that of a parent for their child. Lavinia's dramatic childishness is represented by her dependence on her father; she is speechless and helpless and becomes a spectral reminder of the child that lurks in us all, and to which, in Jacques's terms, we will return: 'The last scene of all | That ends this strange eventful history, | Is second childishness and mere oblivion, | Sans teeth, sans eyes, sans taste, sans everything' (*As You Like It*, 2.7). Suddenly the huge developmental leaps that the infant makes to become an adult seem tenuous, fragile, and relative.

'THOSE THAT DO TEACH YOUNG BABES, | DO IT WITH GENTLE MEANS AND EASY TASKS'

I use Desdemona's remark in *Othello* as a subheading to highlight the dreadful irony with which most children in Shakespeare are taught. Forms of instruction are rarely gentle in Shakespeare and almost never easy. *Titus* is one of the few plays in which he dramatizes, albeit briefly, the materiality of childhood. Immediately following the fly scene is a scene which begins with the young boy, Lucius, running away from his mutilated aunt. The stage direction details that 'the Boy flies from her with his books under his arm', at some point during this entrance he must drop his books, so that the frantic Lavinia can find them. These books, which include Ovid's *Metamorphoses* and Cicero, are educative as well as entertaining and suggest that young Lucius is being schooled in the liberal arts.[36] Terrified of his aunt's reaction, the young child tries to understand her within the context of his education:

> And I have read that Hecuba of Troy
> Ran mad for sorrow. That made me to fear,
> Although, my lord, I know my noble aunt
> Loves me as dear as e'er my mother did.   (4.1.20–3)

Here the child is presented in the stage that Malvolio would disparagingly call 'the standing water, between boy and man' (*Twelfth Night*, 1.5.141).

---

[36] See Charlotte Scott, *Shakespeare and the Idea of the Book* (Oxford: Oxford University Press, 2007) for a detailed discussion of the role of the book in *Titus*.

His understanding of life is determined only by his books and now he is forced to confront experience through textual precedent. Through his reading young Lucius has understood that women can go mad from grief (Hecuba's son was killed); fearing his aunt is insane he runs away from her, but yet is tied to her through the bonds of care he perceives as maternal. The fear and confusion is symbolized through the books that lie centre stage: here are some brief objects that tell us the boy is a child and learning to understand life through forms of education. These books are the relics of that education—both powerfully symbolic and dreadfully inadequate. In this way, the books function on two levels; one to identify the child with the material articles of education and therefore at a particular stage in his life; and two to expose the representative structures through which knowledge is gained. Young Lucius must simultaneously contend with the symbolic and the institutional as his education becomes experience. Lavinia will 'ply' the pages until she finds book 6 of Ovid's *Metamorphoses* and the tale of Philomela, through which she will indicate to her father and uncle that she, too, has been raped and had her tongue cut out. Later in the play she will write the names of the perpetrators in the sand with a stick. But here the narrative turning point centres on the two children—and the books through which they were taught about the past, which has now become their present. The play's conflict with ceremonial structures finds an alternative pressure in the concept of story, both 'pattern' and 'precedent', it becomes a dreadful mediator between the past and the present.

We cannot overestimate the centrality of the child in *Titus Andronicus* and yet, as with many of Shakespeare's plays, there is no structure of childhood to which the play commits. The children in *Titus* are both victims and agents of violence: they win wars as soldiers, destroy lives as rapists; they read books and give comfort, they love their parents and they also devastate them. They are central to a network of love and belonging that is tribal, ferocious, and unconditional but they give us no glimpse into anything that is unique to youth or immaturity. Above all, the power of the child in *Titus* is its effect on the adult. One of the most disquieting and surprising examples of this occurs towards the end of the play, when Aaron, the man who wishes he could do 'a thousand more heinous deeds' than live a day when he 'did not [do] some notorious ill', encounters his newborn baby. As the play's hideous events move towards their climax, the child becomes once again the means of inflicting pain on the adult. To punish Aaron, and force him to admit his crimes, Lucius threatens the infant:

> First hang the child, that he may see it sprawl:
> A sight to vex the father's soul withal.
> Get me a ladder.   (5.1.51–3)

The play has come full circle in its punishment of the parent through the child. Aaron, one of the most rapacious villains in Shakespeare, now has a 'soul' to be vexed. But once again the child does not function as itself or even as an idea of infancy, only as a means of inflicting pain on the parent. What Shakespeare seems most interested in here is not children as a unique life stage but the dramatic depth of the relationship between child and parent. What becomes especially compelling, however, from a theatrical perspective, is how Shakespeare can imagine and rehearse that bond without developing the special character of the child. Shakespeare, it appears, appeals to a bond that he recognizes as both human and humane. There is no greater rebuke to Stone's infamous thesis that the early modern parent was tyrannical and disinclined to love their child than this play. The child in *Titus*, as amorphous as that noun can be, is the emotional centre of the narrative. The play ends as Aaron refuses to die quietly, buried to the neck outside the walls of Rome. 'I am no baby', he declares, 'why should wrath be mute and fury dumb?' (5.3.183,182). This, however, is Aaron's failure: the power of the child in *Titus* is not in their speech or even in their anger, but in the love they produce, which can be both 'mute' and 'dumb'.

'HOW DO I LOVE THEE?'

King Lear is in many ways where we find the culmination of many of the children I have already discussed. Traces of the children in *King John*, *Richard III*, *Romeo and Juliet*, and *Titus Andronicus* reside in the tragedy of the King who risked his future on a love trial of his daughters. It is not just Lear, of course, who has children who want to destroy or protect him: the subplot of the Duke of Gloucester and his legitimate son Edgar, and illegitimate son Edmund, also dramatizes the power of children in their parent's lives. What distinguishes *Lear* from all the plays I have discussed so far is that none of these children is particularly young: some are already married, Goneril and Regan, others are bachelors, Edmund and Edgar, and one gets married early on, and off-stage, Cordelia. Despite the fact that the children in this play are to all intents and purposes 'grown up', their status as 'children', the offspring of parents within the play-world, is absolutely central to the drama. Once again for Shakespeare, the dramatic interest in the child lies in its relational dynamic with the parent, and because of the ages of the characters in this play, there is no sense of childishness or childhood. Instead, what becomes defining for the tragedy is familial love—its representation, expression, betrayal, and need. As the play begins focused on the child's love for the parent, it will end with the parent's love for the child: nowhere does Shakespeare explore paternal love more devastatingly than in *King Lear*.

The opening of the play, in which the aged King Lear decides to divide his kingdom between his three daughters, focuses on the women's ability to describe their love for their father in extravagant terms: 'which of you shall we say doth love us most | That we our largest bounty may extend' (1.1.49–50). As many critics have observed, Lear's behaviour, his 'darker purpose', is apparently odd and unnecessary. He has already divided the kingdom into three equal parts and so his direction to his daughters appears as an afterthought; a game, perhaps, in which the old King asks his daughters to pander to his demanding nature one last time. Such demands are not unusual, we imagine, as Regan later observes: he 'hath ever but slenderly known himself', and yet Cordelia's decision not to play along with her father is a catastrophic one. Unlike any other play by Shakespeare, the opening scene unequivocally establishes, and sets in motion, the narrative and emotional registers of the drama. Lear's shift from demanding father to violent monarch is modulated through the terms of love that he seeks from his daughters, and most especially Cordelia; 'I loved her most, and thought to set my rest | On her kind nursery' (1.1.121–2). The vocabularies of parental love through which the drama opens will change radically and devastatingly as the play progresses and much of the power of this opening comes from raising our expectations about the difference between parent and child.

The jocular exchange between the Earls of Kent and Gloucester, through which the play opens, focuses on the terms of the father. Referring to his illegitimate son Edmund, Gloucester comments that he was once ashamed to acknowledge him and yet now he is hardened to it, to which Kent admits:

I cannot conceive you.

GLOUCESTER: Sir, this young fellow's mother could, whereupon she grew round-wombed and had indeed, sir, a son for her cradle ere she had a husband for her bed. Do you smell a fault?   (1.1.20–3)

Gloucester's merry punning on the word 'conceive', to mean both understand and become pregnant, allows him ample opportunity to jest at Edmund's expense: 'Though this knave came something saucily to the world before he was sent for, yet his mother was fair, there was good sport at his making, and the whoreson must be acknowledged' (1.2.17–21). The jaunty combination of insults and acceptances here presents Gloucester's attitude to parenting as somewhat flippant. Unlike some of Shakespeare's other 'bastards', Edmund is genuinely illegitimate. As *King John* takes pains to explain, the child of an affair is only illegitimate if the mother is unmarried.[37] If the mother is married then the husband is legally obliged to acknowledge the child, even if he suspects it to be fathered by someone else.[38] Despite Gloucester's references to Edmund as a 'knave' and 'whoreson', typically abusive terms for the Jacobeans, his acceptance of the child as his own, and no less dear to him that his legitimate child, make the Earl of Gloucester a somewhat radical father figure within the play-world. Tragically, of course, Edmund's behaviour will vilify such generosity but, at the beginning of the play, Gloucester's attitude strikes a resonant note within the music of fatherhood.

The relationship between the father and the child defines the drama of *King Lear* but what it means to be a father, or a child, in this play is obscure. The parents in *King Lear* appear to believe in an ideology of family that the play cannot bear out. Gloucester and Lear understand their children not as relationships or even characters but as emblems of an order they designate as 'natural'. The bonds they expect from their children come not from the individual relationship but from the conventional doctrines of duty, obligation, expectation, and accord. These are what we might call textbook relationships, ones which are defined by a hypothetical order of law (natural or institutional) rather than unique emotional bonds. As we have seen, all sixteenth- and seventeenth-century parenting books collude on the point of obedience, supporting the will of the father above that of the child. But what many of these texts also acknowledge is the father's 'nature' as well as his 'affection'. As Blower explains:

> Now this calls to mind an other disagréement betwéen the father and the childe, which is the partiall loue of the father towardes his *children*: for in my minde it is a great fault that he should loue one more then an other, and that all being of his flesh and bloud, he should cast a merry countenance vpon some of them, and an angry looke vpon other some. Yet this is the nature of man, that a father loueth not all his *children* alike, and yet he whom he loueth least, cannot iustly complaine of him: for the in-equality of loue is permitted to the fathers affection.[39]

Such 'in-equality of love' is both their failure and their tragedy. Despite Gloucester's assertion that Edmund is 'no less dear' to him than Edgar, both he and Lear fail to understand the office of a parent. Blower acknowledges

---

[37] 'Sirrah, your brother is legitimate; | Your father's wife did after wedlock bear him, | And if she did play false, the fault was hers; | Which fault lies on the hazards of all husbands | That marry wives' (*King John*, 1.1.116–20).

[38] In *The Winter's Tale*, within these terms, whatever Leontes' imaginings, Perdita is legally legitimate.

[39] *THE COVRT OF good Counsell. VVHEREIN IS SET downe the true rules, how a man should choose a good Wife from a bad, and woman a good Husband from a bad* (London, 1607), Gv3.

that it is a 'great fault' of the father to love one child more than another, yet he also understands that it is 'the nature of man' to do so. The contest between 'nature' and decorum is a major preoccupation within the play, and supports the spectral possibility that things could have been different had Lear and Gloucester belonged to a different 'nature'. The forces at work within the play, between an orthodox and a mechanistic nature, focus on the parental relationship as a source of meaning. The complexities of this relationship are further developed by the status of the main children who are also adults: these children are not young nor are they especially vulnerable. They are independent adults who, in most cases, have made their lives distinct from their fathers and yet Lear's actions, and Gloucester's gullibility, change that irrevocably.

Gloucester's jocular introduction of Edmund to Kent is followed by an admission that he has been away 'for nine years, and away he shall again' thereby demonstrating that whatever terms of acceptance Gloucester has offered his illegitimate son they are theoretical rather than emotional. Edmund's intention to slander 'legitimate Edgar' and become the sole inheritor suggest that Gloucester is capable of making Edmund his legal son, if not his most familiar one. Yet the bonds and rights through which parents recognize their children and children recognize their parents become quickly distorted as the play progresses. Even from the outset, however, we question the bonds by which fathers can 'love' (but not know) their children and know (but not love them). From Gloucester's jaunty humiliation of Edmund, we move to Lear's 'darker purpose' to witness the division of the kingdom. The language through which he demands, and his daughters respond, is entirely mediated through the language of familial duty. Goneril speaks first, and declares that she loves Lear 'As much as child e'er loved or father found' (1.1.47); Regan, who goes next, admits that she is 'made of that self mettle as my sister', 'Only she comes too short' (67, 70). The language of love that Lear demands and his elder daughters respond with is defined by their status as children, not as individuals. Exceeding the bounds of romantic love to suggest something more unconditional, Goneril exclaims:

> Sir, I love you more than words can wield the matter;
> Dearer than eyesight, space, and liberty
> Beyond what can be valued rich or rare,
> No less than life;   (1.1.53–6)

The weight of Goneril's assertions will come back to haunt the fathers in the play: Gloucester who will lose his eyesight and Lear who will lose everything. Goneril, as becomes quite clear, does not love her father in this way. The vast unconditional love that she draws on is absent for almost the entire play, glimpsed only, perhaps, at the devastating moment in which Lear holds his dead Cordelia in his arms. But here the high terms of amplification reflect no register of genuine emotion only the possibility of what can but does not exist at this moment. As Regan allies herself with her sister, as well as attempting to outdo her, we understand Cordelia's linguistic reticence. What do words mean now, if they have been shown by her sisters to mean nothing? The resounding nihilism of Cordelia's response to her father registers the deep chasm of meaninglessness into which her sisters have pushed feeling.

> What shall Cordelia speak? Love and be silent.   (1.1.60)

Compared to the extravagant terms of Goneril and Regan, Cordelia's silence seems legible. Cordelia's comment, however, is always marked as an aside, further developing the ways in which the play-world is constructed as inhospitable to love. Cordelia's assertion resides on the periphery of the stage, spoken out to the audience or inwards to herself but never to the space that her father inhabits. What she speaks to her father is 'nothing'—

> CORDELIA: Nothing, my Lord.
> LEAR: Nothing?
> CORDELIA: Nothing.
> LEAR: Nothing will come of nothing. Speak again.   (1.1.85–8)

The vast 'nothing' that Cordelia invokes is the point at which all words become hollow. Her sisters' claims have so extravagantly stretched the terms of meaning that Cordelia is no longer able to use language other than in its strictly utilitarian context. To that end she calls on the language of duty and obligation, an apparently shared language of institutional expectation:

> You have begot me, bred me, loved me.
> I return those duties back as are right fit—
> Obey you, love you, and most honour you.
> Why have my sisters husbands if they say
> They love you all? Haply when I shall wed
> That lord whose hand must take my plight shall carry
> Half my love with him, half my care and duty.
> Sure I shall never marry like my sisters
> To love my father all.   (1.1.94–101)[40]

Cordelia provides her father with an entirely conventional and decorous response to his question, in which she reproduces a widely rehearsed view of the child's duty towards its parent, including the understanding of

---

[40] The final line is in the quarto text only.

marriage as transference of authority from the father to the husband.[41] Lear, it seems, wants more. His parental demands exceed the boundaries of conventional expectations and insist on the exceptional, the unconditional, the rare, and the extraordinary. Shakespeare's interest in Lear is not in him as a father but in someone who exceeds that title, who stretches that role to its limits and who demands more from his children than they are able to give. Cordelia's rational appeal to the language of duty and obedience defines her, for Lear, as 'untender' and unnatural but the play has no 'normal' from which she can be judged to have erred.

King Lear is fascinated by nature—as a landscape, a cosmic order, a familial construct and a coherent set of expectations from which the unnatural is seen to diverge.[42] From the outset, however, our understanding of 'natural' is complicated. Is it 'natural' to love your father more than your life or your eyesight, never mind your husband? Is it natural to disown your daughter for claiming she loves you and returns her duties 'as are right fit'? The bonds of family to which *King Lear* appeals are nowhere in evidence in the play and yet they are constantly invoked as a measure of what we should, or could, expect. As Lear rails against his monstrous and unnatural daughters, the natural manifests in our mind's eye as something other than this. We can only make sense of the terrible events of the play and the grinding nihilism of its resolution if we accept the radically unnatural nature of it all. In this way, perhaps, each character only makes sense if we see them as diverging from their prescribed role, rather than representing it. Father, daughter, brother, husband, wife, sister, or godson do not fulfil or represent their roles but travesty them. This is not to suggest that Shakespeare offers *King Lear* as a critique of family values or behaviour but rather as an exploration of whether indeed there are such things as family values at all.[43]

The idea of family values haunts the play as a question rather than as an assertion. As soon as Lear has rejected Cordelia as his 'sometime daughter', Kent jumps to her defence. In order to assure Lear of his sincerity and

[41] See particularly Charles Gibbons , *A Work Worth the Reading* (London, 1591), in which he discusses, through the form of a dialogue, not only duty but also the extent to which children are entitled to marry for love, rather than 'lucre' and questions of inheritance. Ralph Josselin concludes his sermon in 1669 with the sentence, 'Oh then children, requite your parents for the cost they have laid out about you, follow their counsels, and cheer up their spirits in their gray hairs,' Alan D. J. Macfarlane, *The Family Life of Ralph Josselin, A 17th Century Clergyman: An Essay in Historical Anthropology* (Cambridge: Cambridge University Press, 1970), p. 82.

[42] There is a great deal of fascinating work in this area, but the classic and most enduring study remains John F. Danby, *Shakespeare's Doctrine of Nature* (London: Faber, 1949).

[43] See Bruce Young in *In the Company of Shakespeare: Essays on English Renaissance Literature in Honor of G. Blakemore Evans* (Madison, NJ: Fairleigh Dickinson University Press, 2002) and *Family Life*, Chedzgoy et al. (eds), *Shakespeare and Childhood*.

trustworthiness, Kent reminds Lear that he honours him as a king and 'loved [him] as my father' (1.1.139). In the context of what has just happened it seems a slightly ill-judged comment but the point and effect is to demonstrate to Lear the profound network of loyalty and truth to which Kent belongs. Even as Lear rejects Cordelia as his daughter, Kent allies himself with her as Lear's son. The conflation of familial emotion is confusing and bewildering at this point since Lear relentlessly rejects the idea of love that both Kent and Cordelia represent. For Kent and Cordelia, the role of the child is held up as a touchstone for truth and protection: for Lear, however, it is a sign of insolence and failure. In attempting to offload Cordelia, without a dowry, to Burgundy or France, Lear announces, 'When she was dear to us, we did hold her so; | But now her price is fallen' (1.1.193–4). Lear's staggering failure to uphold the sentiments that he demands from others, to stop loving his daughter for her failure to say what he wants, is symptomatic of the extraordinary confusion of the play's opening. Lear demands the kind of love that he himself cannot show, Cordelia feels the kind of love that cannot be made legible with words, and Kent stands in loyalty through the figure of a child, at precisely the point that the child is no longer admissible to Lear. Only the King of France, one of the briefest of roles of the play, understands:

> Love's not love
> When it is mingled with regards that stands
> Aloof from th'entire point. (1.1.236–8)

It is only this scene that fully engages with Lear as a father and the women as his daughters, his children: from Cordelia leaving for France and Lear relying on Goneril and Regan for hospitality and comfort the roles of father and child become attenuated and perceptual. Only Lear and Gloucester, variously oppressed by their children, continue to identify the suffering or anxiety of the family dynamic. Goneril and Regan rarely refer to Lear in paternal terms and come to increasingly identify him as the King, rather than their father. Cordelia, however, absent for most of the play, but reunited with Lear towards the end, not only insists on the word father but articulates that relationship through a recognition of its deep bonds. Cordelia represents, albeit briefly in terms of the stage presence of her character, unconditional love. All those who observe her understand the love that she shows towards her 'child-changed' father as redemptive. As she kisses him, strokes his white hair, and kneels in tenderness before him Cordelia demonstrates the love she was unable to describe at the beginning of the play. In extremis, the love between father and daughter becomes entirely visible through the heart-breaking analogy of imprisoned birds who will sing to each other in their cage. Lear's happiness at being close to his daughter manifests through a language of reciprocity:

> When thou dost ask me blessing, I'll kneel down
> And ask of thee forgiveness; so we'll live,
> And pray, and sing, and tell old tales, and laugh
> At gilded butterflies... (5.3.10–13)

The fantasy here is one of mutuality and togetherness: gone is the demand for outlandish declarations of superlative love and what remains, endures even, is a belief in belonging and sharing the quotidian aspects of life. The larger, hostile forces at work in this play quickly destroy this brief and wonderful image of familial love, so that being a child or a father is neither a guarantor of love nor an expression of it. Indeed, the play continually begs the question as to what those bonds could or should mean. Both Lear and Gloucester frequently invoke their horror at the betrayal of a familial relationship, and Edmund provides an ironic chorus on the extent to which he can pervert those bonds. Having falsely persuaded Gloucester that his legitimate son Edgar is intending to kill him, betrayed his father to the Duke of Cornwall, betrothed himself to Goneril and Regan, with the intention of having Albany killed, Edmund repeatedly invites comments on his 'natural' behaviour.[44] The impression that he succeeds in giving to the majority of the play-world is one of loyalty, kinship, protection, and honour: these are the qualities associated with the 'natural' affections between family members, even to the extent that Cornwall, delighted to have Edmund on his side, promises him, 'I will lay trust upon thee, and thou shalt find a dearer father in my love' (3.5.20–1).

Throughout the play, the language of kinship is constantly invoked as a representation of loyalty and love and yet much of the play's most shocking action continually confounds this notion. Even as the play unhinges our expectations of the familial relationships it continues to put its faith in them. There is a staggering modernity in *King Lear* in which we observe that there is no such thing as unconditional love or loyalty in parental relationships: all love is predicated on behaviour and circumstance and we are fools to assume otherwise (indeed, Lear's fool provides a continual critique of the kind of stupidity he associates with Lear's failure to 'see better'). The love and endurance that Edgar and Cordelia come to represent shines through the apocalyptic horror of the play not as an emblem of the perfect or natural child but as rare individuals who have the capacity to empathize beyond self-interest. One of the most startling instances of this in all of Shakespeare's drama is the scene in which Edgar, disguised as Poor

---

[44] See especially 3.5.

Tom, leads his blinded father to an imaginary cliff, where he hopes to commit suicide. The idea of loyalty and the bonds of protection are further emphasized in this brief scene by the figure of the old man: a tenant of both Gloucester's and his father, the old man represents a form of fidelity that is feudal but also personal. The ties that bind in this scene are born of a love that transcends circumstance: Edgar, cast out, no longer enjoys the privilege of being Gloucester's son, and the old man, decrepit and unable to work, no longer enjoys the privilege of Gloucester's estate. Witnessing Edgar lead Gloucester to his imaginary death, only to convince him he has been 'miraculously' saved, is a powerful testament to his love for a father who believed him capable of patricide.

What this play so powerfully questions is our belief in human relationships as unconditional. There are exceptions—Cordelia and Edgar—who shine like good deeds in a naughty world but they are exceptions and only one of them survives. Bleakly and fascinatingly, this play questions the right of the family to love and loyalty and gestures towards a mechanistic universe where all relationships are always in the process of being made and unmade. This is not necessarily cynical on Shakespeare's part; he writes to a culture that understands the tenuousness of human bonds but also the necessity of them. When Gloucester, early on in the play, remarks,

> Love cools, friendship falls off, brothers divide, in cities, mutinies; in coun-tries, discord; in palaces, treason; and the bond cracked 'twixt son and father.... The King falls from the bias of nature: there's father against child. We have seen the best of our time   (1.2.98–103)

he appears to understand the breakdown of familial relationships within the larger terms of social discord. It is inevitable, he suggests, that human relationships fail during the pressures of a period of social division. Yet despite Gloucester's insights here, he, and the main protagonists of the play-world, continue to use the language of kinship as a shorthand for love or loyalty. Lear and Gloucester persistently commit themselves to the idea that children should be loving, loyal, and obedient. Faced with their own aberrant children they maintain their horror at their betrayals and yet they cannot, until the end of the play, relinquish the ideology that assumes faith in familial relationships. Gloucester's piercing remark that 'As flies to wanton boys are we to the gods; | They kill us for their sport' (4.1.37–8) paradoxically recognizes the cruelty of children yet lays the blame for his own plight on the gods. The great irony here, of course, is that it is Gloucester's 'boy' who has tormented him, not his god. On the one hand, the play recognizes the mindless cruelty that children are capable of but on the other it seems genuinely appalled when children assimilate those acts of cruelty into their adult lives. In this way the figure of the child becomes an idealized reflection of social cohesion: once 'there's father against child' the future is bleak. Although *King Lear* registers a breakdown of society at profound levels it is unclear as to where or with whom the responsibility for that breakdown ultimately lies.

The play presents various views—both deterministic, in which individuals are responsible for their own lives, and fatalistic, in which individuals are pre-conditioned at birth to behave in certain ways. The play parodies both views: Edmund travesties the fatalistic view (1.2) and Kent champions it (4.3) and yet we are left feeling that there can be no such thing as a 'natural' bond between children and parents when we have witnessed such brutality. Even within the midst of that brutality, however, the context of the child is recalled. When Cornwall's servant, appalled at what he is doing to Gloucester, attempts to stop him he reminds him that he has been in his service since he was a child and 'But better service have I never done you | Than now to bid you hold' (3.7.72–3). The import of his plea lies in the assumed bond that he shares with his master and the trust that he has earned as one who has been with him since he was a child. Recalling the scuffle that then takes place, in which Cornwall is fatally wounded, a messenger explains: 'A servant that he bred, thrilled with remorse, | Opposed against the act, bending his sword | This great master who thereat enraged | Flew at him, and amongst them felled him dead.' (4.2.41–5). The significance here is the relationship between Cornwall and his servant, who having served him since he was a child assumes absolute loyalty to his master to the extent that he wants to save him from himself. Like Cordelia and Edgar, however, his attempts are not rewarded by their father figures, but punished. The play is powerfully confused by its children—both redemptive and revolting, the children in this play are the last hope and an image of the promised end. The play continually returns to the nature of the bond between parent and child, a bond, and a nature, that becomes increasingly attenuated and elusive. Perhaps, unsurprisingly, the great hero of *King Lear* is not a character but a concept—love: the love that Lear so craved he is finally rewarded with in Cordelia but it is a love predicated not on ambition but on that greatest of Christian virtues, Charity.

When Cordelia is reunited with her father she remarks:

> No blown ambition doth our arms incite,
> But love, dear love, and our aged father's right. (4.3.27–9)

Such love, dear love, resonates in forgiveness and is extended to Edmund, too, by his oppressed brother, Edgar:

> Let's exchange charity,
> I am no less in blood than thou art, Edmund. (5.3.156–7)

The relationship between love and charity had been a controversial one since William Tyndale had translated the Greek word, ἀγάπη, understood as 'charity' in the Greek New Testament into Love in the vernacular New Testament. Despite vicious disputes with members of the Catholic church who perceived Tyndale as changing the meaning of scripture, Tyndale maintained that he was above all committed to clarity and to making the text as readable and as understandable as possible.[45] Tyndale's word choice would come to define many of the ideological differences between Protestantism and Catholicism as well as the central focus on interpretation. For Sir Thomas More and the many others who believed in the integrity of the Greek or Latin texts, fixed meaning was central to religious doctrine. Tyndale's belief in interpretation meant that key words, such as love, took hold of their readers individually and variously. Edgar's use of the word charity positions him outside that Reformation context: what he extends to Edmund is forgiveness and Christian kinship, but not, notably, love. Cordelia, on the other hand, offers a love which is individual, idiosyncratic, subjective, and unique: a love that transcends community doctrine and offers intense feeling instead. One of the most affecting non-literary texts of the period, *Newnam's Night crow* (1590), written to mothers and fathers, by a man who has 'suffered' at the hands of a bad stepmother, writes of parents: 'The thing that is most required to be found in them is natural love, augmented and confirmed by the same which Christ so carefully commended to his children...Charitie.'[46]

Familial language is used in this play to register an expectation of empathy and loyalty through which one character may identify with another. Lear's repeated use of the word 'child' or 'daughter' provides him with a shorthand of emotional expectation. When Gloucester or Lear uses the term son or daughter it is usually as a form of amplification: to demonstrate the great kindness or the great horror that such a relationship can perform. When Gloucester observes that 'Our flesh and blood, my lord, is grown so vile | That it doth hate what gets it' (3.4.129–30) he registers a profound rupture in our expectations of kinship. When Lear, raving on the heath, encounters Poor Tom, he assumes that only a family member could have brought a man so low: 'Didst thou give all to thy daughters | And art thou come to

---

[45] In his preface to the reader he writes how he 'had perceived by experience how that it was impossible to establish the lay people in any truth, except the Scripture were plainly laid before their eyes in their mother tongue, that they might see the process, order and meaning of the text', see David Daniel, *Tyndale's Old Testament* (New Haven: Yale University Press, 1994), p. 4; Morna Hooker, 'Tyndale as Translator', Hertford Tyndale Lecture, 19 October 2000.

[46] 'A bird that breedeth braules in many families and households wherein is remembered that kindly and provident regard which fathers ought to have towards their sons', John Newnham, *Newnams Nightcrowe* (London: John Wolfe, 1590), B2v.

this?' (3.4.46–7). Lear obsessively focuses on Poor Tom and whether 'his daughters brought him to this pass', assuming that only children are capable of such destruction: 'Nothing could have subdued nature | To such a lowness but his unkind daughters' (3.4.65–6). Lear's observations reflect the intense egoism of distress but they also register the play's wider exploration of the depths of human suffering. No one, it seems, can hurt you more than your children, and most parents, then and now, would agree. Yet the potential that children have to destroy their parents is inchoate, and equally so in *Lear*: is it love, responsibility, trust, or expectation that makes children so powerful a force in their parents' lives? Lear suggests that you can stop loving your children when they betray you—'our some-time daughter'—but the play does not bear this out, and no amount of cursing or arraigning makes this more convincing. In fact, quite the contrary; it is precisely the violence of Lear's response to his daughters that demonstrates his love for them. When, towards the end of the play, the Gentleman observes that 'the great rage in him is killed' we might assume that Lear has finally let go of the anger—and the love—he felt as a father but the final scene, in which Lear holds the dead body of his daughter in his arms, is the most emotionally devastating scene that Shakespeare would write:

> And my poor fool is hanged. No, no, no, life?
> Why should a dog, a horse, a rat have life,
> And thou no breath at all? Thou'lt come no more.
> Never, never, never, never, never.
> [To KENT] Pray you, undo this button. Thank you, sir.
> Do you see this? Look on her. Look, her lips.
> Look there, look there.   (5.3.280–6)

The Folio version, quoted above, suggests that Lear dies believing his beloved daughter to be still breathing. The earlier quarto version does not contain the last two lines and suggests that Lear dies in a state of extreme distress: 'Pray you undo | This button. Thank you, sir. O, O, O, O!' The emotional intensity of witnessing Lear, bent over his dead daughter, willing her to life again, with the howls of injustice that see a rat or dog 'have life' resonates with anybody who has grieved a loved one. The depth of the emotional anguish, however, seems so uniquely realized in this relationship: whatever emotional engagement we may feel or agonies we may imagine in the deaths of Desdemona or Cleopatra, for example, nothing is as profound or as catastrophic as the death of a child in the arms of a parent. Shakespeare's audience would have been equally devastated, we might imagine, since they would have been expecting a different ending: the ending of Shakespeare's source play, *The True Chronicle History of King*

Leir and his Three Daughters, Gonorill, Ragan, and Cordella, in which father and daughter survive to bring justice to a broken world.[47] Shakespeare, however, denies both fathers the chance to live and see their reviled children happy again. Edgar, reporting the moment he reveals his story to his father, recalls:

> I asked his blessing, and from first to last
> Told him our pilgrimage; but his flawed heart—
> Alack, too weak the conflict to support—
> 'Twixt two extremes of passion, joy and grief,
> Burst smilingly.   (5.3.186–90)

Only a parent's heart could 'burst smilingly': the tragic mixture of joy and grief registers the profound impulses of the parent to hold on to the child they love, but also to let them go. There is no respite in this play from the terrible effects of grief and the agonies that children can bring to their parents, and parents to their children. *King Lear* is not Shakespeare's goriest or most psychologically dense tragedy: it does not stage multiple deaths, involve witches, or the razing of cities and dynasties, but it is without doubt his most distressing tragedy. *King Lear* confronts the most fundamental relationships we have, those of our families, and subjects them to terrifying scrutiny, in which no one is blameless. The most profound tragic impulse comes from the terms of love: the simple question, 'which of you doth love us most?' resonates throughout the drama as meaning everything and nothing. In the process the characters in the play are forced to confront what those relationships mean to them and to society at large. As France so eloquently put it at the beginning of the play, 'Love's not love | When it is mingled with regards that stands | Aloof from th' entire point' (1.1.236–8). The nebulous 'bond' to which Cordelia refers when she tells her father, 'I love your majesty |According to my bond, no more nor less' (1.1.90–1) turns out to be the most important expression of love that the play can contain. That 'bond', between parent and child, is what Lear returns to, broken, diminished, and ravaged at the play's end. But, above all, it is a bond of 'love, dear love', which aims to protect and rescue, to alleviate and to hold: just the same bond that sent the ragged Edgar to rescue his blinded father: the bond that can make a heart 'burst smilingly'.

---

[47] James Shapiro's *1606, The Year of Lear* (London: Faber, 2015), writes especially well on the relationships between the two plays; see pp. 55–74.

4

'Love is proved in the letting go'

Marriage, Space, and Gender in *A Midsummer Night's Dream* and *Much Ado about Nothing*

If the tragic impulse is to divide in death then the comedic impulse is to unite in marriage. Marriage has long been recognized as the defining imperative of comedy and, within these terms, we see how genre functions not as a 'linguistic category defined by a structured arrangement of textual features' but, as Charles Bazerman suggests, 'a socio-psychological category which we use to recognise and construct typified actions within typified situations'.[1] Like genre, marriage functions especially well as a socio-psychological category because it adheres to a set of principles understood as 'typical'. Normative arrangements of gender and sexuality produce apparently linear narratives within the comedies in which marriage becomes the end point at which the couples' lives begin.[2] There are no young children in Shakespeare's comedies, with the exception of William in *Merry Wives of Windsor*, who is of school age.[3] Instead the comedies tend to focus on the lives and loves of young people, most of whom are women of marrying age. Many of the narratives of these plays, *A Midsummer Night's Dream*, *The Merchant of Venice*, *Much Ado about Nothing*, *As You*

---

[1] Charles Bazerman, *Shaping Written Knowledge: The Genre and Activity of the Experimental Article in Science* (Madison: University of Wisconsin Press, 1988), p. 319.

[2] This is not to imply of course that Shakespeare presents or endorses these narratives as uncomplicated. A great deal of scholarship on the subject of sexuality and marriage shows that Shakespeare disrupts normative institutional structures even as he represents them. Catherine Belsey, 'Disrupting Sexual Difference: Meaning and Gender in the Comedies', in John Drakakis (ed.), *Alterative Shakespeares* (London: Methuen, 1985): Lynda Boose, 'Scolding Brides and Bridling Scolds: Taming the Woman's Unruly Member', *Shakespeare Quarterly*, 42.2 (1991), pp. 179–213; Arthur L. Little, '"A Local Habitation and a Name": Presence, Witnessing, and Queer Marriage in Shakespeare's Romantic Comedies', in Evelyn Gajowski (ed.), *Presentism, Gender, and Sexuality in Shakespeare* (London and New York: Palgrave Macmillan, 2009), pp. 207–36. Carol Thomas Neely, *Broken Nuptials in Shakespeare's Plays* (New Haven: Yale University Press, 1985); Valerie Traub, *The Renaissance of Lesbianism in Early Modern England* (Cambridge: Cambridge University Press, 2002).

[3] See also M. M. Mahood, *Playing Bit-Parts in Shakespeare* (Cambridge: Cambridge University Press, 1992), pp. 1–22.

Like It, and *The Taming of the Shrew*, for example, centre on the stories of
fathers marrying off their daughters. The average age for women to marry
in this period was 26 years old, and for men it was about 28 years old, so
we can safely assume that the characters are not children but they are still
young. As with almost all of Shakespeare's plays, the interest and significance lies less in what age the characters are and more in what relationship
they have with their parents (usually fathers) and with themselves. Many
of the comedic plots present marriage as a significant step in the young
person's process of socialization. But beyond the individual relationships
or demands placed on the young woman by the father, the comedic
structure appears to offer marriage as the transition into adulthood where,
we might suppose, the process of socialization is complete. Through the
structure of the comedies this chapter will look at ideas of socialization in
Shakespeare's drama and how growing up becomes akin to being rendered
acceptable by the play-world. This in itself is very revealing since it allows
us to consider what the values of the play-world might be and when a
young person is considered worthy of adopting them.

There is little in Shakespeare's drama that we could recognize as specifically belonging to childhood. There are no material objects through
which we locate the interests of children as distinct from the adult world,
no toys, playthings, or spaces of recreation or amusement; no articles or
areas that belong exclusively to youth. The creation and use of space is
especially revealing in establishing the child as distinct from the adult:
although children obviously inhabit adult spaces, the home, the garden,
the court, for example, they also attempt to take control of those spaces
through their own imaginative identifications or re-creations of adult
behaviour. Although all modern play areas (parks, playgrounds, for example)
are created and directed by adults, how they are used can depend on
the children. Studies in the archaeology of childhood have shown that
children will make their own 'play' areas on the periphery of the domestic
sphere; they will use a vast range of material objects as playthings and they
will tend to create play areas in clusters, rather than randomly.[4] In this
chapter I want to focus on the spaces outside of adult control, in which the
young people of Shakespeare's comedies attempt to establish themselves
as individuals, free of imperial parental control. Alongside the spaces of
individuation, I will examine the role of marriage as an institutional
marker of adulthood and the values it represents as a form of socialization.[5]

---

[4] Baxter, *The Archaeology of Childhood*, pp. 57–75; Julie Wileman, *Hide and Seek*
(Stroud: Tempus, 2005), pp. 155–70; Jane Eva Baxter (ed.), *Children in Action: The
Archaeological Papers of the American Anthropological Association*, No. 15 (2005).

[5] See Ivy Pinchbeck and Margaret Hewitt on the construction of the family and the
institution of marriage as a social, not individual, function, *Children in English Society*,

Gender is central to both these concerns since appropriate socialization is determined on the basis of whether you will grow up to be a husband or a wife. Almost all western toys, clothes, and play rituals have been established on the basis of reinforcing and developing gender expectations.[6]

In many of Shakespeare's comedies gender and childhood are linked through memory and friendship and the shared community of same-sex friendships. Often characters are siblings or cousins (*The Shrew*, *As You Like It*, *Much Ado*) or they present a shared past that simulates familial relations through its closeness. In this way, the idea of the family becomes a revealing metaphor since it assumes not only physical proximity but also tenderness and unity. Familial tenderness should not be assumed, however, since the majority of early modern books on domesticity recognize 'the family' as consisting of certain roles rather than feelings. William Gouge's much cited *Of Domesticall Duties* (1622) establishes:

> Among other particular callings the Apostle maketh choice of those which God hath settled in priuate families, and is accurat in reciting the seuerall and distinct orders thereof, (for a *family* consisteth of these three orders, Husbands, Parents, Masters, all which he Wiues, Children, Seruants, reckoneth vp) yea he is also copious and earnest in urging the duties which appertain to them.[7]

The status of the family is determined by the ways in which certain roles are inhabited and reinforced. There is nothing to suggest that the family provides any special status of feeling but rather a microcosmic structure of social competency. William Perkins explains:

> A Familie, is a naturall and simple Societie of certaine persons, hauing mutuall relation one to another, vnder the priuate gouernement of one. These persons must be at the least three; because two cannot make a societie. And aboue three vnder the same head, there may be a thousand in one familie, as it is in the households of Princes, and men of state in the world... A *Family*, for the good estate of it selfe, is bound to the performance of two duties; one to God, the other to it selfe.[8]

volume I: From Tudor Times to the Eighteenth Century (London: Routledge & Kegan Paul, 1969), pp. 13–23.

[6] Fascinatingly, studies reveal that while many of these consumer choices have been consciously reinforced, ancient mortuary sites show that little girls were given material objects that resembled domestic work while little boys were given objects that could be used as tools. This is, however, culturally specific and many non-western cultures do not, and have not historically, followed the same gender determination. See Baxter, *The Archaeology of Childhood*, pp. 109–15.

[7] Gouge, *Of Domesticall Duties* (London, 1622), Cr.

[8] William Perkins, *Christian Oeconomie* (London, 1609), Bv.

The duty that the family owes to 'it selfe', under the 'priuate gouernement of one', becomes one of the most dominant themes in the comedies precisely for the ways in which those expectations, and roles, are under discussion: on the one hand the children Brisol of the comedies appeal to an idea of family values (proximity, shared spaces, allegiance), while also showing that these values are in an almost constant state of crisis. On the other hand, the comedies fetishize youth (as something past) and yet largely represent adult women. If there are any 'little' people on Shakespeare's comedic stage then they are Titania's fairies in *A Midsummer Night's Dream*; insouciant, ethereal, and at the command of the deeply maternal queen.[9] Elizabethan audiences would have been used to seeing little children take on such mythological or unearthly roles in pageants and masques but beyond the fairies, however, the stages of the comedies are dominated by young couples.[10] Even with the presence of little children on stage, in the role of fairies, however, their representation is not of youth, vulnerability, or even innocence but of the impish and ethereal world of the supernatural. The idea of childhood takes shape in the comedies through its absence: as we witness the narratives of young people determined to make their way in the adult world of marriage the language of childhood creeps in only through reflection or recollection, as something that must be left behind.

Often in Shakespeare's comedies friendship becomes an alternative space of intimacy in which feeling can take shape outside of the prescribed roles of the family. What comes to shape those relationships is a sense of history, of a shared past, and of mutual affection. Frequently the closest we get to a sense of childhood is through friends reminiscing about their youth together. Memory becomes a central medium for the representation of childhood but this also makes it an unstable one.[11] In *A Midsummer Night's Dream*, we meet four young people who are on the cusp on adulthood. The transition to adulthood is marked by marriage and the whole play is framed by the imperatives to celebrate or consummate marriage. Oberon and Titania, the King and Queen of the fairies, divided over their acquisition of a human child, must be reunited and live, albeit unconventionally, as a family. Theseus, the Duke of Athens, and Hippolyta, his Amazonian bride, look forward to celebrating their nuptials, and going to bed together, at the play's end. Before anybody can get married or

---

[9] For a discussion on the size and shapes of fairies in the sixteenth-century imagination, see Katharine Briggs, *The Anatomy of Puck* (Bristol: Routledge and Kegan Paul, 1959), pp.17–33.

[10] Witmore, *Pretty Creatures*, esp. pp. 58–93.

[11] For a broader exploration of memory see Hester Lees Jefferies, *Shakespeare and Memory* (Oxford: Oxford University Press, 2014).

consummate their relationship, however, the young lovers must escape into the wood to find their freedom, their selves, and each other.

From the outset, Hermia is described as a child only, but crucially, to the extent that it makes her the property of her father. The play begins with Egeus demanding that his daughter feel the full force of the Athenian law if she continues to disobey him and marry the man she loves, Lysander, rather than who her father has chosen, Demetrius. Presiding over the argument, Theseus reminds Hermia that

> To you your father should be as a god,
> One that composed your beauties, yea, and one
> To whom you are but as a form in wax
> By him imprinted, and within his power
> To leave the figure or disfigure it.   (1.1.47–51)

Here Theseus conflates several key perceptions about both form and identity: on the one hand, he refers to a conventional belief in the duty and obedience that children owe to their fathers; on the other he brings together two important images within early modern constructions of the self. One is Platonic in that it rehearses the soul as waxen, in which our experiences make imprints of the memories that come to define who we are; two, it calls on a conflicted image of women as unstable and malleable.[12] When Viola, in *Twelfth Night*, reflects on Olivia's attraction to her she observes: 'How easy is it for the proper false | In women's waxen hearts to set their forms! | Alas, our frailty is the cause not we, | For such as we are made of, such we be' (2.2.27–30).[13] The most troubling development on this image, however, is Theseus' claim that because Egeus 'composed' his daughter so he can 'disfigure' her. Despite the prevalence of the waxen image, the impulse is usually to mould rather than disfigure. Robert Cleaver's *A Godly Form of Household Government* (1621) is a typical example of early modern parenting manuals which uses the waxen image to support parental responsibility:

> Parents therefore are herein to respect two points: first, to begin to frame and bend their children in their tender youth to virtue, remembering that a seal entereth deepest into softest wax.[14]

---

[12] 'Let us, then, say that this is the gift of Memory, the mother of the Muses, and that whenever we wish to remember anything we see or hear or think of in our own minds, we hold this wax under the perceptions and thoughts and imprint them upon it, just as we make impressions from seal rings; and whatever is imprinted we remember and know as long as its image lasts, but whatever is rubbed out or cannot be imprinted we forget and do not know.' Plato, *Theateus*, trans. M. J. Levett (Indianapolis: Hackett, 1992), p. 191.

[13] See Wendy Wall on the fascinating mobility of the metaphor of print, especially in relation to questions of gender and autonomy, *The Imprint of Gender, Authorship and Publication in the English Renaissance* (Ithaca, NY: Cornell University Press, 1993).

[14] Cleaver, *A Godly Form of Household Government* (London, 1621), Q5r.

The 'softest wax' appears to be commensurate with age, so that the more 'tender' or younger the child is the more likely they are to receive the right, parental impression. But the fear of over-indulgent parenting runs as a deep vein throughout these texts and even those, like Cleaver's, that seek to emphasize love through fear, also warn against the perils of permissive, almost always maternal, love.[15] The anxiety that maternal love produces socially irresponsible children is expressed in various registers across these texts, and some of them are extreme. One of the most severe is written by John Bradford as advice to a friend, 'Master A.B.', whose apparently over-indulgent attitude has promulgated his son's disobedience. Bradford accuses his addressee of

> a fond love and a foolish affection, which evermore falleth out to be the childs utter destruction: you both have suffered him to pass on pleasantly in his own delights: you have permitted him to run the course of his own will: you have foolishly forbourne to spend the sharp rods of correction upon the naked flesh of his loins: you have fondly pittied to spill some blood of his body with the sharp stripes of chastisement: you have preserved his skin from breaking, his blood from spilling and his loins from smarting.[16]

As we have seen, Bradford's draconian attitude was not endorsed by liberal humanists and teachers who promoted a much more tolerant and even-handed treatment of children. Roger Ascham, Latin Secretary to Mary Tudor and later Elizabeth I's tutor, advocates that the child be taught 'cheerfully and plainly', advising 'cheerful admonishing, and heedful amending of faults: never leaving behind just praise for well doing'.[17] Erasmus was similarly concerned with the well-being of children and supported a learning environment in which a child could be encouraged as well as disciplined. Even the most tolerant, temperate attitudes to children, however, took the Bible as the foundational text and many writers used the New Testament to endorse strict parenting. The Bible is full of proverbs which promote the disciplining and punishing of the child and the epithets 'The rod and correction give wisdom' and 'A child set at liberty maketh his mother shamed' were common parlance for the Elizabethans.[18]

---

[15] Cleaver links mothers who cannot bear to let their children 'be an hour out of their sight' with 'unbridled wantonness and ungraciousness' in children, *A Godly Form of Household Government*, T2r.

[16] John Bradford, *A Letter sent to Master A.B. from the most godly and learned preacher* (London, 1584), Aiiiir.

[17] Roger Ascham, *The Schoolmaster* (London, 1572), 2v.

[18] See Proverbs 22:6; 29:13; 22:4; 'If a man has a stubborn and rebellious son who will not obey the voice of his father or the voice of his mother, and, though they discipline him, will not listen to them, then his father and his mother shall take hold of him and bring him out to the elders of his city at the gate of the place where he lives, and they shall say to the elders of his city, "This our son is stubborn and rebellious; he will not obey our voice; he is

Egeus' threat, however, derives from an ancient law that does not distinguish itself as specifically Christian and appears unique to Athens, but it nevertheless presents a stark and terrifying view of the father's power over his child. Like Lear, Egeus uses the term 'child' to reinforce his parental expectations rather than to denote extreme youthfulness. Hermia is obviously not a child in our modern sense of the word, but she remains a child, the property of her father, until she marries and transfers that obedience to her husband.[19] Despite the structures of power through which the men around her operate, Hermia demonstrates remarkable independence and presence of mind in her commitment to escape her father's threats and fulfil her own desires. The forest, full of fairies and wandering paths, becomes a fascinating place of refuge for the young lovers as a journey away from the areas of adult imperialism and into somewhere without rules, without society, and at the mercy of a sprite with a potion.[20] In *A Midsummer Night's Dream* two fantasies of childhood converge: one is the liberation of the dependent body from the constraints of the parent; and two is the inhabiting of a space without limitation.

'AND THOUGH SHE BE BUT LITTLE, SHE IS FIERCE'

A Midsummer Night's Dream is especially complex in the context of children. It has often been presented as the most accessible of Shakespeare's plays to a young audience because its fairy world presents a context in which young children have been taught the power of escapism as well as authority.[21] Alongside the forest of naughty fairies and lush landscapes lies a much more adult context of desire, aberration, transformation, and sex: the whole play is, in many ways, a homage to the fulfilment of desire, intent as most characters are on consummating their relationships or

a glutton and a drunkard." Then all the men of the city shall stone him to death with stones. So you shall purge the evil from your midst, and all Israel shall hear, and fear,' Deutoronomy 21:18–21. In *Measure for Measure*, the Duke uses the metaphor of a father who only threatens, rather than uses, 'the twigs of birch' as an image of failed authority.

[19] For a range of early modern documents, including *Homily on the State of Matrimony*, see Frances E. Dolan, *The Taming of the Shrew: Texts and Contexts* (New York: Bedford St Martin's, 1996).

[20] See Charlotte Scott, 'Foul Dens and Forests: Titus Andronicus and A Midsummer Night's Dream', *Shakespeare Survey*, 64 (2011), pp. 276–89; Richard Marianstras, *New Perspectives on Shakespeare*, trans. Janet Lloyd (Cambridge: Cambridge University Press, 1995).

[21] Jack Zipes (ed.), *The Oxford Companion to Fairy Tales* (Oxford: Oxford University Press, 2015).

manipulating sexual feelings. It teeters on the edge of bestiality and wilfully
delights in the proximity between sex and violence, wooing and winning.
We might wonder then why children should feel so at home in this seemingly adult world. Partly, I would suggest, it is because the play celebrates
a form of disobedience that will become the mainstay of children's literature. The story of the young lovers centres on a narrative of exploration,
ingenuity, and rebellion in which the young person escapes the adult
world to exercise their own authority and imagination. The threats, fears,
and anxieties that the young person is then subject to, however, are not
resolved by them but by a little magic and the re-entry into the adult
world. Yet this is not a play-world that sits easily alongside the conventional images of children: there is little to suggest innocence here and the
energy of the play is more devoted to leaving that state behind, rather than
celebrating it. What remains in place, however, is the idea of obedience,
which resonates across all Shakespeare's portrayals of children, whether
young or adolescent. A cardinal virtue for the Elizabethans, obedience is
both celebrated as an essential part of social cohesion but also as a poten-
tially dangerous response to tyranny.[22] In many of Shakespeare's comedies
the question of obedience is central to the representation of the young
person's relationship to their father. In some contemporary Christian texts
on household government, the language of duty, fear even, is appropriated
through the terms of the child. Cleaver's *A godly form of household government* takes fear as the presiding context of parenting, in which he explains
that children should not be kept under 'servile or slavish subjection but
rather be a *child*-like and reuerend feare, which both the subiects owe vnto
their Princes, and children vnto their parents; and which both the one and
the other easily obtaine at the hands of such as are vnder their gouernment, by their equall, vpright, and moderate behauiour towards them'.[23]

Even love, for Cleaver, belongs to fear: 'And let all parents always labour,
that their children may rather fear them for love and reverence, then [*sic*]
fear of punishment.' Despite the softening emphasis on love, the organizing principle here is fear, which is reiterated throughout the text in different registers. The structure of the comedy, however, extends the idea of
obedience from the oppressive ties of parental authority to the bonds of
friendship and the desire for affinity. In this way, the language of childhood is modulated through various terms of allegiance—enforced, con-
sensual, or obligatory.

---

[22] See for example Lysimachus Nicanor, *The epistle congratulatorie of Lysimachus Nicanor
of the Societie of Jesu, to the Covenanters in Scotland. VVherin is paralleled our sweet harmony
and correspondency in divers materiall points of doctrine and practice* (London, 1640),
pp. 64–5.
[23] Robert Cleaver, *A Godly Form of Household Government* (London, 1621), V6–7.

The forest becomes a refuge for the lovers precisely because it sits outside the remit of Athenian law and therefore represents a space in which the young people may lay claim to their own desires and wills. As with all such spaces, however, it is perceptual and the lovers inhabit the forest first as a sanctuary, full of liberty and memories and potential; and then as a space of fear and anxiety, from which they want to escape. When Helena follows her dear friend into the forest to find Demetrius we discover that the wood has a history:

> And in the wood where often you and I
> Upon faint primrose beds were wont to lie
> Emptying our bosoms of their counsel sweet.   (1.2.214–16)

Helena will return to this relationship later in the play when she mistakenly interprets the effects of Puck's love potion as Hermia's betrayal of their friendship:

> Is all the counsel that we two have shared—
> The sisters' vows, the hours that we have spent
> When we have chid the hasty-footed time
> For parting us—o, is all quite forgot?
> All schooldays' friendship, childhood innocence?   (3.2.199–203)

Like Bassanio in *The Merchant of Venice* the memory of childhood and the bond between childhood friends becomes fixed through an idea of innocence.[24] The minor details of young friendship are very revealing, since they gives us a rare glimpse into what we might call childhood:

> We, Hermia, like two artificial gods
> Have with our needles created both one flower,
> Both on one sampler, sitting on one cushion,
> Both warbling of one song, both in one key
> As if our hands, our sides, voices and minds
> Had been incorporate. So we grew together,
> Like to a double cherry: seeming parted,
> But yet an union in partition,
> Two lovely berries on one stem.   (3.2.204–12)

This enchanting picture of companionship centres on their togetherness and their leisure; singing, sewing, and sitting 'on one cushion', they did everything as one. This glimpse into the recreational activities of

---

[24] As a marker of his loyalty and love for Antonio, Bassanio invokes a story from their past, claiming: 'I urge this childhood proof, | Because what follows is pure innocence' (*The Merchant of Venice*, 1.1).

aristocratic children is perhaps conventional in what it relates but unique in the way it represents something akin to privacy, as though these two young women shared their past with each other and no one else. The relationship that Helena describes is predicated not only on their shared history but also on their gender: 'And will you rend our ancient love asunder, | To join with men in scorning your poor friend?' (216–17). Childhood and gender become intertwined in the feminine enterprises of sewing and singing. As the play works towards the marriages of the young couples, such companionship, and indeed childhood itself, must be replaced by heterosexual marriage and adulthood.[25] As we will see in *The Winter's Tale*, the adult world of sex and responsibility cannot accommodate the childhood world of innocence and friendship. Here, Helena calls back that childhood world to protect her from the male sexuality that she now feels threatened by, but as confusion abounds, the young lovers do not take comfort in their childhood selves but resort to an unhappy infantilism. Hermia calls her friend 'you juggler, you canker blossom', while Helena retorts that she is a 'puppet'. What then ensues is a series of amusing insults and outrages on the basis of the difference in the women's height. Hermia, we learn, 'though she be but little, she is fierce' (325), while Helena is called a 'painted maypole' (297). The physical characterization of the young women is suggestive of the potential comedy that can be drawn from this scene as well as, perhaps, the statures of the young boys playing these roles:

> And you are grown so high in his esteem
> Because I am so dwarfish and so low?
> How low am I, thou painted maypole? Speak,
> How low am I? I am not yet so low
> But that my nails can reach unto thine eyes.   (3.2.295–9)

This is one of the few instances where Shakespeare characterizes his youth through their dialogue rather than through their status. The young women resorting to physical insults and slurs reveals their immaturity and, in doing so, exposes a vulnerability. Hermia's diminutive shape makes her seem even more childish here and yet, ironically, what this moment marks is the inevitable shift into adulthood that arguing over a boy will bring. Although not irrevocably so, the friendship between the women is strained and what must replace their childish companionship is their sexually independent selves; distanced from each other and available for marriage.

---

[25] R.C., *The School of Vertue* (1621) begins with a verse in which parents are encouraged to look after the 'tender years' and that if the children 'halt' it is the 'tutor's fault'. It's all about how to behave and deport yourself as a child with civilitie and courtesy. The text emphasizes cleanliness, preparation, and behaviour as a rehearsal for adulthood.

At this point in the play, all forms of allegiance are under strain—the child's obedience to the father and the bonds of same-sex friendship. The women's escape into the wood marks a point at which the structures of childhood are systematically broken down but, as in the wider play, such gestures at anarchy are written through a deep pleasure in the comedic potential of chaos.[26]

There is no doubt that the play is a celebration of pleasure—sexual, theatrical, personal, and social—and the various ways in which the characters experience forms of pleasure. If the play's narrative looks towards unity and fecundity, then it also invests in the two narrative frames through which such unity is promoted. The human and the fairy worlds present two versions of cohesion; we learn that not much can go well for the human world unless the fairy world is calm, but Shakespeare departs from conventional narratives of threatening fairies and imps who wreak havoc with human endeavour and presents an altogether more beneficent world of fairy.[27] Beyond the narratives of the young lovers (and how convinced we are that Demetrius loves Helena only by virtue of Puck's potion), the real success story of this play belongs to Oberon and Titania. The values of harmony or cohesion that the play promotes are at their most visible in the picture of the King and Queen of the fairies safely reconciled, as a family, with their Indian boy. The rather dubious explanation initially offered by Puck that Oberon only wants this child for his 'henchman' is modified by Titania, the mother of all fairies, who 'makes him all her joy' (2.1.27). The story of the boy's kidnap is equally ambiguous: according to Puck the 'lovely boy' was 'stol'n from an Indian king... | And jealous Oberon would have the child | Knight of his train, to trace the forests wild' (2.1.22, 23–5) but Titania tells us:

> Set your heart at rest.
> The fairyland buys not the child of me.
> His mother was a vot'ress of my order,
> And in the spiced Indian air by night
> Full often hath she gossiped by my side...
> When we have laughed to see the sails conceive
> And grow big-bellied with the wanton wind,
> Which she with pretty and with swimming gait
> Following her womb then rich with my young squire,

---

[26] C. L Barber's study of the play and its representation of misrule remains one of the most significant works of criticism on this aspect of the play, *Shakespeare's Festive Comedy: A Study of Dramatic Form and its Relation to Social Custom* (Princeton: Princeton University Press, 1959).

[27] See K. M. Briggs, *The Anatomy of Puck: An Examination of Fairy Belief among Shakespeare and his Successors* (London: Routledge, 1959); Roger Lancelyn Green, 'Shakespeare and the Fairies', *Folklore*, 73.2 (1962), pp. 89–101.

> Would imitate and sail upon the land
> To fetch me trifles, and return again
> As from a voyage, rich with merchandise
> But she being mortal, of that boy did die;
> And for her sake do I rear up her boy;
> And for her sake I will not part with him.   (2.1.121–5, 128–37)

This picture of female friendship, maternity, and loyalty strikes a particularly profound chord in a play which explores male authority. Titania's story is both moving and beautiful in its love of female fecundity and the images through which the body and the sea, the wind and the sails are pregnant with futurity. Maternity and protection support Titania's love, while jealousy and annoyance drive Oberon's behaviour. There is something strangely inchoate about the character who wishes to humiliate his Queen by causing her to be devoted to a human, partially transformed into a donkey, so that he can take the beloved child away from her. One the one hand, a silly trick, and on the other a rather sophisticated but troubling example of Oberon's need to be loved more than the boy: like any new father, perhaps, Oberon wants to know he still matters most. Whatever Oberon's motives, the play resolves them through a celebration of the family, represented by the fairy monarchs and their human child. The rather unconventional testimony to heterosexual union is achieved through a restitution of order and obedience played out through adoption and devotion, loyalty and love. As the young lovers emerge from the forest and their experiences there, they look back on that brief time as another childhood, marking their move out of the forest and into married life as one of maturity and rationalization. Demetrius, explaining to Egeus that he no longer loves Hermia, relates:

> But, my good lord, I wot not by what power—
> But power it is—my love to Hermia,
> Melted as the snow, seems to me now
> As the remembrance of an idle gaud
> Which in my childhood I did dote upon,
> And all the faith, the virtue of my heart,
> The object and the pleasure of mine eye
> Is only Helena. To her, my lord,
> Was I betrothed ere I saw Hermia.
> But like in sickness did I loathe this food;
> But, as in health come to my natural taste,
> Now I do wish it, love it, long for it,
> And will for evermore be true to it.   (4.1.161–73)

For Demetrius, loving Helena is akin to growing up: his infatuation with Hermia is remembered now only as an irrational attachment, like a child to a toy. Demetrius's metaphor relies on childhood as a temporary and inadequate rehearsal for adulthood, through which he can dismiss his affection for Hermia as analogous to doting on an 'idle gaud'. Extending the metaphor from childhood to illness, he perceives his current state as one of sagacity and full health. Such states of being are relative and transitional. Childhood and illness become temporary states where right judgements and appropriate responses cannot be made. The understanding that Demetrius has grown up and come to his full senses, and self, is reflected in Theseus's comment that he will overrule Egeus and proceed towards solemnizing their marriages. In this way, childhood is not something to be relished but endured.

Everything that takes place in the forest, including attachments, illusions, and memories, is subject to change. The idea of childhood is implicated in this process since it, too, like the fairy magic, Bottom's transformation, and the lovers' feelings, is a distant memory at the play's close. What replaces those memories is the transition to adulthood marked by marriage: 'For this cause shall a man leave his father and mother and cleave to his wife.' Citing Ephesians 5:3.1, Cleaver provides the caveat:

> Not that marriage exempteth any from their due honour and obedience to parents but to declare that the union between man and wife is greater than between the children and their parents.[28]

Union becomes the dominant model of celebration as each character takes his or her place alongside another. Understanding marriage as a version of social obedience recognizes that these children have grown up and accepted their terms of allegiance in the adult world. As Titania reminds us, 'We are their parents and original' (2.1.117). The 'original' parents bless the lovers and the marriage bed with the help of fairies who bring only perfection:

> And the issue there create
> Ever shall be fortunate.
> So shall couples living three
> Ever true in loving be,
> And the blots of nature's hand
> Shall not in their issue stand.
> Never mole, harelip, nor scar,
> Nor mark prodigious such as are
> Despised in nativity
> Shall upon their children be.   (5.2.35–44)

The play's resolution centres on a vision of fulfilment in which the child is central to both happiness and harmony. The birth of the perfect child,

---

[28] Cleaver, *A Godly Form of Household Government*, M7r.

rendered here as physical conformity to an unmarked ideal, is both a blessing and a reward.

The emphasis on marriage and fertility has led many scholars to suspect that *A Midsummer Night's Dream* was especially commissioned to celebrate a wedding. There is no evidence to support this claim but the play certainly invests in the idea of marriage as a form of social harmony and that children are both a product of that marriage and will themselves grow towards marriage as an ideal form of socialization. There is little space in *Dream* for anxieties about sexual appetite, the corruption of innocence, or romantic failure that attend many of the daughters of Shakespeare's comedies. *Dream* is unique in its unrestrained representation of heterosexuality; similarly, there is little anxiety in this play about female innocence. Many of Shakespeare's comedies depend on the tensions between innocence and experience, loquaciousness and silence, and define their women according to how well they can or cannot relate to ideas of female purity. The marriages of the young couples in *Dream*, however, appear to attest to a successful transition from child to adult through forms of social acceptance.

'KNOW THE WORLD'

When in *The Merry Wives of Windsor* Mistress Quickly remarks, ''tis not good that children should know any wickedness. Old folks, you know, have discretion, as they say, and know the world' (2.2.115–17), she reflects on the child's inability to manage the social code of what to say and when. It is not that the child should be kept from 'wickedness', per se, more that the child would not know how to keep it to themselves! The joke here is that she, Mistress Quickly, has little discretion, as she puts it, and that the adult world of sexual intrigue she attempts to keep William from is not for his sake, but for hers. Nevertheless, she speaks to a difference between the adult and the child that resonates throughout Shakespeare's work: the difference between innocence and experience. The young child in Shakespeare has a unique relationship to the quality of innocence as we saw in the history plays of Chapter 2, and as I will return to in the final chapter, but as Shakespeare's children are a little older in the comedies, usually young adults or adolescents, that idea of innocence becomes particularly equated with female sexuality. In *The Taming of the Shrew*, for example, Lucentio finds Bianca's quietness especially attractive when he translates it into innocence. Reflecting on the difference between the two women, the 'shrewish' Katherine and the 'fair' Bianca, he exclaims: 'But in the other's silence do I see | Maid's mild behaviour and sobriety' (1.1.70–1). Bianca's 'silence' makes her sexually attractive precisely because it suggests, to

Lucentio at least, that she is restrained and gentle. Construing her as a 'maid' also suggests that she is a young woman, perhaps even a 'girl'.[29] A housewifery manual of the mid- to late seventeenth century explicitly identifies adolescent women as 'maids', especially through the onset of puberty: 'maids have their terms at fourteen years old, and they cease at about fifty, for they want heat and cannot breed much good blood nor expel what is too much.'[30] In this way, the body produces a life cycle that is understood as linear through which children must be both taught and affirmed. Lucentio's desire for Bianca is reaffirmed through his recognition that she is at an appropriate age to marry and demonstrates the behaviour he would expect in a wife. Her 'silence' reflects a version of subservience that many of Shakespeare's most attractive women contest.

In a fascinating except from an early modern jest book, the author narrates a story of a young child:

> A Girl about ten years old, had got a trick of confidently staring in mens faces when they were talking; for which her mother reproved her, saying Daughter, our Sex enjoins us Modesty, and you ought to be bashful, and look down-ward when you are looking in mens company, and not to stand gazing and gaping as if you were looking babies in their eyes: to which the pert girl replied, This lecture forsooth, should have been read in my former ignorant Ages, but every age grows wiser and wiser; that maids of every age know better: Men indeed may look down on the primitive dust, from whence they were taken, but Man being our original, I will stare in their faces, say what you can to the contrary.[31]

This wonderfully precocious child suggests that she is now too old to learn an appropriate form of submission because she has the prudence to question that judgement rather than simply adopt it. Many of Shakespeare's greatest young women take a similar position, although they are most likely older than 10. But the discourse of innocence continues to surround them, and, in exceptional cases, devastate them.

Like the sisters in the *Taming of the Shrew*, the young women in *Much Ado about Nothing* are characterized through contrast: Beatrice, 'Lady Disdain', and Hero, 'a modest young lady'. Both unmarried and eligible,

---

[29] Jennifer Higginbotham explores how 'girlhood' was simultaneously understood to reflect a time in a woman's life but also as a marker of 'unruly femininity', *The Girlhood of Shakespeare's Sisters*, esp. pp. 62–75. Deanne Williams also approaches the category of the girl as culturally specific in *Shakespeare and the Performance of Girlhood* (Basingstoke: Palgrave, 2015).

[30] Jane Sharp, *The Midwives Book, or the whole art of midwifery* (1671), ed. Elaine Hobby (Oxford: Oxford University Press, 1999), p. 69.

[31] J.S., *England's Merry Jester: or Court, City and Country Jests, New and Suitable to the Times* (London, 1693), sig. Cv–C2r. See Higginbotham, *The Girlhood of Shakespeare's Sisters*, pp. 62–3.

the narrative of the play's action centres on the relationships between men and women. While the main plot focuses on the comedy of manipulation wherein Beatrice and Benedick are brought to believe that they love each other, the subplot focuses on Hero and her victimization by various men in her life, including her fiancé, her father, and a malcontent. Much of the play's humour comes from the overarching investment in misunderstanding: gestured at in the play's title, the 'nothing' to which it refers can mean 'women' (those with no thing) and noting (including multiple forms of interpretation). Hero's victimization in the play is largely made possible through her characterization as the opposite to Beatrice. In fact we see very little of who Hero is but we know that she is *not* Beatrice and so by extension we perceive her as quiet, submissive, and dutiful. The scene in which she is brought to the altar to marry Claudio, having been set up to appear adulterous by her waiting woman, Margaret, is entirely dependent upon forms of perception and the interpretation of innocence. It is in this scene that Hero is her most childlike; on the threshold of marriage, between her father and her would-be husband, she is reduced to a travesty of male anxiety, as she is systematically shamed and brutalized by the two men who marked her child and adult selves. Believing her to have seduced another man, Claudio declares:

> There, Leonato, take her back again.
> Give not this rotten orange to your friend!
> She's but the sign and semblance of her honour.
> Behold how like a maid she blushes here.
> O, what authority and show of truth
> Can cunning sin cover itself withal!   (4.1.31–6)

Returning her back to her father through the image of unwanted produce, Claudio insults Hero with the language of her perceived failure. She is not what she seems, he insists: 'Behold how like a maid she blushes here.' The great agony for Claudio is that Hero appears to blush like the young virgin she should be but in fact it is an elaborate attempt to perform innocence:

> Comes not that blood as modest evidence
> To witness simple virtue? Would you not swear—
> All you that see her—that she were a maid,
> By these exterior shows? But she is none.
> She knows the heat of a luxurious bed.
> Her blush is guiltiness not modesty.   (4.1.37–42)

Calling on his wedding guests to witness her blushing body, Claudio instructs his audience on how to read her: she looks like a maid—here construed as a young female virgin—but she is quite the opposite, 'She knows the heat of a luxurious bed.' 'Her blush is guiltiness not modesty': Claudio's rendition of events and what he perceives in Hero's face completely dismantles the relationship between the body and the mind, between innocence and experience. All the landmarks of youth and innocence are violated here as neither Hero's age nor her physical responses protect her from accusations of licentiousness. According to Claudio we can no longer read the innocence of young women in their responses or their status, for they are capable of the most artful forms of manipulation—using the apparatus of innocence to conceal sin. It is a fascinating and vertiginous moment in the theatre since, if we follow Claudio's logic, there is no security in meaning since all forms of innocence can be performed. The great agony for Claudio is not only Hero's perceived betrayal but also her ability to cover it up. For the audience, however, who know that Hero is the victim of a cruel trick, we see innocence in that blush and we see modesty in her face. But Claudio has let the possibility of interpretation into the theatrical space; he has voiced the prospect that women can pretend to be something other than they are and this unleashes a torrent of male anxiety. Don Pedro, assuming Hero to be lying, says, 'you are no maiden', reiterating the persistent fear that she is not a virgin. Believing his daughter to be guilty Leonato attempts to remove all paternal bonds:

> Could she here deny
> The story that is printed in her blood?
> Do not live, Hero, do not ope thine eyes...
> Grieved I, I had but one?
> Why ever wast thou lovely in my eyes?
> Why had I not with charitable hand
> Took up a beggar's issue at my gates,
> Who smirched thus, and mired with infamy,
> I might have said 'No part of it is mine;
> This shame derives itself from unknown loins.'
> But mine, and mine I loved, and mine I praised,
> And mine that I was proud on; mine so much
> That I myself was to myself not mine,
> Valuing of her—why she, O she has fallen
> Into a pit of ink, that the wide sea
> Hath drops too few to wash her clean again,
> And salt too little which may season give
> To her foul, tainted flesh.   (4.1.121–3; 127–43)

Leonato embarks on a fantasy of rejection in which he imagines Hero to have been adopted so that at this moment he could unflinchingly claim no paternal responsibility. The horror that Leonato feels is predicated partly on his love for Hero but also on his paternity—'But mine, and mine I loved'—and the betrayal that such an attachment can bring. He cannot disentangle Hero's behaviour from his status as her father and the amplified and repetitive language of possession signifies the extent to which the child remains attached to the parent until they marry. The accusations against Hero are catastrophic—they have stained her soul and tainted her flesh—and as far as Leonato is concerned they are 'confirmed' by her bodily responses. The bond of the father it seems remains intact so long as the child adheres to, and represents, their value system. If the child fails in this regard their life is no longer valuable:

> For did I think thou wouldst not quickly die,
> Thought I thy spirits were stronger than thy shames,
> Myself would, on the rearward of reproaches,
> Strike at thy life.   (4.1.124–7)

There is no parental bond in Shakespeare that can transcend perceived wrongdoing on the part of the child. Although the majority of early modern texts to address parenting agree that the office of a parent is to love and care for their child there are moral limits to this. Many texts that discourse on the nature of sin present an argument for learned rather than inherited behaviour. Many of these texts recognize that virtuous and morally stable parents can produce deviant children just as morally deviant parents may produce virtuous children. All these texts acknowledge the point at which an individual must protect the moral and Christian integrity of themselves, irrespective of external influences, including parents. Daniel Tuteville's illuminating book, *St Pauls threefold cord wherewith are severally combined, the mutual oeconmical duites betwtixt husband wife. Parent childe. Master. Servant*, makes the bold claim that 'The word is indefinite and without all exemption or limitation. Children Obey' but he goes on to explain that if children are encouraged to evil by their parents they have a god given duty to refuse.[32] Almost all of these texts observe that the parent has supreme authority over the child but they differ in how that authority should be used and the extent to which the child can be punished by the parent. One of the most brutal attitudes in this respect is reflected in Bradford's letter, which includes a section, 'Touching the Correction of children' (1548): He advises that the child be stripped naked and whipped until all their skin is broken. He then goes on to take a passage from the Bible in which it is outlined that if children go on disobeying their parents they will be brought to the City Fathers and stoned to death, through which their evil will be removed. He cites this as an example to show that 'no

---

[32] p. 143. The 'threefold' distinction that he makes is that when your parents urge you to **good** things they must be obeyed, when they urge you to **evil** things they must **not** be obeyed and when they urge to things that are neither good nor bad ('of an indifferent strain') then they must be obeyed, see pp. 162–3.

years are excepted'.[33] Although most writers will agree that the moral upbringing of children rests with the parent, when a child errs the parent has a right to punish them in whatever ways they deem fit. Many writers cautioned against corporeal punishment and advocated kindness and tenderness but others, like Bradford, were unrestrained in the abuse of the child.[34] What resonates throughout these texts is an almost obsessive anxiety about forms of obedience. The authority of the father is continually reaffirmed by the obedience of the child: if the child is judged to have strayed from their duty of obedience then there is no limit to the punishments possible. Such profound anxieties about disobedience manifest in many of Shakespeare's comedic fathers and remain unresolved. Egeus, after all, does not retract his earlier threats but subsumes them through Demetrius's desire to marry Helena. Similarly, Leonato accepts his daughter again because she is proved innocent.

Within this context Leonato's rejection of Hero is not unusual since she can be understood to have betrayed his parental values but the swiftness with which he reacts and the violence of his response makes him exceptional in terms of early modern parenting.[35] Only the friar, who has been standing silently until now, takes a risk on the young woman's body and believes in her:

> By noting of the lady, I have marked
> A thousand blushing apparitions
> To start into her face, a thousand innocent shames
> In angel whiteness beat away those blushes,
> And in her eye there hath appeared a fire
> To burn the errors that these princes hold
> Against her maiden truth.   (4.1.158–64)

The friar instantly rewrites the body of Hero: not only does he promote her from 'child' to 'lady' but he reinstates her as a 'maiden'. The friar's speech focuses on the same bodily responses that Claudio noted but interprets them very differently: here, the blush is not of shame or guilt but of innocence and injustice. Hero is no longer treated as an indictment on those who once loved her (her father and Claudio) but as an individual woman

---

[33] John Bradford, *A Letter Sent to Master A.B.* (London, 1584), Biir. Cf. Deuteronomy 21:18–21.
[34] See Rebecca Bushnell, *A Culture of Teaching: Early Modern Humanism in Theory and Practice* (Ithaca, NY: Cornell University Press, 1996), pp. 23–56.
[35] Bruce Young and Deborah Shuger make similar points on King Lear and in the period more generally: 'One of the most striking features of the Renaissance image of fatherhood—largely ignored or misrepresented in contemporary criticism—is its association with kindness, nurturing, and generous self-giving. Lear's actions in the play's first scenes are calamitous not because they fit contemporary expectations for fatherhood, but because they violate them,' *In the Company of Shakespeare*, p. 46; Deborah Shuger, *Habits of Thought*, pp. 218–50.

who has been wronged. The friar's response to Hero is fundamentally important within the context of the play-world since it amplifies two key aspects of the drama. The friar has no more information to go on than that which Claudio has presented but unlike Leonato he believes in Hero's truth and virtue. This is a wonderful moment of meta-theatricality where Shakespeare points to the very instability of interpretation and the cata-strophic consequences misinterpretation can have. The other important factor here is that the friar does not treat Hero as a child: by engaging with her as an adult, by trusting her virtue, and by observing her responses as those of a wronged woman he distinguishes her from the male networks that seek to control her. She is neither daughter nor wife, but a 'lady' struggling to contain her anger and sadness at such slanders. The play never resolves the issues it raises around kinship, possession, and male networks of authority but it rehearses the fantasy of abandonment as well as the terms of restitution.

Forcing Leonato to engage with Hero once again as his daughter, the friar resolves to keep her secretly hidden and assumed dead:

> For it so falls out
> That what we have we prize not to the worth
> Whiles we enjoy it, but being lacked and lost,
> Why, then we rack the value, then we find
> The virtue that possession would not show us
> While it was ours.   (4.1.217–22)

Here Shakespeare adumbrates one of the great themes of the late plays—loss, regret, and remorse. The friar's point is that we do not know what we have got until it is gone and that by simulating this experience for Claudio it will make him remember the Hero he loved, not the Hero he defamed. The electrifying power of theatre is that, unlike life, it can turn back time, feign death, enforce structures of regret and mourning, and manipulate characters' emotions for the betterment of their moral selves. Hero never moves beyond her characterization as a young woman, a maid, who is manipulated and condemned by the men who purport to love her: that she ends up marrying one of those men is deeply problematic but the play is less interested in the emotional lives of its characters and more invested in structures of possession. The emphasis in the comedies on marriage as a unifying organization of social cohesion allows Shakespeare to explore forms of obedience through the transition from child to adult, father to husband. Many of the issues raised by the comedies' representation of these power dynamics are never resolved: as a virtue, obedience is never directly critiqued nor endorsed but exposed as a quality capable of both destruction and unification. That it haunts the child in Shakespeare's drama provides us with an arresting glimpse into expectations of authority.

5

'Time is chasing us'

Regret, Time, and the Child Eternal in the Late Plays

There is no greater testimony to the power of time and the role of the child than the collection of plays that Shakespeare wrote between 1606 and 1611, commonly referred to as the late plays or the Romances. Shakespeare would write other plays during this period, notably *All is True*, and *The Two Noble Kinsmen*, but *The Winter's Tale*, *The Tempest*, *Cymbeline*, and *Pericles* converge around the same theme: a beloved child, loss, and the fantasy of recovering the past.[1] The plays I will examine here, *The Winter's Tale*, *Pericles*, and *The Tempest*, bring together all the concerns I have so far discussed: innocence, father–daughter relationships, and growing up. Collectively they are a deep swan-song to the power of childhood, to memory, to love, and to the terrible awareness that only age brings of the preciousness of time. There is no doubt that these plays are written by a man who is getting older and who has loved his children, his youth, and lost both. There is an acute sensitivity to loss and to the dream of recovery: nowhere more beautifully and devastatingly expressed than in *The Winter's Tale*. All three plays, however, share a central concern with the father and daughter, and that relationship defines the narrative and emotional scope of the plays.[2]

It was once fashionable to imagine that Shakespeare wrote *The Tempest* as a valediction to the theatre and to his role as the master conjuror, or playwright.[3] Prospero, the illusionist, who could suspend time, conjure spirits, and manipulate action, was the consummate playwright whose beautiful speech to Ferdinand about the transitory nature of both life and

---

[1] Shakespeare also wrote *Cymbeline* during this period and it is usually grouped with the late plays as it shares many features but my concern in this last chapter is with childhood which is relatively less significant in this play.

[2] In her introduction to *Pericles*, Suzanne Gossett perceives a direct link between the play and Shakespeare's emotional state: 'pouring his grief over the deaths of Edmund and infant son [Hamnet], his fears for Susanna and his delight at his grand-daughter's [Elizabeth] birth into the scenes of birth and apparent deaths in the third and fourth acts. By March 1608 Shakespeare was writing the father–daughter reunion scene of the fifth act' (London: Arden, 2004), p. 61.

[3] Edward Dowden, *Shakespeare: A Critical Study of his Mind and Art* (Oxford: Blackwell, 2003), pp. 328, xiii; *Collected Works of Samuel Taylor Coleridge* (London: Routledge and Kegan Paul, 1978).

art became a lucid reflection on the temporality of everything, not least of all the theatre. Within this image of Prospero as Shakespeare we could understand the combination of rage, frustration, resignation, and insight that characterizes so much of who he is. Prospero's unique blend of cynicism and hope, anger and love, makes him a compelling figure who can fit our fantasies of the middle-aged playwright, having enjoyed a hugely success-ful career, getting ready to enjoy his home town and his sizeable assets. Whether Shakespeare considered himself like Prospero is perhaps no more relevant than, or equally relevant as to, whether he considered himself like Hamlet or Othello, but whatever Shakespeare's personal engagement with his characters there is no doubt that the father/child relationship is central to this collection of plays. There is an emotional intensity to this relation-ship that gestures towards experience if not necessarily biography.

The Tempest opens with the drama of a storm: thrust into the middle of this experience we, too, feel the anxiety of the Boatswain's cries, the fear in the shrieks of those on board the ship, and the visceral description of lash-ing winds and raging waters. All those on board, the mariners and the party returning from the wedding of the King's daughter, believe that they will drown and the short scene ends with Gonzalo begging for dry land. The next scene opens with Miranda, Prospero's 13-year-old daughter, sug-gesting to her father that 'If by your art, my dearest father, you have | Put the wild waters in this roar, allay them' (1.2.1–2). Miranda's awareness that her father has created an illusory storm does not mitigate her empathy which is fully realized through her description of watching those on board the ship: 'O I have suffered | With those that I saw suffer!' (5–6). Prospero's justification for wrecking the ship is that everything he has done has been 'but in care of thee, | Of thee, my dear one, thee, my daughter' (16–17). Prospero then reveals that Miranda knows nothing of their past, of who her father was and why they are living together on this 'bare isle'. Recreating their history, Prospero discloses to his daughter that he is more than just her father, 'master of a full poor cell', he is the usurped Duke of Milan, 'A prince of power' (55). At this early point in the play, Prospero offers to Miranda a collection of memories that define the events between her infancy and the twelve years they have been living on the island. The his-tory is entirely focused on what led them there, namely Antonio's usurp-ation of Prospero and his subsequent escape, with his library and his infant daughter, on a boat pushed out into the Mediterranean. Miranda's responses to her father's story are characterized by her empathy and love for him, rather than her own loss or suffering:

> O my heart bleeds
> To think o'th'teen that I have turned you to,
> Which is from my remembrance. Please you, farther.　(1.2.63–5)

Miranda feels sorrow for something that she cannot remember but something that she can imagine. There is no suggestion that she was a trouble to her father but she imagines that she might have been and that is enough to make her heart bleed. Miranda's staggering empathy emerges from a sense of what might have happened—to those on board the ship or to her father as a single parent—and engages her emotions to the extent that she cannot distinguish the actual from the possible. The dramatic and emotional relationship between what is and what *might* have happened is intensified throughout the play through the use of Prospero's magic but here it works to shape Miranda's memory and her deep sensitivities to the power of art. Prospero's description of his escape recalls how, 'I'th' dead of darkness, | The ministers for the purpose hurried thence | Me and thy crying self' (1.2.130–3) to which Miranda again responds with her empathetic imagination:

> Alack, for pity!
> I, not remembr'ing how I cried out then,
> Will cry it o'er again; it is a hint
> That wrings mine eyes to't.   (1.2.133–5)

Miranda snatches at the bits of her father's story in which she sees herself and attaches to their memory, recreating who she was through who she is now. Rehearsing these brief glimpses into her childhood she identifies with her father's memory to reclaim herself. Experiencing her heritage for the first time she enunciates a value system in recognition of the complexities of good and evil:

> I should sin
> To think but nobly of my grandmother.
> Good wombs have borne bad sons.   (1.2.118–20)

From the isolation of the island, Miranda now has an uncle and a grandmother with whom she attempts to relate, imagining the one as good and the other as bad. Her identification with her past and her father, however, is constantly reiterated through the possibility that she was a burden: 'Alack, what trouble | Was I then to you!' (1.2.151–2) to which her father touchingly responds:

> O, a cherubin
> Thou wast that did preserve me. Thou didst smile,
> Infused with a fortitude from heaven,
> When I have decked the sea with drops full salt,
> Under my burden groaned; which raised in me
> An undergoing stomach, to bear up
> Against what should ensue.   (1.2.152–8)

Here the familial roles become conflated: Miranda, the child, becomes the strength through which the father, also figured as the mother through his 'burden', is sustained. As Miranda weeps now for the past in which she might have caused her father trouble, so Prospero wept then for the trouble they were in. Only the infant Miranda, smiling through the stormy seas, kept her father afloat. The conflation of the emotional and the experiential shapes the relationship between father and child which is entirely defined in these brief memories of distress and companionship. Miranda's childhood, such as it was, and the twelve years spent on the island, are mapped in four lines as Prospero announces:

> Sit still, and hear the last of our sea-sorrow.
> Here in this island we arrived, and here
> Have I thy schoolmaster made thee more profit
> Than other princes can, that have more time
> For vainer hours and tutors not so careful.   (1.2.171–5)

Despite their circumstances Prospero has instructed his daughter in the education that befits her status. Her education creates a unique link to Prospero beyond the environment of the island and suspends any notion of childishness or childhood. Beyond the memories of her crying, infant self there is nothing that suggests Miranda lived as a child: there is no childish companion or 'play', no toys or domestic space; only Prospero's 'utensils' and the 'full poor cell' that is their home. Dramatically, what makes her a child in this play is the intensity of her relationship with her father. Miranda and Prospero are unique, however, in the later plays, precisely because of their relationship. The control that Prospero exerts and the means he uses to orchestrate her destiny, as well as the reactionary responses he demonstrates in anger and in love, make him a powerful example of the patriarch. In many ways Prospero is closer to the early modern idea of fatherhood than any other father on Shakespeare's stage as he represents a range of parental values, including tenderness, nurture, authority, punishment, education, and protection.[4] His paternal role, although deeply troubling at times, extends to both Ariel and Caliban, to whom he is both carer and punisher. The now notorious observation he makes of Caliban—

> A devil, a born devil, on whose nature
> Nurture can never stick; on whom my pains,
> Humanely taken, all, all, lost, quite lost   (4.1.188–90)—

---

[4] Anthony Fletcher, *Gender, Sex and Subordination in England 1500–1800* (New Haven: Yale University Press, 1995), pp. 297–321.

establishes Prospero as the instructor/father who organizes his relationships on the island through identification with the paternal self. Having
conflated the role of the tutor and father with Miranda he extends it to
Caliban, so that the 'pains' he takes become 'humane' only to the extent
that they attempt to include the servant in his island family. But unlike
Miranda, Ariel and Caliban rebel against him so that Prospero's authority
becomes shaped by pain and punishment. The threat that he will return
Ariel to the 'cloven pine' from whence he rescued him is somewhat akin to
the fantasy that you can return the child to the womb. But Prospero's
relationship with both Ariel and Caliban is a horrifying mix of love and
anger, punishment and reward. Both characters are enslaved to Prospero
and in this way they retain the status of the child who was often analogized
to the slave through shared processes of obligation, duty, and obedience.
Vives and Erasmus both make the claim that 'willing service' instils the
greatest bonds and therefore instruction should start with love but keep
the rod 'in sight'.[5] Rebecca Bushnell explains: 'Teachers should abjure violence, thus, because it makes children, like slaves, at once too servile and
not servile enough.'[6] Despite the shared space of servility that children and
slaves occupied in relation to their master or father, a distinction between
fear and love remained central to many Christian texts on the subject.
Arthur Hildersam's lectures, published in 1635, attempt to discriminate
between forms of servile fear:

> As their love to God is not a fellow-like familiarity, as is among equalls but is
> (out of an apprehension of his greatnes and holinesse, and justice) tempered
> with feare, and a dreadfull awe of him; so neither is that feare of God that is
> in them, a servile feare, like that of the *slave*, that hath nothing to move him
> unto duty but the feare of the whip, but is (out of an apprehension and
> assurance of his goodnesse) mixed with love. Like the feare that ought to be
> in every good *child*, towards his parents.[7]

Joseph Hall makes a similar distinction when he claims that 'the
good *child* is afraid of displeasing his father, though he were sure not to be
beaten; whereas, the *slave* is only afraid of stripes, not of displeasure.'[8]
Such attitudes to service suggest that the slave, unlike the child, could
never hope to be loved and so that their forms of service could only be
bound by fear of pain rather than displeasure. The distinctions between

---

[5] Vives, *De Tradendis*, Bk 2, p. 285. See Bushnell, *A Culture of Teaching*, p. 32.
[6] *A Culture of Teaching*, p. 33.
[7] Arthur Hildersam, *CLII lectures vpon Psalme LI preached at Ashby-Delazouch in Leicestershire* (London, 1635), p. 383.
[8] Joseph Hall, *The remedy of prophanenesse. Or, Of the true sight and feare of the Almighty A needful tractate. In two books* (London, 1637), pp. 152–3.

fear and love become increasingly complex in the dynamics of the family. If the semantic relationship between child and slave was based on the extent to which true obedience could only be instilled by love and respect, rather than fear and punishment, the role of anxiety in supporting submission becomes progressively hard to justify.[9] Unlike Machiavelli's famous observation that fear is more powerful than love, liberal humanists understood love as a far more binding emotion than fear.[10] Yet for Prospero, as many early modern texts would suggest, fear and love go hand in hand, and become inextricably linked in his role as both magus and father. In fact, much of his magic depends on creating fear and anxiety, rather than pleasure or celebration.[11] But this was not always the case: as Prospero tells his history to Miranda he reveals that his magic began, not in asserting power, but in avoiding it: 'Me, poor man, my library | Was dukedom large enough' (1.2.109–10). Later in this scene we also discover that Caliban was not always his detested slave but his companion, having lived together with Prospero in his 'cell' until he tried to violate Miranda. Prospero iterates Caliban's move from family member to servant when he exclaims, 'Thou most lying slave, | Whom stripes may move, not kindness' (1.2.348–9). Reflecting early modern attitudes to the subject, Prospero expels Caliban from the space of kinship on the basis, not only of what he attempted to do to Miranda, but also according to what drives his allegiance. Recognizing that Caliban can only respond to punishment rather than kindness Prospero dismisses him from the bonds of love that distinguish the child from the slave. But despite Prospero's differentiations, and Caliban's professed loathing of his master, the relationships between kindness and 'stripes', love and service, become inextricably intertwined. The island's history belongs, it seems, to a culture of service in which the child and the

---

[9] The link between children and service goes much deeper in terms of social history since children would leave their parental home in order to take up a position in service or as an apprentice. The child would enter the household of another family, often at a very young age, and remain in a subordinate position for their rest of their life, Krausman Ben-Amos, *Adolescence and Youth*, pp. 156–82. The Bible also talks about children and slaves in the same ways, Ephesians 6:1–24.

[10] Niccolo Machiavelli, 'Men are less hesitant about injuring someone who makes himself loved than one who makes himself feared, because love is held together by a chain of obligation that, since men are a wretched lot, is broken on every occasion for their own self-interest; but fear is sustained by a dread of punishment that will never abandon you,' *The Prince*, trans. Peter Bondanella (Oxford: Oxford University Press, 2005), p. 58.

[11] The exception to this is the masque which involves Ceres and Iris, in celebration of the union between Miranda and Ferdinand. There is no doubt that even here, in the context of pleasure, Ferdinand is made decidedly anxious by the illusion. For the creation of anxiety as central to mechanisms of power see Michel Foucault, *Power/Knowledge: Selected Writings, 1972–1977* (New York: Pantheon, 1980).

slave are interwoven. Lecturing a peevish Ariel on his obligation to Prospero, he reminds him of Sycorax, Caliban's mother:

> This blue-eyed hag was hither brought with child,
> And here was left by th' sailors. Thou, my slave,
> As thou report'st thyself, was then her servant;
> And for thou wast a spirit too delicate
> To act her earthy and abhorred commands,
> Refusing her grand hests, she did confine thee
> By help of her more potent ministers,
> And in her most unmitigable rage,
> Into a cloven pine...
>   This was then the island—
> Save for the son that she did litter here,
> A freckled whelp, hag-born—not honoured with
> A human shape.   (1.2.271–9; 283–6)

The pregnant witch, herself aided by 'ministers' or servants, enslaves Ariel and gives birth to Caliban who, in turn, is 'in service' to Prospero. Part of Prospero's narrative in the play is the process of relinquishing—Ariel, Caliban, and, finally, Miranda. Prospero's agreement to release Ariel in two days' time, his departure from the island, which remains as Caliban's home, and the marriage of Miranda to Ferdinand (as well, of course, as the drowning of his books) register the role of the parent as one who must let go. Tom MacFaul puts it very well when he writes: 'In abandoning his magic and acknowledging his mortality, Prospero is shuffling off the sacred element of his paternity, leaving himself with the full pathos of his position as a private—and deprived—father.'[12] Unlike the master, who maintains his servants for their lifetime, the father relinquishes his child to marriage, service, or labour. Loss is the chorus that joins these late plays together but what is actually at stake for each of the fathers in these plays is very different.

Prospero's failure, and loss, as a parent has begun before the play begins. His relationship to Caliban is described in terms that situate Prospero within an educative tradition, which, like his relationship to Miranda, is determined by both process and success. Rehearsing Caliban's spectacular fall from grace, from loved companion to 'poisonous slave', we gather that Prospero once 'made much of' him, 'strok'st' him and fed him 'water with berries in't' (1.2.236, 237). But, unlike the relationship between father and daughter, there was reciprocity between Caliban and Prospero. Where

---

[12] McFaul, *Problem Fathers in Shakespeare and Renaissance Drama* (Cambridge: Cambridge University Press, 2012), p. 161.

Miranda feared she was nothing but a trouble to her father, Caliban describes how he 'showed thee all the qualities o'th'isle': 'For I am all the subjects that you have, | Which first was mine own king' (1.2.344–5). Despite Caliban's change in status, from king to subject, he remembers a love for Prospero that was both generous and dutiful. But both Prospero and Caliban rewrite their relationship: where Prospero once loved and nurtured Caliban he now inflicts pain on him and keeps him in service; where Caliban once loved Prospero and shared his island with him, he now would disempower and kill him. The change that takes place between them is very revealing since it sets out the relationship between nurture and behaviour. Prospero's draconian treatment of Caliban stems, it seems, from a profound sense of loss, as well as betrayal. Retaliating against Caliban's accusations of imprisonment, Prospero declares:

> Thou most lying slave,
> Whom stripes may move, not kindness! I have used thee,
> Filth as thou art, with human care, and lodged thee
> In mine own cell, til thou didst seek to violate
> The honour of my child.   (1.2.348–51)

The early modern slippage between human and humane is well documented and here Prospero invokes both meanings—treating Caliban, the son of a witch, as a human—but also humanely indicates a degree of attachment between the characters, especially within the context of their makeshift domesticity.[13] Prospero's attempts to include Caliban in his life on the island are elaborated on by Miranda who suggests that she, like her father to her, took on the role of tutor:

> I pitied thee,
> Took pains to make thee speak, taught thee each hour
> One thing or other. When thou didst not, savage,
> Know thy own meaning, but wouldst gabble like
> A thing most brutish, I endowed thy purposes
> With words that made them known.   (1.2.356–61)

Miranda extends the role of tutor into something much more maternal—teaching the child to speak and to make themselves understood is a fundamental stage in the narrative of human development.[14] Miranda

---

[13] Kiernan Ryan, *Shakespeare's Universality: Here's Fine Revolution* (London: Bloomsbury Publishing, 2015), p. 84. See also Christian Hogel, *The Human and the Humane: Humanity as Argument from Cicero to Erasmus* (Göttingen: V&R unipress GmbH, 2015).

[14] Thomas Thomas's Latin/English dictionary describes *infantia* in the following terms: 'infancie, babeship, childhood: also foolishness, lacke of utterance, lack of eloquence or grace to tell his tale' (Cambridge, 1587). As this definition implies, it is not just the acquisition of speech that defines the development into adulthood but also the eloquence and grace of expression.

specifically identifies this process with agency as she reminds Caliban that she 'endowed thy purposes | With words that made them known'. Caliban's now famous retort, 'You taught me language, and my profit on't | Is I know how to curse' (366–7), defies any suggestion that language is power.[15] To the contrary, he suggests, there is no meaningful advantage for him in sharing Miranda's language. Much has been written on the relationships between Caliban and Prospero through the discourse of post-colonialism and the extent to which Prospero's role is both exploitative and imperial.[16] The intense domestic environment through which Caliban and Miranda 'grow up' shifts the conversation away from colonial strategies of power and onto the ways in which the family unit reproduces as well as creates networks of dependency and authority, which may replicate colonial incentives but are not exclusively informed by them. Like Prospero, Miranda reveals a sense of betrayal—that she had invested in Caliban only to be assaulted by him. At the centre of both her and her father's complaint is a revulsion that 'nature', or 'race', as Miranda puts it, cannot be altered.[17] Both father and daughter appear to have changed their view of human nature and of education. Prospero admits that he cannot change Caliban, despite his 'pains humanely taken'; and Miranda cannot liberate him from his 'savage' impulses, despite her attempts at language:

> Abhorred slave,
> Which any print of goodness wilt not take,
> Being capable of all ill!   (1.2.354–6)

The debate between nature and nurture, as we term it, was deeply relevant to the early modern period since it resonated with varying beliefs in the doctrine of original sin. While many believed that Adam and Eve condemned all humans and therefore that no person was innocent, or free of sin, others understood that infants could not be held responsible for their parent's crimes, let alone those of their Christian ancestors. The debate took several forms and was often presented as such through the humanist tradition of dialogue. A text from the mid-seventeenth century explores the hereditary relationship between parents and children in these terms:

> First I deny the consequence, which is if a soul begets a soul, then a learned man must beget a learned child, and so of grace as well as on sin, because if

---

[15] Stephen Greenblatt, *Learning to Curse: Essays in Early Modern Culture* (London: Routledge, 1990).

[16] Ania Loomba, *Colonialism/Postcolonialism* (London: Routledge, 1998); Meridith Anne Skura, 'Discourse and the Individual: The Case of Colonialism in *The Tempest*', *Shakespeare Quarterly*, 40 (1989), pp. 42–69.

[17] The *OED* cites the first use of this term to mean 'a group of people, animals or plants connected by common descent or origin' as 1547. Miranda's use of the word is modified by the adjective 'vile', but the emphasis falls on 'vile' rather than 'race', 1.2.361.

the soul do beget a soul then it is to be supposed that it begets such a soul in likeness as it was in nature's being, and not such a one as it was by art or by gift but learning is artificial and grace is a gift: but sin is natural for it is the corruption of nature and did enter in on the world of one man over all men, Rom. 5. 12 and therefore we are by nature the children of wrath, Euph, 2.3., and not by accident. (C2r).[18]

Hotham's point here is that humans are naturally inclined to sin but they can rise above that sin through education and grace. Hotham perceives such gifts as intellect and virtue as learned therefore they could not be inherited, only developed or accomplished. Many of the texts to address the question of original sin, however, remain ambiguous as to the moral status of the child. John Weems, for example, understands original sin as hereditary, as Adam bequeathed it to humankind: 'This originall sinne the Lord may punish the *children* for it, if hee would deale in judgement with them, because it is found in all *children* transmitted from their parents' but he also understands that children cannot be punished for the sins of their parents: 'the *children* shall not be put to death for their fathers offences'.[19] According to Weems, 'There are two sorts of children: children by nature and children by imitation'; while 'nature' condemns all humans to sin, imitation provides an opportunity to renounce that sentence or reaffirm it.

Miranda's denunciation of Caliban does not necessarily distinguish him from anybody else, in that all humans may be sinful, but it is his apparent inability to learn that makes him despicable. Prospero's instruction of his daughter, and her subsequent tutoring of Caliban, recognizes the value of learning and knowledge beyond the capacity of the island's structures. Caliban's apparent refusal to move beyond his 'nature' and embrace his 'nurture' ruptures the foundations on which Prospero organizes both his island and his self. Prospero's incessant punishment of Caliban registers an intense unease about the threat he poses to Prospero's paternal self. Prospero rules by fear and control but he also equates this process with love. As we know, many early modern texts on education are divided in their approach to punishment but however liberal we may consider some writers now—Ascham and Mulcaster, for example—in their cautioning against corporeal punishment, almost all educational theorists accept that

---

[18] Charles Hotham, *An introduction into the Tutonick philosophy* (1650). See also Thomas Lamb, *A treatise of Particular Destination* (1642).

[19] John Weems, *An exposition of the morall lavv, or Ten Commandements of almightie God set dovvne by vvay of exercitations, wherein is contained an explanation of diverse questions and positions for the right understanding thereof, together with an explication of these scriptures which depend upon, or belong unto every one of the commandements, all which are cleared out of the originall languages, the customes of the Iewes, and the distinctions of the schoolemen* (London, 1632), pp. 123, 124.

if a child will not respond to kindness, coercion, and instruction then physical pain is the only alternative. Returning to *Newnams Nightcrowe* (1590) we observe two fundamental points: one is that parents have a duty to love and care for their children; and two, they teach by example not by punishment: 'Good examples do edify and uphold, ill examples do destroy and confound. Humanity is taught by the law of nature.'[20] In this case the 'law of nature' is, in fact, nurture where the 'natural' bond between parent and child promotes virtue, which in turn produces a stable and cohesive society. Caliban's departure from the law of nature, where he refuses to learn beyond the remit of cursing or sexual assault, is registered by Prospero as extreme failure: 'A devil, a born devil, on whose nature | Nurture can never stick on whom my pains | Humanely taken, all, all lost, quite lost' (4.1.188–90). The idea of nature—as a set of unalterable characteristics— is controversial, even within the remit of the play-world, but the possibility registers a deep unease, conveyed by Prospero's magic, that people can only be changed through coercion or art. The loss that Prospero speaks of here is only one version of the deprivations that resonate throughout the play. It is not entirely clear, however, what Prospero is lamenting: his own disappointment as a father/tutor or Caliban's character? The two become deeply entangled for Prospero—he is only as good as his magic or only as successful as his children's future.

It is unclear in the scene in which Miranda meets Ferdinand whether the attraction they feel towards each other is 'natural' or manufactured by Prospero: 'It goes on, I see | As my soul prompts it' (1.2.422–3). The word 'prompt', intriguing in a play so concerned with the power of illusion and theatre, is instructive since it suggests that Prospero is inciting or urging the attraction.[21] 'Soul', too, suggests something deeper than desire or wish; something corresponding to the innermost part of Prospero that is attached to his life, and by extension, his daughter. Prospero's role as a father cannot be separated from his role as a magus and the idea of power, paternal, princely, or magic, at its most potent, comes to involve all three. Prospero's greatest effects, however, manifest through the play's intense movements between loss and gain. 'Something stained | With grief', believing his father to be drowned, Ferdinand is brought into sight of Miranda. Prospero's contrivance of their romance leads him to threaten Ferdinand with shackles, drinking salt water, and forced labour. At the

---

[20] *Newnham's Nightcrowe*, B2v.

[21] That this should come from his soul is less convincing, however, since Prospero has never allied his magic to his soul, only his learning. The distinction between soul and body is often opaque in Shakespeare and so it is perfectly possible that Prospero uses the term to refer to his thoughts as well as his actions.

briefest sign of resistance Prospero puts his future son-in-law under a spell where everything except Miranda fades into insignificance:

> My father's loss, the weakness which I feel,
> The wreck of all my friends, nor this man's threats
> To whom I am subdued, are but light to me,
> Might I but through my prison once a day
> Behold this maid.   (1.2.491–5)

The obedience that Prospero seeks from Ferdinand is similar to that which he demands from his slaves and his daughter: it is the register through which Prospero understands his own authority but also his own affections. The process of forced labour through which Ferdinand is made subservient to Prospero causes the young lovers deep distress—Ferdinand is in pain from the hauling of logs and Miranda 'weeps when she sees...[him] work'. The scene in which Ferdinand works and Miranda weeps culminates in their betrothal and in this way connects obedience and servitude with love.[22] Just before this scene, however, we had witnessed another version of love and servitude, parodied through Caliban's meeting with Stephano and Trinculo, as well as his discovery of alcohol.

The pattern of compliance and distress is so deeply ingrained in Caliban that when he meets Stephano and Trinculo he assumes they are Prospero's minions sent to punish him: 'Do not torment me, prithee! | I'll bring him home faster' (2.2.68–9). This subplot of insurrection and exploitation uses alcohol to amplify the play's interest in the relationship between submission and love. Forcing drink on Caliban initiates a form of obeisance, as he pledges his duty to these men as gods: 'These be fine things, an if they be not spirits. | That's a brave god, and he bears celestial liquor. | I will kneel to him' (2.2.108–10). Caliban's dutiful but inebriated subjection parodies Prospero's production of human bonds as both circumstantial and contrived. Focusing on forms of love, coerced, fabricated, or illusory, many of the plays that involve children interrogate the extent to which this love, too, is contingent or unconditional. The child, like the servant or the drunkard, is a moment of being and offers no more allegiance to the parent than the servant to his master, or the drunkard to his bottle. What so many of these plays seem to engage with, though, and especially these late plays, is the extent to which loss, even imagined loss, can challenge the contingency of feeling. Despite the overarching sense of grief that accompanies the figure of the child in these late plays, the deepest grief belongs to the parent and not the child.

---

[22] David Schalkwyk, *Shakespeare, Love and Service* (Cambridge: Cambridge University Press, 2008), pp. 16–56.

Despite his changed expression, Ferdinand seems to accommodate the loss of his father far more readily than his father can assimilate the loss of his son. Equally, Caliban seems happy to murder his one-time companion, Prospero, yet the magus appears genuinely conflicted in his liberation of Caliban: 'This thing of darkness I acknowledge mine.' The play's exploration of forms of attachment (memory, service, labour, dependency, love) is at its most complex in the figure of the child.

'TRULY THOUGH OUR ELEMENT IS TIME . . .'

One of the most surprising moments in this highly theatrical play is the use of the space at the back of the stage (often called the discovery space) to reveal Ferdinand and Miranda playing chess to an audience, including Ferdinand's father, who until now believed his son to be dead. Prospero's show here relies on one of the central themes of the late plays, which is the return of someone you thought dead or lost. No one can rehearse losing someone they love and yet this is what the plays simulate: the forced grief of deprivation and the changes in behaviour that a resurrection would bring. It is the greatest magic of all—godlike in its capacity to offer salvation, hope, and relief—but highly immoral in its manipulation and abuse of human emotion.

On the whole, however, the plays suppress any hint at the unethical use of deception. *The Tempest* comes closest to allowing its audience to critique the use of magic as a source of power precisely because of the dubious ways in which Prospero uses his art to control, subdue, and punish. Who is he, we might ask, to assume such a godlike power? But even within our unease at the poetic justice that the play celebrates, everyone in the end is largely happy, and the structures of illusion to which the play pays homage prevent us from becoming censorious or taking that power too seriously: it is, after all, 'an insubstantial pageant' (4.1.155) which 'leave[s] not a rack behind' (156). But the play also acknowledges the power of that pageant: 'We are such stuff | As dreams are made on, and our little life | Is rounded with a sleep' (156–8). Those dreams are in all of us: and it is this devastating awareness of the dreams of the past and the shadows of mortality that makes the child such a complex and compelling figure in the late plays.

When Prospero has tormented his enemies into submission, and revealed the living Ferdinand to his grief-stricken father, Alonso, the King of Naples, is so overwhelmed and delighted that he immediately agrees to the union with Miranda:

> I am hers.
> But O, how oddly will it sound, that I
> Must ask my child forgiveness. (5.1.199–201)

To which Prospero responds: 'There, sir, stop. | Let us not burden our remembrance with | A heaviness that's gone' (5.1.203–5). Like many afflicted fathers before him, Alonso prostrates himself before his son and prospective daughter-in-law as a father seeking forgiveness. The forgiveness he seeks from Miranda is on behalf of her father, Prospero, and the networks of obligation and intimacy become inextricably linked through remorse and 'remembrance'. Prospero's comment is deeply ironic and important within the context of these plays, since it is precisely the 'burden' of 'remembrance' that drives both the action and the resolution. Prospero makes two claims within the play that he cannot substantiate: one is that our dreams 'leave not a rack behind'; and the other is that we can forget the 'heaviness that's gone'. The wonder of these plays is that everything leaves something behind and we are all made up of the 'heaviness that's gone'. The 'heaviness' of grief, loss, or torment may pass but it never truly goes: that is the power to which Prospero appeals in his art and on the island. Ultimately, of course, Prospero can no longer refer to magic, since he has drowned his books, so he appeals to the next best thing—faith: the belief that we can be forgiven and forgive. As Hilaire Belloc would write many years later:

> They say that in the unchanging place
> Where all we loved is always dear
> We meet our morning face to face
> And find again our twentieth year.[23]

'MINDING TRUE THINGS BY WHAT THEIR MOCKERIES BE'

The father figure dominates the action of the late plays but each play negotiates this relationship in different ways. Underpinning that relationship, however, is a deep theatrical investment in the child as healing or curative. The child functions restoratively in different ways: partly through a unique relationship to the parent in which their love or bond can neither be replicated nor replaced; but also as a more generic figure of hope to which the present may appeal in lieu of the future. The child as future depends heavily on a sense of restitution; that somehow the figure can atone for, or change, the past. In this way, children become symbolic registers of failure as well as hope. *Pericles* is perhaps the boldest representation of the recuperative powers of the child: Marina, who begins her role as a baby, without

---

[23] Hilaire Belloc, *They say that in the unchanging place*.

a mother and left by her father to the charge of the Governor of Tarsus, falls into the hands of pirates, bawds, and false friends, only to convert the lascivious visitors to the brothel and to recuse her father from a grief-induced torpor.[24] The play begins, however, with a sinister glimpse into the different possibilities of the father/child relationship.

The King of Antioch has devised a riddle in order to prevent any marriage of his beautiful daughter, with whom he is having an incestuous relationship. The riddle, which is meant to entrap suitors into losing their lives, centres on the allegorical 'I' as both father and daughter, action and intention:

> I am no viper, yet I feed
> On mother's flesh which did me breed.
> I sought a husband, in which labour
> I found that kindness in a father.
> He's father, son, and husband mild;
> I mother, wife, and yet his child.
> How they may be, and yet in two,
> As you will live, resolve it you.   (1.1.65–72)

The mellifluous way in which the relationships are conflated and iterated seems especially repellent, particularly within the context of Jacobean conventions in which 'son' is also used for son-in-law. In this riddle the first person begins as Antiochus (feeding on the flesh he bred) and then becomes his daughter (who is, incidentally, never individualized through a name in the play). Both father and daughter become one through the act of incest as well as kinship: all familial relationships are collapsed into the two bodies of lover and beloved. The most shocking aspect of this riddle is not the revelation of incest itself but the ways in which it is characterized. Speaking as the daughter, the 'I' claims that she sought a husband but 'found that kindness in a father': the abuse of the term kindness is one of the most disturbing in the period since it plays on the multiple meanings of kinship, sexual favour, generosity, and gentleness; that these should reside in a sexual relationship between father and daughter defies the dominant use of the word 'kindness' to mean social harmony and affiliation. Such an abuse of the term kindness, however, is not unique to the riddle. Later in the play, Dionyza, left to bring up Marina, decides to have her murdered because she thinks she is compromising the future of her own daughter:

> None would look on her,
> But cast their gazes on Marina's face,

---

[24] The extent of Shakespeare's involvement in *Pericles* has long been debated. There is no doubt that the play is either co-authored or adapted in transcription and that Shakespeare is not responsible for all of it. For a recent discussion of the authorship question see Brian Vickers, *Shakespeare Co-Author* (Oxford: Oxford University Press, 2002), pp. 219–32.

> While ours was blurted at, and held a malkin,
> Not worth the time of day. It pierced me through.
> And though you call my course unnatural,
> You not your child well loving, yet I find
> It greets me as an enterprise of kindness
> Performed to your sole daughter.   (4.3.32–9)

The perverse value system through which Dionyza determines that Cleon, her husband, is failing his daughter by resisting the murder of Marina extends again to this term 'kindness', which is here recast as an act of maternal love 'performed to your sole daughter'. Only Pericles will return the word to its normative use at the end of the play, but much of the narrative in between is focused on the bonds, social and familial, that bind people in virtue rather than deviance.

Having solved the riddle, and in horror at its meaning, Pericles leaves in fear of his life. Arriving fortuitously at Tarsus, Pericles learns that they are in the grip of famine:

> Those mothers who to nuzzle up their babes
> Thought naught too curious are ready now
> To eat those little darlings whom they loved.
> So sharp are hunger's teeth that man and wife
> Draw lots who first shall die to lengthen life.   (1.4.42–6)

The provisional nature of familial bonds is central to Shakespeare's dramatization of the parent/child relationships but *Pericles* is unique in presenting a range of parents—incestuous, cannibalistic, and ambitious—through which the eponymous hero emerges as unique in his absolute commitment to unconditional love.

Much of the play will focus on Pericles and his lost daughter Marina and, although we never return to the King of Antioch, the play's harsh moral lesson with which it begins remains like a spectre throughout the play. Shakespeare, we assume from *The Winter's Tale*, is not especially interested in incest, since he did not retain Greene's concern in his source material, *Pandosto*. Many scholars believe Shakespeare to be responsible for only the last three acts of the play, but there is no doubt that, framed by the threat of Antioch, what it means to love your child and to be a father is central to the justice of Shakespeare's narrative. As we saw in some of Shakespeare's comedies, sexuality is intimately tied not only to definitions of innocence but also to status. In contrast to Antioch's daughter, 'Bad child, worse father', Marina is sexually innocent. Despite the effects she produces in other people, largely on the premise that she is a virgin, she responds without any sexual impulse of her own: to the contrary, the muse most constantly invoked is Diana, the goddess of chastity, and Marina spends most of her time at the brothel proselytizing. Although she is technically still very young her innocence is not characterized by her youth but by her character. Most of the scenes in the brothel are taken up with Marina's 'peevish chastity' where those who arrive for sex leave instead hoping to 'hear the vestals sing' (4.5.4–5). The almost comic insistence that Marina's 'preaching' can convert hardened brothel-goers is balanced by the bewitching scene with her father. Brought to Pericles by Lysimachus, Marina is charged with the task of bringing a man stupefied with grief back to consciousness:

> I am a maid,
> My lord, that ne'er before invited eyes,
> But have been gazed on like a comet. She speaks,
> My lord, that maybe hath endured a grief
> Might equal yours, if both were justly weighed. (5.1.83–7)

Identifying herself as a virgin, and as a young woman, Marina speaks with that greatest of all Shakespearian qualities—empathy.[25] Identifying herself with Pericles, she reaches out to him through a shared understanding of suffering and of loss. Marina has no information to base this on, but such is the bond of father/child that her affiliation with the broken man in front of her transcends both time and place. Pericles responds:

> Prithee speak.
> Falseness cannot come from thee, for thou lookest
> Modest as justice, and thou seemest a palace
> For the crowned truth to dwell in. I will believe thee,
> And make my senses credit thy relation
> To points that seem impossible, for thou lookest
> Like one I loved indeed. (5.1.119–25)

The faith that Pericles puts in her is the absolute trust that emanates from a remembrance of one he loved. Carrying the burden of remembrance towards Marina, Pericles can cross that impossible space between his past and her present. This devastatingly moving scene in which, bit by bit, Pericles discovers the daughter he thought dead draws its entire emotional range from the audience's faith in parental love. Revealing that 'this is Marina', confirmed through recalling the name of her apparently dead mother, Thaisa, Pericles performs his own resurrection:

> Rise; thou art my child.
> Give me fresh garments...
> She shall tell thee all;

[25] The term 'maid' as discussed by Williams, *Shakespeare and the Performance of Girlhood*, pp. 30, 43–4, could apply to either a virgin or a young girl or both: given the play's intense interest in sexuality it is likely that Marina attempts to establish herself as sexually innocent despite the many eyes who gaze on her.

> When thou shalt kneel; and justify in knowledge
> She is thy very princess.   (5.1.214–19)

The dialogue tells us that first Marina kneels and then rises, and then
Pericles' trusted aid, Helicanus, will kneel. The characters' movement
between images of faith and benediction, or supplication and devotion,
makes this a highly charged scene to watch. Despite the pagan gods to
which many of the characters appeal, there is a deep sense of spirituality in
this play, and in many of the late plays, in which faith—in God, each other,
hope, love, or kindness—shapes the fulfilment of individual fantasies.

Only Pericles will return the word kindness to its normative use at the
end of the play, when, reunited with his lost wife and daughter, he exclaims:

> No more, you gods; your present kindness
> Makes my past miseries sports; you shall do well
> That on the touching of her lips I may
> Melt, and no more be seen.   (5.3.40–3).

The 'kindness' that the gods have shown in bringing Pericles back to his
family restores our faith in the word and the bonds of kinship. As with so
many of Shakespeare's fathers, it is at this supreme moment of happiness
and union that Pericles lets go. Happy to die or leave—to 'melt'—now he has
felt the embrace of his wife and daughter shows the audience that the point
of absolute fulfilment is of holding those whom you loved and thought lost.
The extraordinary theatrical power that Shakespeare gives to the reunion
between parent and child demonstrates the vast capacities of the affective
landscape to which he appeals. The burden of remembrance that Prospero
talks of shows us the unique power of the past to attach like a shadow to the
present. The theatre, these late plays suggest, can simulate the fantasy of time
travel, so that we *can* 'call back yesterday, bid time return' (*Richard II*) and
make peace with the present. Where Prospero's confrontation with the past
enables him to find liberation, rather than failure, in death: 'And thence
retire me to my Milan, where | Every third thought shall be my grave'
(5.1.313–14); Pericles' melting into the ether of the past marks his new beginning. Calling for a razor and new clothes he becomes the man he was fourteen years ago: 'I'll beautify,' he declares in a rare and wonderful homage to
the future. *Pericles* is, however, unique in this way: it takes its child forward
with a sense of unity and compassion that is nowhere matched in Shakespeare.

THE END OF INNOCENCE

The Winter's Tale is the culmination of all Shakespeare's writing on children. There is less hope here than in *Pericles* but perhaps more magic; there
is more grief but perhaps less suffering. *The Winter's Tale* is the greatest of

Shakespeare's symphonies to the power of time and the devastating hold that the past has on us. But *The Winter's Tale* produces the most profound fantasy of all: to bring back the dead and say sorry. If children are spectres of the past than the recovery of that past becomes the greatest debt that Shakespeare pays to the children of his stage. Children and what they represent to the adults that were once children and the adults who beget children fascinate the play. Of all the plays discussed in this book, *The Winter's Tale* comes the closest to imagining a stage we might call childhood, and for valuing that stage as unique in the human life cycle.

The Winter's Tale opens with a discussion of the friendship between the two kings of Bohemia and Sicilia. Camillo, Lord to Leontes' court, admits that

> Sicilia cannot show himself over-kind to Bohemia. They were trained together in their childhoods, and there rooted betwixt them then such an affection which cannot choose but branch now. (1.120–3)

Camillo uses a conventional horticultural metaphor to suggest not only the idea of childhood, whereby children may be 'cultivated' and 'trained', but also an intermingling of roots, so that, according to Camillo, nothing could separate them.[26] For those familiar with the story, Camillo's observation is poignantly ironic but it suggests, albeit briefly, that the men share a bond, unique to childhood, which is, or should be, unshakeable. Moving from the kings as children, Polixenes' attendant Lord, Archidamus, refers to Leontes' son Mamillius: 'You have unspeakable comfort of your young prince Mamillius. It is a gentleman of the greatest promise that ever came into my note,' to which Camillo replies:

> It is a gallant child, one that, indeed, physics the subject, makes old hearts fresh. They that went on crutches ere he was born desire yet their life to see him a man. (1.1.32–3; 36–8)

'Would they else be content to die?' asks Archidamus: 'Yes, if there were no other excuse why they should desire to live,' responds Camillo (39–41). The movement from the kings' childhood to the son of the king quickly establishes the child as a locus of value within the play-world. The terrible irony here is that Camillo suggests that without Mamillius there is little desire for the aged to go on living. The hope and faith that Camillo attributes to Mamillius's life will be shortly taken away with the death of the young prince. The optimism and joy expressed through the figure of the child, and childhood, is instantly established in order to unequivocally

---

[26] See Rebecca Bushnell, *Green Desire: Imagining Early Modern English Gardens* (Ithaca, NY: Cornell University Press, 2003), Scott, *Shakespeare's Nature*, and Scott, 'Incapable and Shallow Innocents', in Richard Preiss and Deanne Williams (eds), *Childhood, Education and the Stage in Early Modern England* (Cambridge: Cambridge University Press, 2017), pp. 74–99.

determine the devastating consequences of Leontes' actions. Meeting the kings in the next scene we observe the strength of those bonds in action: Leontes refers to Polixenes as 'brother' and Hermione observes that the reason Polixenes strains to leave Sicilia is that he 'longs to see his son were strong' (1.2.15, 34). Friendship is cemented through the bonds of family, by which love is both shared and understood. Defining the bonds of love as familial, and then extending those bonds to childhood friends, develops a network of emotion across the relationships.

Beginning with the kings as young boys, 'trained together in their childhood', ascertains the child as the central emotional register through which attachments can be developed. Crucially, however, in terms of the play's wider narrative of guilt and sin, the child belongs to a specific discourse of innocence, which, unlike the past, can never be recovered. Recalling their shared histories, Polixenes declares, 'We were, fair Queen, | Two lads that thought there was no more behind | But such a day tomorrow as today, | And to be boy eternal' (1.2.61–4). The memory of childhood emerges from this concept of liberty where there is no apprehension, no anxiety, and no responsibility: the child's ability to live in an eternal present frees them from the great shadow that hangs over so many of these plays—age and mortality:

> We were as twinned lambs that did frisk i'th'sun,
> And bleat the one at th'other; what we changed
> Was innocence for innocence—we knew not
> The doctrine of ill-doing, nor dreamed
> That any did.   (1.2.66–70)

Polixenes' representation of the past combines both pre- and post-lapsarian images of innocence—one, pre the Fall, untainted by sexuality; and the other, post the Fall, but with the promise of salvation in the figure of the lamb. The synthesis here of innocence and redemption supports his view of childhood as wholly distinct from the adult world of experience. The 'doctrine of ill-doing' to which Polixenes refers seems to include any form of harm or injury associated with Christian conceptions of sin. The formative dynamic of innocence through which the boys interacted imagines childhood as a unique space of development, over which the child retains complete control. Polixenes' view of childhood allies him with a certain strand of Christianity in which the child represents innocence and purity in relation to the adult world. In this way, the term 'child' becomes a synecdoche for innocence, as John Downe, in *A Treatise of the true Nature and Definition of Justifying Faith* (1635), explains:

> To that our saviour where he seem expressly to affirm that little ones believe:
> I answer first, that those Little-ones are not Infants properly, but such men

as resemble little Children in holy Innocence & Simplicity: in regard whereof they are elsewhere called by Christ, that is Infants. Secondly, grant it that Children bee also meant, yet not such Children as are infants, but growne to some stature and capacity. For although the Child whom Christ tooke in his armes, be called a little Child: yet was hee both a follower and hearer of Christ, and such a one as in some measure could vnderstand, such as were those little children whom Saint John thought it not unfit to write.[27]

The idea of the child becomes bound to networks of innocence established by faith in Christ. This comparative, or relative, view of the child is further informed by a biblical narrative which identifies Christ's purity in images of infancy as well as the sacrifice that so many babies were forced to make in Herod's Massacre of the Innocents. Within this context the term innocent absorbs a number of different meanings: not only does it suggests the element of purity which Polixenes refers to, which is a mind without sin, but it also implies a key concept within the play—'not guilty'. All these terms are relative, of course: we can only recognize innocence in relation to sin, as we can only give the verdict 'not guilty' as a negation rather than an assertion.[28] The semantic dynamic of difference in which we locate meaning through what it is not is central to the play's discourse of childhood as well as inno-cence. In this scene Polixenes remembers the past he shared with Leontes through its difference from the adult world: they did not, he assures us, know the 'doctrine of ill-doing'. To name it as such they must now recognize:

> Had we pursued that life,
> And our weak spirits ne'er been higher reared
> With stronger blood, we should have answered heaven
> Boldly, 'not guilty', the imposition cleared
> Hereditary ours.   (1.2.70–4)

Imagining the hypotheses that they remained 'boy eternal' clears both men from the mortal indictment of the Fall. Polixenes' suggestion of an imaginary trial, whereby he could answer heaven 'not guilty', is deeply ironic within the context of Hermione's experiences later in the play but once again the emphasis is on the relative positions between the boys and their 'hereditary' imposition. As Hermione rightly points out, 'By this we gather | You have tripped since' (73–4). The gently mocking tone of

---

[27] John Downe, *A treatise of the true nature and definition of justifying faith together with a defence of the same, against the answere of N. Baxter. By Iohn Downe B* (London, 1635), pp. 198–9.

[28] In fact the many definitions of innocence in this period tend to conflate the idea of 'puritie', associated with children, and 'unguiltinesse, harmlessness', associated with sin or criminality, cf. Randle Cotgrave, *A Dictionary of the French and English Tongues* (London, 1611). Etymologically, the term 'innocent' derives from the Latin prefix *in* as an expression of negation and the present participle of *nocēre*, meaning to hurt or injure.

Hermione highlights the audacity of Polixenes' fantasy but it also locates
the idea of sin as explicitly sexual. Hermione uses the word trip to mean
stumble, as though the kings have lost their footing, metaphorically, on their
life of innocence, but Polixenes understands her meaning as sexual and
women as 'temptations'.[29] Hermione, carefully goading Polixenes, insists:

> Yet go on;
> Th' offences we have made you do we'll answer,
> If you first sinned with us, and that with us
> You did continue fault, and that you slipped not
> With any but us.   (1.2.81–5)

By contrast, then, the adult world becomes one of 'offences', sins and slips
which are teasingly contained within the boundaries of marriage. For all
the gentle and amused reflection in this exchange the world of adult
sexuality looms large over the memory of the uninhibited innocence
of childhood. In this conversation between Hermione and Polixenes we
observe how the idea of innocence becomes acutely contested: to be not
guilty and to be free from sin are not the same things. Here, however,
innocence is explicitly tied to a pre-sexual period in which friendship
performs love and affection without sex. This is the innocence to which
the kings can never return: as Leontes will shortly declare: 'I have seen the
spider.' Leontes' powerful response to his wife's success in persuading
Polixenes to stay is entirely informed by the conflation of sex and love.
Leontes believes, in his adult mind, that affection and sex are inextricably
linked and therefore 'Too hot, too hot! | To mingle friendship far is min-
gling bloods' (1.2.108–9). The discrepancy between the adult and child
worlds is amplified further in this scene through the use of Mamillius.
Leontes' behaviour confirms Polixenes' point that since they did not
remain boy eternal they cannot answer heaven 'not guilty': and now guilt
will shape the rest of the drama.

   Leontes' sudden determination that his wife has been unfaithful to him
and that is why Polixenes concedes to her request to stay longer in Sicilia
is played out through the figure of Mamillius. Like the worst of adult
divorces the child becomes a testing ground for moral value and emotional
punishment. According to the stage direction, Mamillius enters with his
parents and Polixenes at the beginning of the scene, in which case he
would have been present for all the conversations so far. Theatrically this is
important since if we are looking on the body of a child during the time in
which Polixenes describes his childhood, those vocabularies of reference
become more meaningful. Imaging the young boys exchanging 'innocence

[29] The *OED* lists no definition of the word 'tripped' as sexually motivated or implied.

for innocence' allows us to transfer those qualities onto Mamillius and observe him within those terms. Within the dynamic of the stage space the figure of the child is the central point through which the fantasy of the past is maintained: we cannot help but look longingly at the idea of innocence when it is presented in such resonant terms. How far Mamillius is engaged in this conversation is directorial but Leontes brings him into the central stage space as soon as he articulates the fear of his wife's infidelity:

> Why, that's my bawcock—what, hast smutched thy nose?
> They say it is a copy out of mine. Come, captain,
> We must be neat—not neat, but cleanly, captain.
> And yet the steer, the heifer and the calf
> Are all called neat.—Still virginalling
> Upon his palm?—how now, you wanton calf,
> Art thou my calf?   (1.2.119–26)

Leontes' broken thought processes manifest in his movement from his son's nose to their resemblance, to cows, to watching Hermione, to questioning his paternity. The speech is a fascinating exercise in word association whereby we observe Leontes' now troubled mind move through an image of tenderness—we must be neat—to a bovine animal (the steer, heifer, and calf) to a term of endearment (Art thou my calf?). In this process we observe Leontes begin to dismantle himself and to involve Mamillius:

> Yet they say we are
> Almost as like eggs—women say so,
> That will say anything. But were they false
> As o'er-dyed blacks, as wind, as waters, false
> As dice are to be wished by one that fixes
> No bourn 'twixt his and mine, yet were it true
> To say this boy were like me. Come, sir page,
> Look on me with your welkin eye. Sweet villain,
> Most dear'st, my collop—can thy dam, may't be
> Affection!—thy intention stabs the centre.   (1.2.128–37)

Searching his son's face for a semblance of himself, Leontes digresses into the sexual control of women. Taking Mamillius into the heady world of adult anxiety, suspicion, and sexual licence he pushes his child into a history very different from his own. Here is not the pre-lapsarian world of boyish innocence but the ravings of a father who implicates all women, including the child's mother, in faithlessness. Observing a change in Leontes, Hermione asks him what troubles him, to which he replies:

> Looking on the lines
> Of my boy's face, methought I did recoil

> Twenty-three years, and saw myself unbreeched ,
> In my green velvet coat, my dagger muzzled
> Lest it should bite its master and so prove,
> As ornaments oft do, too dangerous.   (1.2.152–7)

Leontes' mendacious reply is in itself very revealing: he may well have been thinking of himself as a child but this is not the reason he appears distressed. Either way, however, Leontes represents his emotional well-being through the idea of the child—himself and Mamillius—and recalls a moment in which the adult world looms menacingly at the door of childhood. The dagger, so often a phallic symbol in Shakespeare, is central to Leontes' remembrance of innocence: here, in his memory, manufactured or real, it is muzzled, protected, 'Lest it should bite its master and so prove, | As ornaments oft do, too dangerous'. The toy and the penis become symbols of danger for Leontes and in his way the world of the child is no longer distinct but powerfully and devastatingly entwined with that of the adult.

Mamillius becomes imbricated into Leontes' fantasies of sexual infidelity through the aggressive insistence that he continue his speech despite the child's continued presence:

> Go play, boy, play—thy mother plays, and I
> Play too, but so disgraced a part, whose issue
> Will hiss me to my grave; contempt and clamour
> Will be my knell. Go play, boy, play. There have been,
> Or I am much deceived, cuckolds ere now,
> And many a man there is, even at this present,
> Now, while I speak this, holds his wife by th'arm,
> That little thinks she has been sluiced in's absence,
> And his pond fished by his next neighbour, by
> Sir Smile, his neighbour—

This is the only instance in Shakespeare where the word 'play' is used in relation to children's recreation. Leontes' demand that his son 'Go play' is quickly qualified by his insistence that his 'mother plays, and I | Play too'. Taking the verb out of the context in which Mamillius recognizes it demands that he take part in the elliptical world of adult ambiguity. Taking the word from childish entertainment, to sexual dalliance, to forced performance, wrenches Mamillius away from the fixed world of childish innocence, where words remain stable and meaning fixed, into the vertiginous world of adult euphemism. Double meaning is, of course, another legacy of the Fall, as described in the Book of Genesis, when a united humanity migrated from the east to Shinar and decided to settle, building what was known as the Tower of Babel. Such ambition enraged God who punished the people by creating a profusion of languages, so that nobody could understand each other or succeed in their shared ambitions. In this way, misunderstanding, ellipsis, and multiple meanings have often been associated with sin. Leontes' wilful manipulation of the word 'play', particularly within the context of the child, seems an especially violent attempt at destabilizing the child's world. The description of infidelity which follows his injunction to play is one of the most invidious and repellent in Shakespeare: imagining the female genitals as sluice gates, opened, as the metaphor suggests, to let the water out, he extends the watery analogy to a fish pond, where the generic neighbour, Sir Smile, finds his rod imagined as a penis. The intense disgust of women that this image betrays extends to all men, Leontes imagines, as he takes perverse comfort in knowing that most wives cuckold most men. At the end of this speech, Leontes turns to his son and asks, 'How now, boy?', as though breaking from his hideous reverie to find out how the child is. Mamillius's response is that 'I am like you, they say' (206) as if he wants to ally himself with his father out of reflex loyalty. Shakespeare reveals a deep perception in his presentation of Mamillius here: it is unclear the extent to which the boy understands or even listens to his father's ramblings but his identification with him, however inchoate, puts him very touchingly on his father's side. It is in no way a moral response but simply a deep connection with the power of association and familiarity. The identification that Leontes feels with his son extends to his need to separate the child from his mother and the next time we see Mamillius will be the last. The brief vignette into the child's world, nurtured by women who love him, by stories, and by intimacy, is all the more intense for the violent way in which Mamillius is seconded by his father. Softly telling his heavily pregnant mother a sad tale of a man who dwelt in a churchyard once again returns us to the vertiginous distance between the adult and child worlds. This 'sad tale', will come to life in the form of his grief-stricken father visiting Mamillius's and Hermione's graves every day for sixteen years. For this brief moment it is a diverting story that allows Mamillius to be close to his mother; shortly it will become the narrative into which he has been fatally cast.

Wrenching him from his mother, 'Give me the boy,' Leontes forces Mamillius to stand between him and Hermione as he publicly vilifies her. The 'innocence for innocence' that the young kings shared now seems an impossible vision of a childhood that his son will never experience: 'Bear the boy hence; he shall not come about her. | Away with him, and let her sport herself | With that she's big with, for 'tis Polixenes | Has made thee swell thus' (2.1.59–62). Telling the child that his mother is carrying another man's baby seems a terrible destruction of the innocence celebrated at the opening of the play. This is the last that Mamillius will see of his mother and the play's deep-seated conflicts with both justice and innocence

are taken up by Hermione and then Perdita. The question of innocence—
what it means and to whom it is applicable—is central to the trial scene.
Passing the newborn infant, out of the prison and to Paulina, Emilia,
Hermione's gentlewoman, quotes her mistress:

> The Queen receives
> Much comfort in't, says 'My poor prisoner,
> I am innocent as you.'   (2.1.25–7)

Hermione conflates the notion of purity, usually attributed to babies, with
that of being not guilty. Hermione may be innocent of the crime she has
been accused of but she is not innocent in the ways associated with children. Polixenes had already introduced the synthesis of these uses in his
description of his childhood—a stage in which he was both pure and 'not
guilty', but the play never resolves what the word means. Hermione is
indeed not guilty, and in this way she is entirely innocent; Perdita, too, is
innocent, both of the supposed crimes of her mother and as a newborn
baby, who enters the world free of sin. But Leontes will not accept either
form of innocence and so it becomes a highly contested concept within
the play-world. The extent to which Leontes has strayed from the values of
his world is most starkly dramatized by his response to the baby. Paulina,
convinced that the sight of the child will soften him, declares:

> We do not know
> How he may soften at the sight o' th' child—
> The silence often of pure innocence
> Persuades when speaking fails.   (2.2.37–40)

Leontes does not 'soften'; quite the reverse. He orders that the child be
destroyed and the last vestige of hope that Paulina had is gone. Leontes'
absolute inability to recognize innocence condemns him and those around
him to unmitigated misery, even death. Although those who loved him—
Polixenes, Camillo, Paulina, Hermione, Antigonus—understand the deep
power, magic even, of innocence Leontes refuses to acknowledge the quality, or even the concept. Paulina presents the baby to him on the understanding that a child's innocence—state of purity or lack of sin—is so
affecting that it can bridge the terrible distance that Leontes has created
between himself and those around him. For Paulina, that distance is
reached through the 'silence' of the pre-linguistic state that defines infants
as distinct from the slippery world of adult language.[30] The idea of 'pure

---

[30] Writing on *The Tempest*, Garber asserts: 'the condition of full humanity is clearly and
repeatedly equated in the play with the proper use of speech', *Coming of Age in Shakespeare*,
p. 101.

innocence' resides in Paulina's antithesis: the difference between silence and speaking is also the difference between innocence and sin; we recognize one because it is not the other. The baby Perdita is powerful precisely because she remains distinct from the torrid climate of her father's 'dreams'. Leontes' inability to speak the language of reason, of sense, of emotional attachment is in evidence for much of the first half of the play but it comes to its climax in the trial scene, in which Hermione exclaims:

> Sir,
> You speak a language that I understand not,
> My life stands in the level of your dreams,
> Which I'll lay down.   (3.2.78–80)

Hermione's failure to understand her husband's accusations is registered through the overwhelming distance between them: they no longer speak the same language and her life is no longer shared with him but at the mercy of his imagination. Leontes has strayed so far from the reasonable shore that he cannot inhabit, let alone recognize, the quality of innocence. Hermione has no defence but language and yet it is one her husband no longer shares. Bereft of all she loves and publicly vilified, Hermione can do nothing but lean on the words her husband no longer accepts. Reiterating the abject horror of the position she is now in, she laments:

> My third comfort,
> Starred most unluckily, is from my breast,
> The innocent milk in its most innocent mouth
> Hailed out to murder.   (3.2.96–9)

Powerfully identifying herself as innocent through the image of the nursing infant, Hermione brings both their bodies together (milk and mouth) as guiltless and pure. The innocence of the child—however culturally we imagine that—is the idea through which certain values can be expressed. We do not know what innocence is—we only know what it is not. Hermione is not guilty and the baby is free from any sin because it has not inhabited the world long enough to engage in any action we consider sinful. Leontes' refusal to allow Hermione her maternal rights further threatens the very values that Leontes appears to uphold. In a powerful defence of women, entitled *A Womans Worth*, Alexandre de Pontaymeri addresses the paradox of man:

> Hee will like wise confesse, that woman was giuen him for his eternall good, and the house is not blessed where she wanteth. By her is this huge masse subsisted, cōmonweales made immortal, citties peopled, Realmes strengthened, Kings assured, and subiects maintained. By her it is, that we liue

againe in our children, posterity haue knowledge of vs, and our memory is
continued. It is by her, that we remember our houses, and respect our families... It was she that had her birth in the terrestrial paradise, and not man.[31]

In establishing the extraordinary role of women in strengthening realms,
upholding kingdoms, and immortalizing commonwealths, Pontaymeri
also observes the position of procreation and children in the preservation
of both memory and posterity. As the keeper of both memory and children, Hermione becomes a powerful testimony to what is actually under
threat in this play. Born as a woman from her own terrestrial paradise she
brings another female into the world only to be vilified and condemned.[32]
In many ways radical, the play shows us that these values are not fixed: they
are relative and conditional. When the news of the Oracle is delivered and
Hermione pronounced 'chaste' and the child 'an innocent babe truly
begotten', Leontes refuses to accept it. In the hostile world of Leontes'
mind and authority, the terms of innocence are no longer recognized.

Polixenes' great claim for childhood that it is both innocent and not
guilty has no place in Sicilia now. The hideous refusal of any terms of
justice other than his own is violently condemned, as it is also symbolized,
in the death of Mamillius. This is the end of innocence precisely because
those terms of reference are no longer understood in Leontes' court. With
innocence goes the child as well as its mother: Mamillius dies and Perdita
is banished. When Antigonus leaves the newborn baby on the shores of
Bohemia to be 'nursed' by chance or violence we realize that there is
nothing left of the childishness that the kings once remembered. All that
remains for Leontes is his grief, accompanying him like a violent shadow
for sixteen years.

The transition to Bohemia marks the great gap of time in which Perdita
grows up. The idea of childhood once so lovingly described by Polixenes is
only a memory but it is also a possibility that the play denies us. In the
opening of the play we were given a glimpse into a state of liberty—both
spiritual and emotional—that the play will never allow again. Instead the
children on this stage have to grow up very quickly—either symbolically

---

[31] Alexandre de Pontaymeri, *A Womans Woorth, defended against all the men in the world
Prooving them to be more perfect, excellent, and absolute in all vertuous actions, then any man
of what qualitie soeuer. Written by one that hath heard much, seene much, but knowes a great
deale more* (London, 1599), pp. 61r–v.

[32] Richard A. Carr asserts that 'It would be a mistake to assume that Pontaymeri is
merely replacing a male-dominated hierarchy with a new one in which woman is the dominant figure; he is not so ingenious. Having witnessed the devastation caused by religious
and political division, Pontaymeri is instinctively conciliatory. In the new world emerging
from civil strife, he sees women playing a new and vital role, that of a civilising force.' 'The
Resolution of a Paradox: Alexandre de Pontaymeri's Response to the Querelle des Femmes',
Renaissance Studies (June 2003), p. 254.

through the experiences they have, like Mamillius who is dragged into the seamy world of Leontes' fetid imagination; or Perdita, whose first few days are taken up by ravens and bears and the rest we do not see. Although Bohemia is characterized by summer flowers, a sheep-shearing festival, and the energies of young love, it is not without its shadows. Polixenes' anger towards both his son and Perdita prompts their escape and the shepherd and his son have their own worries about money and then about the threat to their lives for Perdita's apparently insouciant ambitions in loving Florizel. Even accepting these blots, however, Bohemia is largely typified as a place of pleasure and freedom in contrast to the frozen and retarded emotional world of Sicilia. As is so typical with Shakespeare we proceed though a set of contrasts by which we identify central elements to the play's narrative. Yet these contrasts do not provide moral absolutes; they are much more suggestive than that: good and bad do not sit in opposition to each other but rather as relative versions of the other.

NOBODY'S PERFECT

As the Oracle foretold, nothing can be restored until that which is lost is found. The emphasis here on the restitution of Perdita has led to certain cynical readings of the play in which the end of the play is only successful insofar as it gives Leontes an heir and restores some dynastic stability to Sicilia.[33] Within the terms of the Oracle, finding that which has been lost appears to override or negate the initial loss. Such pragmatic interpretations do not acknowledge any of the attendant emotions or implications of loss, it is simply a process of filling a gap that has been made. Within these terms finding Perdita is perfectly successful since the body that was once 'lost' is now inhabited and returned. What the play never resolves, however, are the very many losses that accompany the beginning of the play—Mamillius, Antigonus, and sixteen years of Hermione's and Perdita's lives. The greatest loss, it seems, is not only childhood—both Mamillius's and Perdita's—but what that symbolized for the two kings at the beginning of the play. The idea of innocence and guiltlessness so winningly expressed by Polixenes in the images of himself and Leontes holding up their heads to heaven to answer 'boldly' 'not guilty' is an image that the play can no longer sustain. The adults in this play are all guilty of something—deception, suffering, subterfuge, or manipulation—the children, on the other hand, are not. As is so often the case with Shakespeare's children they are victims of circumstances: innocent bystanders to an adult

---

[33] See Orgel's introduction, especially pp. 47–50.

world they can neither comprehend nor control. But the innocence here is always relative—they are innocent only to the extent that they are not yet embroiled in the complex world of adult behaviours. Mamillius dies as a result of adult failure, Perdita survives but not as the woman she could have been. For better or worse she has lost the identity, the parenting, the context into which she was born: Hermione, too, has lost both her children and a great part of her own life in which she has been sequestered. What is found at the end of this play is not childhood or even innocence but the body of the woman who was once a child, and the image of a woman who has been denied being a mother. For all its apparent resolution there is something deeply tragic about the end of this tale.[34]

When Paulina asks us to awake our 'faith' and watch the statue of Hermione move, as if the dead can return to life, she asks us to rehearse the greatest fantasy of all: that we can turn back time; that we can bring back the dead. *The Winter's Tale* is a powerful aria to the power of time to divide and to destroy. Just as Leontes and Polixenes had changed—'by this we gather you have tripped since'—so all human life is subject to change, loss, grief, and transition. Even with the greatest faith in the world we cannot call back yesterday and bid time return: even Paulina's magic cannot erase the passage of sixteen years on Hermione's care-worn face, nor can it arrest the moment and return her to her children as they once were. The play tries with all the hope and tragedy of human frailty to do its best at celebrating a version of restoration but most is left to our imaginations. We do not see the moment when Leontes realizes that Perdita is his daughter, whom he left for dead on the wild shores; we do not hear or see the conversations that might take place between mother and child, between husband and wife. All such pleasure is left to our own creativity, our own experiences of loss, our own hopes of restoration, and our own fantasies of childhood. Referring to the reunited Queen with her daughter and husband, Paulina declares:

> Go together,
> You precious winners all; your exhalation
> Partake to everyone. (5.3.130–3)

But there are no winners in this play: every character is touched by the loss or grief of something whether it is their own history or someone else's. This is Shakespeare's greatest play of childhood precisely because it acknowledges the fantasy in all of us for a time elsewhere—a time of freedom, perhaps, or emotional and moral liberty; a time where we could all answer

---

[34] Stanley Cavell writes very eloquently on this loss in *Disowning Knowledge* (Cambridge: Cambridge University Press, 1987), p. 193.

heaven 'boldly, not guilty'. Above all, childhood comes to us in this play as the past and that past is both collective and individual, imagined and real; it resonates in all of us as a time we could return to, as children ourselves or the youth of our own children; to return to our parents or to be different parents ourselves. Whatever that time is, *The Winter's Tale* finds a past in all of us and gives both the pain and joy of imagining its return:

> Good Paulina,
> Lead us from hence, where we may leisurely
> Each one demand and answer to his part
> Performed in this wide gap of time since first
> We were dissevered.   (5.3.151–5)

But, of course, the 'wide gap of time' can never be 'performed' or returned to; it can be imagined and that is the as much as we can hope for. Perhaps the only real winner in *The Winter's Tale* is the truth: the only thing that can be told or restored and the only thing that gives anyone a vestige of victory. The child is associated with the truth in Shakespeare because it represents a period in human life that is distinct from the adult world, and for this it is both condemned and celebrated.

6

'Prevent it, resist it, let it not be so, | Lest child, child's children, cry against you woe!'

Even in *Richard II*, which does not represent any children on stage, the idea of the child remains central to the play's moral vision. Every action of kings challenges the children of the future and every unborn child is marked by the present. As images of past injustices or testimonies of the future, the child haunts Shakespeare's dramatic imagination as a spectre of human responsibility. History matters, so the plays suggest, only to the extent that it affects the child and the child's children. But history itself is always in contention: as a story, a chronicle, a narrative sequence, or a memory, the role of the child in determining that history tells us something about the form itself. The child dominates Shakespeare's history plays precisely because it engages with the emerging complexities of the genre. In the chronicles of English kings the dialectic between memory and forgetting governs the narrative's awareness of its own status. From Bolingbroke's deposition of Richard II to Henry VI's loss of France, history is told through the dual processes of remembering and forgetting.[1] Within the dialectic of history, the child becomes the single most powerful emblem of memory; not only in relation to what has happened in the past but also in respect of what should not happen in the future. The spectre that haunts history is that of the child.

When Macbeth returns to the weird sisters for reassurance of his future he is confronted with three apparitions, two of which are children. The second apparition, 'more potent than the first', is a bloodied child who tells him that 'none of woman born | Shall harm Macbeth' (4.1.79–80), while the third, wearing a crown on his 'baby brow' and holding a tree in

[1] Two famous and eloquent discourses on the nature of history are Friedrich Nietzsche, 'The Use and Abuse of History' and Karl Marx, 'The Eighteenth Brumaire of Louis Bonaparte'. See also Hayden White, *Metahistory* (Baltimore: Johns Hopkins University Press, 1973); A. P. Rossiter, 'The Dialectic of the Histories', in *Angel with Horns: Fifteen Lectures on Shakespeare* (London: Longman, 1989).

his hand, exclaims: 'Macbeth shall never vanquished be, until | Great Birnan wood to high Dunsinane Hill | Shall come against him' (4.1.91–3).[2] As we have seen, children are often harbingers of truth and Macbeth understands them as such. Taking from their words and presence a belief in his own invincibility Macbeth enters the fray only to be vanquished by a camouflaged, moving army and a man born by caesarean section. Even to the last, however, Macbeth will not give up. Faced with the prospect of his imminent death he exclaims:

> I will not yield
> To kiss the ground before young Malcolm's feet,
> And to be baited with the rabble's curse.
> Though Birnam wood be come to Dunsinane,
> And thou opposed being of no woman born
> Yet I will try the last.   (5.10.27–32)

Macbeth dies recalling the words of the children who came to remind him of his past as well as his future. The dead children of *Macbeth*, like the ghosts of the young Princes in *Richard III*, are the last images on the heroes' minds. Despite the spectacle of the supernatural there is nothing triumphant or even transcendental about the representation of these little bodies. The phantom children are grotesque testimonies to the moral failures of the play-worlds; their lives may have been extinguished but their shadows remain as a challenge to the immediate future. Such spaces are Shakespeare's greatest testimony to the power of the child. Fragile, frightening, beautiful, mutilated, anguished, innocent, precocious, or credulous the child moves through the plays as a marker of social value. How the play-worlds accommodate their children, what spaces they make available to them, and how they are remembered reveals a great deal about the affective landscape of their narratives. Though not all so grisly or portentous as Hecate's visions, a great many children manifest on the stages of Shakespeare's plays. Many of those children are the dead bodies of an untold history, whose memories lie on the peripheries of the sad stories of the death of kings. Some of those children remain central to the moral outrages of the past, to the records of responsibilities, political failures, and the individual misdeeds. A few of those children, the young Princes in *Richard III*, have been annexed by history into another story of human monstrosity: while others have grown up, Henry VI, or been subsumed by adult anxieties, Arthur. But these children remain as the grief that fills up

---

[2] Following Taylor's work, this scene is now widely attributed to Middleton. Gary Taylor, 'Empirical Middleton: Macbeth, Adaptation and Microauthorship', *Shakespeare Quarterly*, 65.3 (2014), pp. 239–72.

the room; the vast, creeping absence of something that seeps into every corner of these plays and reminds us of what we loved:

> Grief fills the room up of my absent child,
> Lies in his bed, walks up and down with me,
> Puts on his pretty looks, repeats his words,
> Remembers me of all his gracious parts,
> Stuffs out his vacant garments with his form;
> Then, have I reason to be fond of grief?
> Fare you well: had you such a loss as I,
> I could give better comfort than you do.
> I will not keep this form upon my head,
> When there is such disorder in my wit.
> O Lord! my boy, my Arthur, my fair son!
> My life, my joy, my food, my all the world!
> My widow-comfort, and my sorrows' cure!   (3.4.93–105)

Constance's extraordinary rendition of loss imagines her anguish as usurping the space of her absent son. Taking on his figure, his body, his form, Arthur's absence becomes a personification of grief itself, haunting the spaces where she saw him last. Grief becomes inextricably linked to the figure of the child through Constance's memory, reinvigorating, cherishing, and rehearsing the thing she is without. This devastating picture of sorrow shines out of this awkward play as an extraordinary moment of clarity through which Shakespeare articulates an image that would continue to preoccupy his drama. Shakespeare's children are powerfully linked to memory, loss, love, and comfort as they are also always receding from our view. The absence that Constance conjures here is the long shadow of a lost presence, which dominates the representations of children in Shakespeare.

The grisly images of Hecate's conjuring or the ghosts of the dead Princes before the battle of Bosworth produce spectral children who remind the play worlds of their injustices as well as their legacies. But many of Shakespeare's children remain as memories without supernatural intervention: whether it is the 'childhood of our joy', as Romeo puts it, the sun under which Leontes and Polixenes frolicked as 'twin lambs', or the single cushion on which Hermia and Helena sat to sew their samplers, childhood is 'melted as the snow' to become a remembrance which, 'like an idle gaud', was doted on. The child's relation to memory becomes a dominant motif for Shakespeare, not only in the hold that they can retain over the play-worlds but also in the ways in which his children are always in the process of moving away from us. Watching the children of the plays die or grow up becomes a powerful rehearsal for the legacies of the stories they tell. How we perceive Shakespeare's children, how we maintain them as little people, transition them into adults, or remember them as ghosts, rehearses the dominant values not only of Shakespeare's worlds but of our own.

Throughout this book I have focused on the figure of the child through the effects and dynamics it produces on stage and within the play-worlds. As I have tried to show, children are everywhere in Shakespeare, not just as little bodies, but as adults or adolescents in relation to their parents; as memories, as past lives and selves, and as images of a yet unlived future. The idea of the child, as well as its representation on stage, produces a vast network of contextual concerns, including questions of obedience, obligation, possession, punishment, and, most centrally, love. The fascination with children in this period, evinced by their popularity as actors as well as their presence in the plays, extends beyond the figure of the young body to the special status of the subject in relation to authority as well as to their parents. The early modern preoccupation with the status of children clusters around questions of authority precisely because such questions rehearse the governing values through which societies organize their histories. But the elasticity of the term child, that extends beyond age and life stage, to relationships, histories, friendships, and memories, retains the figure of the child as central to all our selves, either as parents or children or both.

Jacques's now famous speech about the 'seven ages of man' envisages the child as both the beginning and end of our human existence:

> All the world's a stage,
> And all the men and women merely players.
> They have their exits and their entrances,
> And one man in his time plays many parts,
> His acts being seven ages. At first the infant,
> Mewling and puking in the nurse's arms.
> Then the whining schoolboy with his satchel
> And shining morning face, creeping like snail
> Unwilling to school. And then the lover,
> Sighing like furnace, with a woeful ballad
> Made to his mistress' eyebrow...
>   The sixth age shifts
> Into the lean and slippered pantaloon,
> With spectacles on nose and pouch on side,
> His youthful hose, well saved, a world too wide
> For his shrunk shank, and his big, manly voice,
> Turning again toward childish treble, pipes
> And whistles in his sound. Last scene of all,
> That ends this strange, eventful history,
> Is second childishness and mere oblivion,
> Sans teeth, sans eyes, sans taste, sans everything.

(*As You Like It*, 2.7.138–48; 156–65)

The child dominates the parts we play, not only in both our entrance and our exit, but in the ways in which childishness is both something devoutly to be wished and feared. Youth remains 'well saved' in the image of the shining morning face or the hose, now, a 'world too wide', as though it is something precious and yet the return to oblivion, 'sans everything', records the body's failure rather than its inception. Childishness hangs over Jacques's stage of life as both a beginning and an end; a perfect memory and a shuddering loss of 'everything'. The existential impulse of this speech leans towards the image of the child, and of youth, as the best of times, and the worst of times: and the children of Shakespeare's drama might well agree. Jacques's paradox of the child is written deep into much of the literature of this period and finds a similar expression in Erasmus's Folly, who, reflecting on youthful nonchalance declares:

> And where does this youthful grace come from? Why, it comes from no one but me, by whose special favour the young have so little knowledge and by the same token are so ingratiating. But when they have grown a little older, learned a little the way of the world, and started to acquire the disciplines of men, call me a liar if their bright and shining faces don't get duller, their quick minds don't slow down, their wit doesn't grow cold, their energy doesn't start to flag. The further they depart from me, the less they really live, until they are overtaken by 'hateful old age'—hateful not only to others but to themselves as well. And old age would really be unendurable to everyone, were it not that I am once again at hand to take pity on its troubles. As the gods of the poets always save the perishing with a timely metamorphosis, so I come to the aid of those with one foot in the grave, and return them, if only for a brief moment, to their infancy. These are the oldsters who are said, quite rightly, to be in their 'second childhood'.[3]

The first and second childhoods, however 'brief', are characterized by the folly that is both remembering and forgetting, delusion and reality. Erasmus's ebullient personification records childhood as a time of 'little knowledge' and of 'shining faces': it is, as Mistress Quickly tells us, 'not good that children should know any wickedness'. Many of Shakespeare's children stand in opposition to the worlds of wickedness in which they are manifest: and many of 'the old folks' who remember those children and themselves as children ask the same question as Edward IV: 'Now tell me...do you love your children?' The children of Shakespeare's plays are loved and despised; destroyed and remembered, but they are everywhere in the poetics of the plays' spaces as testimonies to the presiding impulses

---

[3] Desiderius Erasmus, *The Praise of Folly and Other Writings*, trans. Robert M. Adams (London and New York: Norton, 1989), p. 14.

of love and loss.[4] As the grief that fills up the room the memories of children and childhoods seep into the inner corners of Shakespeare's stage. Many, many years later Charles Dickens would remind us of that inner corner where the child remains in every story they inhabit. Following the death of little Paul Dombey, Dickens recalls Constance in the poetics of the spaces of children, which are filled by both darkness and the morning sun:

> After dark there come some visitors—noiseless visitors, with shoes of felt—who have been there before; and with them comes that bed of rest which is so strange a one for infant sleepers. All this time, the bereaved father has not been seen even by his attendant; for he sits in an inner corner of his own dark room when anyone is there, and never seems to move at other times, except to pace it to and fro. But in the morning it is whispered among the household that he was heard to go upstairs in the dead night, and that he stayed there—in the room—until the sun was shining.[5]

---

[4] On space, see Gaston Bachelard, *The Poetics of Space* (New York: Penguin, 2014).
[5] Charles Dickens, *Dombey and Son* (Basingstoke: Penguin, 1970), p. 310.

Bibliography

Adelman, Janet, *Suffocating Mothers: Fantasies of Maternal Origin in Shakespeare's Plays, Hamlet to The Tempest* (London: Routledge, 1997).

Anonymous, *A Strange Report of Sixe most notorious Witches, who by their diuelish practises murdred aboue the number of foure hundred small Children: besides the great hurtes they committed vpon diuers other people: Who for the same, and many other like offences, were executed in the princely Cittie of Manchen in high Germanie the. 29. of Iuly. 1600* (Printed at Nuremberge by Lucas Mayr Ingrauer, dwelling in Kramergesle: and now translated out of Dutch, according to the same Coppy there imprinted. At London, Printed by W. W. for T. Pauier, dwelling at the signe of the Cat and Parrets neare the Exchange. 1601).

Anonymous, *Natures Cruell Step-Dames: OR, Matchlesse Monsters of the Female Sex; Elizabeth Barnes, and Anne Willis. Who were executed the 26. day of April, 1637. at Tyburne, for the unnaturall murthering of their owne Children. Also, herein is contained their severall Confessions, and the Courts just proceedings against other notorious Malefactors, with their severall offences this Sessions. Further, a Relation of the wicked Life and impenitent Death of Iohn Flood, who raped his own Childe* (Printed at London for Francis Coules, dwelling in the Old-Baily, 1637).

Aries, Philippe, *Centuries of Childhood: A Social History of Family Life*, trans. Robert Baldick (New York: Knopf, 1962).

Ascham, Roger, *The Schoolmaster* (London: Cassell and Company, 1572).

Aughterson, Kate (ed.), *Renaissance Women: Constructions of Femininity in Early Modern England* (London: Routledge, 1995).

Avery, Gillian and Julia Briggs, *Children and Their Books: A Celebration of the Work of Iona and Peter Opie* (Oxford: Clarendon Press, 1989).

Bachelard, Gaston, *The Poetics of Space* (New York: Penguin, 2014).

Barber, Cesar L., *Shakespeare's Festive Comedy: A Study of Dramatic Form and its Relation to Social Custom* (Princeton: Princeton University Press, 1959).

Batt, Barthelemy, *The Christian Man's closet* (London, 1581).

Baxter, Jane Eva, *The Archaeology of Childhood: Children, Gender, and Material Culture* (Walnut Creek, Calif.: Altamira Press, 2005).

Baxter, Jane Eva (ed.), *Children in Action: The Archaeological Papers of the American Anthropological Association*, No. 15 (2005).

Bazerman, Charles, *Shaping Written Knowledge: The Genre and Activity in the Experimental Article in Science* (Madison: University of Wisconsin Press, 1988).

Belsey, Catherine, *Shakespeare and the Loss of Eden: The Construction of Family Values in Early Modern Culture* (London: Macmillan, 1999).

Belsey, Catherine, 'Disrupting Sexual Difference: Meaning and Gender in the Comedies', in John Drakakis (ed.), *Alternative Shakespeares* (London: Methuen, 1985), pp. 169–93.

Bellamy, John, *Strange Inhuman Deaths: Murder in Tudor England* (Stroud: The History Press, 2005).

Ben-Amos, Ilana Krausman, *Adolescence and Youth in Early Modern England* (New Haven: Yale University Press, 1994).

Berry, Helen and Elizabeth Foyster, *The Family in Early Modern England* (Cambridge: Cambridge University Press, 2007).

Berry, Ralph, 'Andrew Gurr: The Shakespearean Stage 1574–1642', *Notes and Queries*, 58.4 (2011), p. 475.

Bevington, David, *This Wide and Universal Theatre: Shakespeare in Performance Then and Now* (Chicago: University of Chicago Press, 2009).

Blake, Ann, 'Children and Suffering in Shakespeare's Plays', *The Yearbook of English Studies*, 23 (1993), pp. 293–304.

Blower, Ralph, *The Court of Good Counsel* (London, 1607).

Boose, Lynda E., 'Scolding Brides and Bridling Scolds: Taming the Woman's Unruly Member', *Shakespeare Quarterly*, 42.2 (Summer, 1991), pp. 179–213.

Boswell, John, *The Kindness of Strangers: The Abandonment of Children in Western Europe from Late Antiquity to the Renaissance* (Chicago: University of Chicago Press, 1998).

Bradford, John, *A Letter sent to Master A.B.* (London, 1584).

Bradley, A. C., *Shakespearean Tragedy: Lectures on Hamlet, Othello, King Lear and Macbeth* (London: Macmillan, 1904).

Briggs, Katharine Mary, *The Anatomy of Puck: An Examination of Fairy Beliefs Among Shakespeare's Contemporaries and Successors* (London: Routledge and Kegan Paul, 1959).

Brooks, Christopher W., *Law, Politics and Society in Early Modern England* (Cambridge: Cambridge University Press, 2008).

Bullein, William, *The Gouernment of Health: A Treatise* (London, 1595).

Burton, William, *Conclusions of peace between God and Man* (London, 1594).

Bushnell, Rebecca W., *A Culture of Teaching: Early Modern Humanism in Theory and Practice* (Ithaca, NY: Cornell University Press, 1996).

Butler, Katherine, *Music in Elizabethan Court Politics* (Woodbridge: Boydell, 2015).

C.I., *A Handkercher for Parents Wet Eyes, upon the death of Children. A Consolatory Letter to a Friend* (London: Printed by E.A. for Michael Sparkes, dwelling at the blue Bible in Greene Arbour, 1630).

Carr, Richard A., 'The Resolution of a Paradox: Alexandre de Pontaymeri's Response to the Querelle des Femmes', *Renaissance Studies*, 17.2 (2003), pp. 246–56.

Cavell, Stanley, *Disowning Knowledge in Seven Plays of Shakespeare* (Cambridge: Cambridge University Press, 1987).

Chambers, E. K., *The Elizabethan Stage* (Oxford: Oxford University Press, 1923).

Chambers, E. K., *The Mediaeval Stage*, vol. 1 (Oxford: Clarendon Press, 1903).

Chedgzoy, Kate, Susanne Greenhalgh, and Robert Shaughnessy (eds), *Shakespeare and Childhood* (Cambridge: Cambridge University Press, 2007).

Clinton, Elizabeth, *The Countess of Lincoln's Nurserie* (London, 1622).

Coleridge, Samuel Taylor, *Collected Works of Samuel Taylor Coleridge* (London: Routledge and Kegan Paul, 1978).

Colon, R. A. and P. A. Colon, *A History of Children: A Socio-Cultural Survey Across Millennia* (Westport, Conn.: Greenwood Press, 2001).

Cotes, William, *A Dialogue of Diverse Questions demanded of the children to their father* (London, 1585).

Cotgrave, Randle, *A Dictionary of the French and English Tongues* (1611; Georg Olms Verlag, 1970).

Crawford, Patricia, *Blood, Bodies and Families in Early Modern England* (London: Routledge, 2014).

Cunningham, Hugh, *Children and Childhood in Western Society since 1500.* (London: Longman, 1995).

Danby, John F., *Shakespeare's Doctrine of Nature* (London: Faber, 1949).

Daniel, David, *Tyndale's Old Testament* (New Haven: Yale University Press, 1994).

Danson, Lawrence, *Shakespeare's Dramatic Genres* (Oxford: Oxford University Press, 2000).

Davies, Robertson, *Shakespeare's Boy Actors* (London: Russell & Russell, 1939).

Davis Ford, Oliver, *Shakespeare's Fathers and Daughters* (London: Bloomsbury, 2017).

DeMause, Lloyd (ed.), *The History of Childhood: The Evolution of Parent–Child Relationships as a Factor in History* (London: Souvenir Press, 1976).

Dolan, Frances E., *Dangerous Familiars: Representations of Domestic Crime in England, 1550–1700* (Ithaca, NY: Cornell Press, 1994).

Dolan, Frances E., *The Taming of the Shrew: Texts and Contexts* (New York: Bedford St Martin's, 1996).

Dolan, Frances E., 'Shakespeare and Marriage: An Open Question', *Literature Compass*, 8.9 (2011), pp. 620–34.

Dowden, Edward, *Shakespeare: A Critical Study of his Mind and Art* (Oxford: Blackwell, 2003).

Elyot, Thomas, *The Book Named the Governor* (1531), ed. S. E. Lehmberg (London: Everyman's Library, 1962).

Enterline, Lynn, *Shakespeare's Schoolroom: Rhetoric, Discipline, Emotion* (Philadelphia: University of Pennsylvania Press, 2012).

Erasmus, Desiderius, *The Ciuilitie of Childehode, with the discipline and institucion of Children, distributed in small and compedious chapters* (London, 1560).

Erasmus, Desiderius, *The Praise of Folly and Other Writings*, trans. Robert M. Adams (London: W. W. Norton, 1989).

Erikson, Erik, *Childhood and Society* (London: Norton, 1963).

Euripides, *Medea and Other Plays*, trans. Philip Vellacott (London: Penguin, 1963).

Ezell, Margaret, *The Patriarch's Wife: Literary Evidence and the History of the Family* (Chapel Hill: University of North Carolina Press, 1987).

Farley-Hills, David, 'The Bad Quarto of Romeo and Juliet', *Shakespeare Survey*, 49 (1996), pp. 27–44.

Fletcher, Anthony, *Gender, Sex, and Subordination in England 1500–1800* (New Haven: Yale University Press, 1995).

Foakes, R. A. (ed.), *Henslowe's Diary* (Cambridge: Cambridge University Press, 2002).

Fowler, Alistair, *Kinds of Literature: An Introduction to the Theory of Genre and Modes* (Oxford: Oxford University Press, 1985).

Foucault, Michel, *Power/Knowledge: Selected Interviews and Other Writings, 1972–1977* (New York: Pantheon, 1980).

Fripp, Edgar Innes, *Shakespeare, Man and Artist*, vol. 2 (Oxford: Oxford University Press, 1938).

Frye, Susan, 'Maternal Textualities', in Naomi Miller and Naomi Yavneh (eds), *Maternal Measures: Figuring Caregiving in the Early Modern Period* (Aldershot: Ashgate, 2001), pp. 224–36.

Fudge, Erica, *Brutal Reasoning, Animals, Rationality and Humanity in Early Modern England* (Ithaca, NY: Cornell University Press, 2006).

Gair Reavely, W., *The Children of Paul's: A Story of a Theatre Company, 1553–1608* (Cambridge: Cambridge University Press, 1982).

Galus, Evaldus, *PVERILES Consabulatiunculae: Or Childrens Dialogues, Little conferences, or talkings together, or little speeches together, or Dialogues fit for children* (London, 1617).

Garber, Marjorie (ed.), *Cannibals, Witches and Divorce: Estranging the Renaissance* (Baltimore: Johns Hopkins University Press, 2003).

Garber, Marjorie, *Coming of Age in Shakespeare* (London: Routledge, 2013).

Gavin, Adrienne (ed.), *The Child in British Literature: Literary Constructions of Childhood, Medieval to Contemporary* (New York: Springer, 2012).

Gibbons, Charles, *A Work Worth the Reading* (London, 1591).

Grant, Ed (trans,), *A President for Parentes, Teaching the vertuous training vp of Children and holesome information of yongmen. Written in greke by the prudent and wise Phylosopher Choeroneus Plutarchus* (London, 1571).

Goodenough, Elizabeth and Mark A. Heberle, *Infant Tongues: The Voice of the Child in Literature* (Detroit: Wayne State University Press, 1994).

Goodwin, Thomas, *A Child of Light Walking in Darkness, Or a Treatise Showing the causes by which God leaves his Children to Distress of Conscience* (London, 1636).

Gowing, Laura, 'Secret Births and Infanticide in Seventeenth Century England', *Past and Present*, 156 (1997), pp. 87–115.

Gowing, Laura, *Domestic Dangers: Women, Words and Sex in Early Modern London* (Oxford: Oxford University Press, 1996).

Gray, Patrick and John D. Cox (eds), *Shakespeare and Renaissance Ethics* (Cambridge: Cambridge University Press, 2014).

Greenblatt, Stephen, *Learning to Curse: Essays in Early Modern Culture* (London: Routledge, 2007).

Greenham, Richard, *A Godlie Exhortation and fruitful donation to virtuous parents and modest matrons* (London, 1584).

Greven, Philip, *The Protestant Temperament: Patterns of Childrearing, Religion, Experience, and the Self in Early America* (New York: Knopf, 1977).

Guillemeau, Jacques, *Child Birth or The Happy Delivery of women* (London, 1612).

Gurr, Andrew, *The Shakespeare Company, 1594–1642* (Cambridge: Cambridge University Press, 2004).

Halliwell, Stephen, *The Poetics of Aristotle: Translation and Commentary* (Chapel Hill: UNC Press Books, 1987).

Harbage, Alfred, *Shakespeare and the Rival Traditions* (New York: Macmillan, 1952).

Harrison, G. B., 'Shakespeare's Topical Significances', *Shakespearian Criticism*, 3 (1919), pp. 271–91.

Heywood, Colin, *A History of Childhood: Children and Childhood in the West from Medieval to Modern Times* (Oxford: Blackwell, 2001).

Higginbotham, Jennifer, *The Girlhood of Shakespeare's Sisters: Gender, Transgression, Adolescence* (Edinburgh: Edinburgh University Press, 2013).

Hillebrand, Harold Newcomb, *The Child Actors: A Chapter in Elizabethan Stage History* (London: Russell, 1926).

Hobbs, Sandy and David Cornwell, 'The Lore and Language of Schoolchildren: A Study of Scholars' Reactions', *Folklore*, 102.2 (1991), pp. 175–82.

Hoffer, Peter C. and N. E. H. Hull, *Murdering Mothers: Infanticide in England and New England, 1558–1803* (New York: New York University Press, 1981).

Høgel, Christian, *The Human and the Humane: Humanity as Argument from Cicero to Erasmus*, vol. 8 (Göttingen: Vandenhoeck & Ruprecht, 2015).

Holmes, Martin Rivington, *Shakespeare and Burbage: The Sound of Shakespeare as Devised to Suit the Voice and Talents of his Principal Player* (Bognor Regis: Phillimore & Company, 1978).

Hooker, Morna, The Annual Hertford Lecture (Oxford, 19 October 2000).

Hotham, Charles, *An Introduction into the Tutonick Philosophy* (London, 1650).

Houlbrooke, Ralph, *The English Family: 1450–1700* (London: Longman, 1984).

Hubert, William, *An Apologie of Infants in Sermon: Prouing, by the reueal will of God, that children preuen d by death of their Baptisme, by Gods election, may be saued* (London, 1595).

Hunt, Alice, *The Drama of Coronation: Medieval Ceremony in Early Modern England* (Cambridge: Cambridge University Press, 2008).

Hutson, Lorna, *The Usurer's Daughter* (London: Routledge, 1994).

Jackson, Russell, *Romeo and Juliet: Shakespeare at Stratford Series* (Cengage Learning EMEA, 2003).

Jackson, Russell (ed.), *The Cambridge Companion to Shakespeare on Film* (Cambridge: Cambridge University Press, 2007).

Jimenez, Ramon, 'The Troublesome Raigne of John, King of England Shakespeare's First Version of King John', *The Oxfordian*, 12 (2010), pp. 21–55.

Kahn, Coppelia, *Roman Shakespeare: Warriors, Wounds, and Women: Feminist Readings of Shakespeare* (London: Routledge, 1997).

Kastan Scott, David, *Shakespeare and the Shapes of Time* (London: Macmillan, 1982).

Kathman, David, 'How Old Were Shakespeare's Boy Actors?', *Shakespeare Survey*, 58 (2005), pp. 220–46.

Kathman, David, 'Grocers, Goldsmiths and Drapers, Freemen and Apprentices in the Elizabethan Theater', *Shakespeare Quarterly*, 55.1 (Spring, 2004), pp. 1–49.

Keenan, Siobhan, *Acting Companies and their Plays in Shakespeare's London* (London: Bloomsbury Publishing, 2014).

Kerrigan, John, *Shakespeare's Binding Language* (Oxford: Oxford University Press, 2016).

Knights, L. C., *How Many Children Had Lady Macbeth?: An Essay in the Theory and Practice of Shakespeare* (London: Haskell House, 1933).

Knowles, Katie, 'This Little Abstract: Inscribing History upon the Child in Shakespeare's King John', *Esharp*, 10 (2007), pp. 1–24.

Knowles, Katie, *Shakespeare's Boys* (Basingstoke: Palgrave, 2015).

Knutson, Roslyn Lander, *Playing Companies and Commerce in Shakespeare's Time* (Cambridge: Cambridge University Press, 2001).

Kristeva, Julia, Michael Marder, and Patricia I. Vieira, 'Adolescence, a Syndrome of Ideality', *The Psychoanalytic Review*, 94.5 (2007), pp. 715–25.

Lamb, Edel, *Performing Childhood in the Early Modern Theatre: The Children's Playing Companies (1599–1613)* (New York: Palgrave Macmillan, 2009).

Lamb, Thomas, *A Treatise of Particular Destination* (London, 1642).

Lancelyn Green, Roger, 'Shakespeare and the Fairies', *Folklore*, 73.2 (1962), pp. 89–103.

Laslett, Peter, *The World We Have Lost* (London: Methuen, 1971).

Laslett, Peter, *Household and Family in Pastime* (Cambridge: Cambridge University Press, 1972).

Lees-Jeffries, Hester, *Shakespeare and Memory* (Oxford: Oxford University Press, 2013).

Leigh, Dorothy, *The Mother's Blessing* (London, 1616).

Lenman, Trevor, 'The Children of Pauls, 1551–1582', in David Galloway (ed.), *The Elizabethan Theatre II* (London: Macmillan, 1970), pp. 35–56.

Little, Arthur, '"A Local Habitation and a Name": Presence, Witnessing and Queer Marriage in Shakespeare's Romantic Comedies', in Evelyn Gajowski (ed.), *Presentism, Gender and Sexuality in Shakespeare* (New York: Palgrave, 2009), pp. 207–36.

Loomba, Ania, *Colonialism/Postcolonialism* (London: Routledge, 1998).

Lyster, John, *A Rule on how to bring up Children* (London, 1588).

MacFarlane, Alan D. J., *The Family Life of Ralph Josselin, a 17th Century Clergyman: An Essay in Historical Anthropology* (Cambridge: Cambridge University Press, 1970).

MacFarlane, Alan, *Marriage and Love in England: Modes of Reproduction 1300–1840* (Oxford: Basil Blackwell, 1986).

MacFaul, Tom, *Problem Fathers in Shakespeare and Renaissance Drama* (Cambridge: Cambridge University Press, 2012).

Machiavelli, Niccolo, *The Prince: A New Translation by Peter Bondanella* (Oxford: Oxford University Press, 2005).

Marienstras, Richard and Janet Lloyd, *New Perspectives on the Shakespearean World* (Cambridge: Cambridge University Press, 1985).

Marx, Karl, *The Eighteenth Brumaire of Louis Bonaparte* (Moscow: Progress, 1937).

Masek, Rosemary, *Audrey Eccles: Obstetrics and Gynaecology in Tudor and Stuart England* (Kent, Oh.: Kent State University Press, 1982).

Martin, Randall, *Women and Murder in Early Modern News Pamphlets and Broadside Ballads 1573–1697* (Aldershot: Ashgate, 2005).

Mellys, John, *The True description of two monstrous children* (London, 1566).

Middleton, Henry, *Certain short questions and answers (for children about godly and Christian matters)* (London, 1580).

Miller, Naomi and Naomi Yavneh, *Maternal Measures: Figuring Caregiving in the Early Modern Period* (Aldershot: Ashgate, 2001).

Miller, Naomi J. and Naomi Yavneh (eds), *Gender and Early Modern Constructions of Childhood* (Aldershot: Ashgate Publishing Ltd, 2011).

Morrice, Thomas, *An Apology for School-Masters, Tending to the aduauncement of Learning, and to the vertuous education of Children* (London, 1619).

Mulcaster, Richard, *Positions* (London, 1581).

Munro, Lucy, *Children of the Queen's Revels: A Jacobean Theatre Repertory* (Cambridge: Cambridge University Press, 2005).

Neely, Carol Thomas, *Broken Nuptials in Shakespeare's Plays* (New Haven: Yale University Press, 1985).

Newnham, John, *Newnham's Nightcrowe* (London: John Wolfe, 1590).

Nichols, John, *Progresses and Processions of Elizabeth* (London, 1823).

Nietzsche, Friedrich, *The Use and Abuse of History*, trans. Adrian Collins (Eastford, Conn.: Martino, 2015).

Orgel, Stephen, *The Illusion of Power: Political Theatre in the English Renaissance* (Berkeley: University of California Press, 1975).

Orlin, Lena Cowen, 'Rewriting Stone's Renaissance', *Huntington Library Quarterly*, 64.1–2 (2002), pp. 189–230.

Opie, Iona and Peter Opie, *The Lore and Language of Schoolchildren* (Oxford: Oxford University Press, 1959).

Packard, Bethany, 'Richard III's Baby Teeth', *Renaissance Drama*, 41.1/2 (2013), pp. 107–29.

Partee, Morriss Henry, *Childhood in Shakespeare's Plays* (Oxford: Peter Lang, 2006).

Paster, Gail Kern, *Humoring the Body: Emotions and the Shakespearean Stage* (Chicago: University of Chicago Press, 2010).

Pendleton, Thomas A., 'Shakespeare's Children', *Mid Hudson Language Studies*, 3 (1980), pp. 39–55.

Petowe, Henry, *The Countrey Ague. OR, London her Welcome home, to her tyer'd retired Children* (London, 1625).

Pinchbeck, Ivy, 'State and the Child in Sixteenth Century England', *British Journal of Sociology*, 7 (1956), pp. 273–85.

Pinchbeck, Ivy, *Children in English Society: From Tudor Times to the Eighteenth Century* (London: Routledge and Kegan Paul, 1969).

Pollock, Linda, 'Childbearing and Female Bonding in Early Modern England', *Social History*, 22 (1997), pp. 286–306.

Pollock, Linda A., *Forgotten Children: Parent–Child Relations from 1500 to 1900* (Cambridge: Cambridge University Press, 1983).

Preiss, Richard and Deanne Williams (eds), *Childhood, Education and the Stage in Early Modern England* (Cambridge: Cambridge University Press, 2017).

Raber, Karen, *Animal Bodies, Renaissance Culture* (Philadelphia: University of Pennsylvania Press, 2013).

Rawson, Beryl and Thomas Wiedemann, *Adults and Children in the Roman Empire* (New Haven: Yale University Press, 1989).

Rhodes, Hugh, *The book of nurture for men servants and children* (London, 1560).

Rosenberg, Marvin, 'The Myth of Shakespeare's Squeaking Boy Actor—or Who Played Cleopatra?', *Shakespeare Bulletin*, 19 (2001), pp. 5–6.

Rossiter, A. P., *Angel with Horns: Fifteen Lectures on Shakespeare* (London: Longman, 1989).

Rutter, Carol Chillington, *Shakespeare and Child's Play: Performing Lost Boys on Stage and Screen* (London: Routledge, 2007).

Rutter, Carol Chillington, 'Remind Me How Many Children Had Lady Macbeth?', *Shakespeare Survey*, 57 (2004), pp. 38–53.

Ryan, Kiernan, *Shakespeare's Universality: Here's Fine Revolution* (London: Bloomsbury Publishing, 2015).

Saccio, Peter, *Shakespeare's English Kings: History, Chronicle, and Drama* (Oxford: Oxford University Press, 2000).

Schalkwyk, David, *Shakespeare, Love and Service* (Cambridge: Cambridge University Press, 2008).

Scott, Charlotte, *Shakespeare and the Idea of the Book* (Oxford: Oxford University Press, 2007).

Scott, Charlotte, 'Still Life? Anthropocentrism and the Fly in Titus Andronicus and Volpone', in Peter Holland (ed.), *Shakespeare Survey*, vol. 61 (Cambridge: Cambridge University Press, 2008), pp. 256–68.

Scott, Charlotte, 'Dark Matter: Foul Dens and Forests', *Shakespeare Survey*, 64 (2011), pp. 276–89.

Scott, Charlotte, *Shakespeare's Nature: From Cultivation to Culture* (Oxford: Oxford University Press, 2014).

Scott, Charlotte, 'Incapable and Shallow Innocents', in Richard Preiss and Deanne Williams (eds), *Childhood and Education on the Early Modern Stage* (Cambridge: Cambridge University Press, 2017), pp. 58–78.

Shakespeare, William, *The Complete Works of William Shakespeare* (New York: W. W. Norton and Company, 1997).

Shakespeare, William, *Pericles*, ed. Suzanne Gossett, The Arden Shakespeare, 3rd series (London: Routledge, 2004).

Shakespeare, William, *Titus Andronicus*, ed. Jonathan Bate, The Arden Shakespeare, 3rd series (London: Routledge, 1995; repr. 2003).

Shapiro, James, *1606: The Year of Lear* (London: Faber, 2015).

Sharp, Jane, *The Midwives Book: Or the Whole Art of Midwifry Discovered* (Oxford: Oxford University Press, 1999).

Sharpe, J., 'Domestic Homicide in Early Modern England', *The Historical Journal*, 24.1 (1981), pp. 29–48.

Shuger, Debora K., *Habits of Thought in the English Renaissance: Religion, Politics, and the Dominant Culture*, vol. 13 (Toronto: University of Toronto Press, 1997).

Skura, Meredith Anne, 'Discourse and the Individual: The Case of Colonialism in *The Tempest*', *Shakespeare Quarterly*, 40.1 (1989), pp. 42–69.

Smith, Emma, *Shakespeare's First Folio: Four Centuries of an Iconic Book* (Oxford: Oxford University Press, 2016).

Stallybrass, Peter, 'Transvestism and the "Body Beneath": Speculating on the Boy Actor', in Susan Zimmerman (ed.), *Erotic Politics: Desire on the Renaissance Stage* (London: Routledge, 1992), pp. 64–83.

Stockwood, John, *A Bartholomew's Fairing for Parents* (London, 1589).

Stone, Lawrence, *The Family, Sex and Marriage, 1500–1800* (London: Harper and Row, 1977).

Taylor, Gary, 'Empirical Middleton: Macbeth, Adaptation and Microauthorship', *Shakespeare Quarterly*, 65.3 (2014), pp. 239–64.

Taylor, John, *The Unnatural Father* (London, 1621).

Thomas, Thomas, *Latin/English Dictionary* (Cambridge, 1587).

Thomas, Keith, 'Children in the Early Modern Period', in Gillian Avery and Julia Briggs (eds), *Children and Their Books* (Oxford: Oxford University Press, 1989), pp. 45–77.

Traub, Valerie, *The Renaissance of Lesbianism in Early Modern England* (Cambridge: Cambridge University Press, 2002).

Travitsky, Betty, 'Child Murder in English Renaissance Life and Drama', *Medieval and Renaissance Drama*, 6 (1993), pp. 63–84.

Tribble, Evelyn, *Early Modern Actors and Shakespeare's Theatre: Thinking with the Body* (London: Bloomsbury, 2017).

Tribble, Evelyn, 'Pretty and Apt: Boy Actors, Skill and Embodiment', in Valeri Traub (ed.), *The Oxford Handbook of Shakespeare and Embodiment* (Oxford: Oxford University Press, 2017), pp. 628–40.

Tribble, Evelyn, 'Marlowe's Boy Actors', *Shakespeare Bulletin*, 27.1 (Spring, 2009), pp. 5–17.

Tuteville, Daniel, *St Paul's Threefold Cord* (London, 1635).

Van Es, Bart, *Shakespeare in Company* (Oxford: Oxford University Press, 2013).

Vickers, Brian, *Shakespeare, Co-Author: A Historical Study of Five Collaborative Plays* (Oxford: Oxford University Press on Demand, 2004).

Vickers, Brian (ed.), *The Complete Works of Francis Bacon* (Oxford: Oxford University Press, 2008).

Wall, Wendy, *The Imprint of Gender, Authorship and Publication in the English Renaissance* (Ithaca, NY: Cornell University Press, 1993).

Warkentin, Germaine, *The Queen's Majesty's Passage & Related Documents* (Ontario: Centre for Reformation and Renaissance Studies, 2004).

West, Richard, *The School of Virtue, the second part or the young scholar's paradise* (London, 1616).

White, Hayden, *Metahistory: The Historical Imagination in Nineteenth Century Europe* (Baltimore: Johns Hopkins University Press, 1975).

Wiedemann, Thomas, *Adults and Children in the Roman Empire* (London: Routledge, 1989).

Wileman, Julie, *Hide and Seek* (Stroud: Tempus, 2005).

Williams, Deanne, *Shakespeare and the Performance of Girlhood* (Basingstoke: Palgrave Macmillan, 2014).

Witmore, Michael, *Pretty Creatures: Children and Fiction in the English Renaissance* (Ithaca, NY: Cornell University Press, 2007).

Wolveridge, James, *Speculum Matricis* (1671; EEBO Editions, ProQuest. 2011).

Wright, Leonard, *The Pilgrimage to Paradise. Compiled for the direction, comfort, and resolution of Gods poore distressed children, in passing through this irkesome wildernesse of temptation and tryall* (London, 1591).

Wrightson, Keith, *English Society: 1580–1630* (London: Hutchinson, 1982).

Wrightson, Keith, 'Infanticide in European History', *Crime and Punishment, History*, 132 (2015), pp. 1–20.

Young, Bruce W., 'King Lear and the Calamity of Fatherhood', in Thomas Moisan and Douglas Bruster (eds), *In the Company of Shakespeare: Essays on English Renaissance Literature in Honor of G. Blakemore Evans* (Madison, NJ: Fairleigh Dickinson University Press, 2002), pp. 43–64.

Young, Bruce Wilson, *Family Life in the Age of Shakespeare* (Westport, Conn.: Greenwood Publishing Group, 2009).

Zimmerman, Susan (ed.), *Erotic Politics: Desire on the Renaissance Stage* (London: Routledge, 1992).

Index